Praise for *Moral Intelligence*

"*Moral Intelligence* is excellent reading for new entrants to the business world as well as experienced managers. I found numerous examples that were right on point with actual events that I have experienced in over 40 years of managing. It was also helpful to have the topics presented in the context of current events that hold the readers' interest. This book should be on the reading list of every student regardless of their career choice."

—Larry Pinnt, Chairman, Cascade Natural Gas

"At a time when capitalism faces questions of legitimacy brought on by poor leadership behaviors, this book provides a healthy way of thinking of the internal compass that can avoid corporate atrocities."

—Mike McGavick, CEO & Chairman of Safeco Corporation

"This book identifies the traits which identify value-oriented corporate leaders and provides a practical primer to a business person to identify and emulate these critical traits. It is essential reading for anyone who believes that this is the way the world is going."

—Mike Phillips, Chairman, Russell Investment Group

"In their new book, Doug Lennick and Fred Kiel bring to the business world a much needed moral guidance system. Given the worldwide erosion of trust in American business, the authors' user-friendly tools and concepts arrive not a moment too soon."

—Keith Reinhard, Chairman, DDB Worldwide and President, Business for Diplomatic Action

Moral Intelligence

Moral Intelligence

Enhancing Business Performance and Leadership Success

Doug Lennick • Fred Kiel Ph.D.

Library of Congress Number: 2004117574

Vice President, Publisher: Tim Moore
Associate Publisher and Director of Marketing: Andrea Neidlinger
Executive Editor: Jim Boyd
Editorial Assistant: Pamela Boland
Development Editor: Russ Hall
Marketing Coordinator: Megan Colvin
Cover Designer: Alan Clements
Managing Editor: Gina Kanouse
Senior Project Editor: Kristy Hart
Copy Editor: Chrissy Andry
Indexer: Julie Bess
Compositor: Jake McFarland
Manufacturing Buyer: Dan Uhrig

Wharton School Publishing offers excellent discounts on this book when ordered in
quantity for bulk purchases or special sales. For more information, please contact U.S.
Corporate and Government Sales, 1-800-382-3419, corpsales@pearsontechgroup.com. For
sales outside the U.S., please contact International Sales at international@pearsoned.com.

Printed in the United States of America

Fourth Printing January 2009

ISBN-10: 0-13-234986-8
ISBN-13: 978-0-13-234986-4

Pearson Education LTD.
Pearson Education Australia PTY, Limited.
Pearson Education Singapore, Pte. Ltd.
Pearson Education North Asia, Ltd.
Pearson Education Canada, Ltd.
Pearson Educatión de Mexico, S.A. de C.V.
Pearson Education—Japan
Pearson Education Malaysia, Pte. Ltd.

To our wives, Beth Ann Lennick and Sandy Kiel, who have helped us fine-tune our own moral compasses over the years—and to our children, who always lovingly challenge us to live in alignment! Alan, Mary, and Joanie (Doug) and Kelly, Amy, Bryn, Anna, Jordan and Freda (Fred)—and to our parents, whose early nurturing provided our foundation—Albert and Martha (deceased) Lennick and Orville and Mabel Kiel (both deceased).

Contents

Foreword xxi

Introduction xxix

PART ONE • MORAL INTELLIGENCE . . . .

1   Good Business 3

2   Born to Be Moral 19

What the Best Leaders Believe 20

A Visit to the Nursery .21

Nature Versus Nurture 22

Growing Up Moral 23

Learning to Be Responsible 23

When Things Go Wrong 24

Inside Your (Moral) Brain 25

It's All in Your Head 26

The Moral Map of Your Brain 29

Why We're Good and Why We're Bad 30

So What Went Wrong? 31

Moral Software 33

3 Your Moral Compass **37**

    Embracing Universal Principles 41

    Discovering Your Values 43

    The Morality of Values 45

    Beliefs 49

    Identifying Your Beliefs 51

    Goals 53

    Why Leaders Love Goals 57

    Your Goals 58

    Put It in Writing 58

    Behavior 59

4 Staying True to Your Moral Compass . . .**63**

PART TWO • **DEVELOPING MORAL SKILLS** . . .

5 Integrity **79**

    Acting Consistently with Principles, Values,
    and Beliefs 80

    Telling the Truth 82

    Standing Up for What Is Right 87

    Keeping Promises 89

6 Responsibility **93**

    Taking Responsibility for Personal Choices 95

    Admitting Mistakes and Failures 97

    Embracing Responsibility for Serving Others . .100

7   Compassion and Forgiveness **105**

   Actively Caring About Others 106

   Letting Go of Your Own Mistakes 109

   Letting Go of Others' Mistakes 112

8   Emotions **115**

   Self-Awareness 117

   Understanding Your Thoughts 119

   Personal Effectiveness 121

   Deciding What to Think 121

   Self-Control 123

   Nurturing Emotional Health 123

   Interpersonal Effectiveness 127

   Empathy 128

   Misplaced Compassion 129

   Respecting Others 132

   Getting Along With Others 135

PART THREE • MORAL LEADERSHIP . . . .

9   The Moral Leader **141**

10 Leading Large Organizations **157**

   The Fabric of Values 157

   Is There Such a Thing as a Morally
   Intelligent Organization? 159

   The Morally Intelligent Organization—
   An Aerial View 160

Morally Intelligent Policies 161

The Principles that Matter Most 163

Organizational Integrity 163

The Responsible Organization 166

The Compassionate Organization 173

The Forgiving Organization 176

Recruiting for Values .178

Reinforcing Values Starts at the Top 179

The Power of Formal Rewards 180

Success Stories 182

Ideal Versus Real 183

Values and the Global Organization 183

11 **Moral Intelligence for the
    Entrepreneur** **. .185**

Moral Values in Small Organizations 190

Last Words About Business Start-Ups 204

**Epilogue: Becoming a Global
Moral Leader 207**

Raising the Stakes 208

Watch Your Wake 209

Give Back 210

Create the Future 211

A Global Business Opportunity 212

Conclusion 214

**Epilogue: Update on *Moral
Intelligence*'s Cast of Characters 215**

Where Have All the Scandals Gone? 216

Good Leaders—Good Results 221

In Their Own Words: Selected Moral
Leaders Two Years Later 227

Where We Stand Now 237

A   Strengthening Your Moral Skills 239

A Look in the Mirror 240

Using the MCI 241

The Right Frame of Mind for Completing
the MCI 241

Scoring and Interpreting Your MCI 241

Prioritizing Your Moral Development Efforts . . .242

The Road Less Traveled 243

The 80/20 Rule 243

Your Moral Development Plan 244

Putting Your Moral Development Plan
into Practice 246

Breaking Bad Habits 247

Reward Yourself for Positive Change 247

Surround Yourself with Positive People 248

Do I Really Need to Change? 248

Books, Audio, and Video Media 249

Workshops 250

Personal Counseling 250

Executive Coaching 250

B   Moral Competency Inventory (MCI)   . .251

C   Scoring the MCI 259

Moral Competencies Worksheet 262

What Your Total MCI Score Means 262

D   Interpreting Your MCI Scores 265

Total MCI Score (Alignment Score) 266

Highest and Lowest Competency Scores 267

Individual Item Scores 267

Reality Testing 268

Do Your Scores Matter? 269

Now What? 270

Index 273

About the Authors

Doug Lennick

Doug Lennick's career as an executive, sales manager, and a developer of people is legendary. Today, in addition to his work as a founding member of the Lennick Aberman Group, Doug continues to work directly with Ken Chenault, CEO of American Express and Jim Cracchiolo, CEO of Ameriprise Financial, formerly American Express Financial Advisors. Although no longer full time, Doug retains the title of EVP at Ameriprise Financial. As a senior advisor to Ken and Jim, Doug's focus is on workforce culture and performance. As a leader, a coach, and a mentor, Doug has taught thousands how to be successful in both their personal and professional lives.

In the early 1990s, Doug was one of two (the other being Jim Mitchell) senior managers at American Express responsible for championing, developing, and implementing the Emotional Competence training program that was recognized by the Consortium for Research on Emotional Intelligence in Organizations as a model program. Doug's work and American Express's Emotional Competence program were recognized in Daniel Goleman's *Working with Emotional Intelligence* and in Tony Schwartz' *Fortune* magazine article on the same topic. In *The Power of Purpose,* Richard Leider referred to Doug as the "spiritual leader" of the company.

Doug lives in Edina, Minnesota, with his wife, Beth Ann. Their youngest daughter, Joan, attends Stonehill College in Easton, Massachusetts. Their oldest daughter, Mary, works in a leadership position for Trader Joe's in the Minneapolis area. Doug's son Alan is an actor and a financial advisor, and is living in Minneapolis with his teacher/actor wife Sari, and thrie son, Dylan.

lennickaberman.com
612-333-8791
dlennick@lennickaberman.com

Fred Kiel, Ph.D.

One of the "founding fathers" of the field of executive coaching, Fred began challenging senior executives in the mid-1970s to improve their leadership skills. Trained as a Ph.D. counseling psychologist, he left the private practice world in the mid-1980s and has since devoted his full-time career to the field now known as executive coaching. He serves as the coach to several CEOs. He is working on his next book, *What CEOs Believe and How It Impacts the Bottom Line*.

In 1987, he formed a partnership with Eric Rimmer in the UK and by 1991, he and Eric joined forces with Kathryn Williams to form KRW International, which has grown into a boutique of mostly Ph.D.-level coaches, internationally recognized for their expertise in the leadership demands of the C-Suite.

Fred lives on his organic farm in Southeastern Minnesota, in the midst of cold running trout streams and Amish farms, along with his wife, Sandy and youngest daughter, Freda. Sandy is the innkeeper for the Inn at Sacred Clay Farm—their country inn bed and breakfast with five luxury guest rooms and meeting space for small groups.

krwinternational.com
612-338-3020
kiel@krw-intl.com

Acknowledgments

Special Acknowledgment for Our Collaborating Writer

Kathleen Jordan, Ph.D.

Kathy has worked with us over the past two years and without her special help, we would not have been able to complete this book. Kathy has brilliantly taken our ideas and rough drafts and worked her magic so that we have one "voice." She is an extraordinary person and personally demonstrates a great deal of moral intelligence.

Kathy has a Ph.D. in Counseling and Human Systems from the University of Florida. After working for large organizations (AT&T Bell Laboratories and later Harvard Business School Publishing Corporation) she has flourished as an independent consultant and is now a partner with the Lennick Aberman Group.

Kathy lives and kayaks in the Boston area. Her daughter Erin is a senior at Vassar.

We wish to give a special thanks to Orlo Otteson, our original "crackerjack" researcher who, over four years, helped us successfully tackle the mountainous job of reviewing the vast literature on this subject.

We wish to thank all of our colleagues and friends who have been so important in helping us sharpen our thinking on moral intelligence. Just as important, they encouraged us to continue our research efforts when the word "moral" was not a word one easily used in public discourse.

These people also inspired us by their own demonstration on a day-to-day basis of what it means to live in alignment!

A partial list from Doug: Kay May, my assistant and friend for a quarter century and now one of my business partners; John Wright, the best man at my wedding and my partner in launching my writing career more than 20 years ago with *The Simple Genius (You)*; the CEOs I have been fortunate to work for and learn from—in order of their appearance, they include Harvey Golub, Jeff Stiefler, Dave Hubers, Jim Cracchiolo, and now Ken Chenault; my partners at Lennick Aberman—Rick Aberman, Jim Choat, Kathy Jordan, Kay May, Fred Mandell, Judy Skoglund, Ben Smith, and Chuck Wachendorfer; the talented team of senior executives I was privileged to lead at American Express Financial Advisors before changing roles in September 2000—Teresa Hanratty, Brian Heath, Jim Jensen, Marietta Johns, Steve Kumagai, Becky Roloff, Sam Samsel, Norm Weaver, and Mike Woodward; Steve Lennick, my cousin, friend and confidant; Carol Lennick, my sister; Bob Day and Tom Turner, the two men who took a chance on me when I was eager to start my business life at the ripe old age of 21—they trained and developed me; Roy Geer, Row Moriarty, Richard Leider, Larry Wilson, and Doug Baker Sr—all five are mentors and friends for many years; and, very importantly, all the people I've had the opportunity to serve as either their leader or their follower or both.

A partial list from Fred: Kathryn Williams, Eric Rimmer, and Kelly Garramone, my partners at KRW International and my other valued KRW colleagues—Meg Armstrong, Randi Birk, Cari Bixel, Lauren Culbert, Tom Crystal, Ann Depta, Mark Edwards, Dolly Etheridge,

John Ficken, Dannie Kennedy, Rita Mendenhall, Kim Merrill, TC Moore, Marsha Nater, Nikky Shaffer, Liz Shamla, Alison Sharpe, Heather Smallman, Ed Starinchak, Mark Tobin, and Don Waletzko and my close personal friends of many years—Frank Verley, Tom McMullen, John Manz, Dwight Cummins, Paul Harris, Bruce McManus, Michael Nation, Paul Brown, and Dave Strofferahn.

Finally, we wish to acknowledge each other, Esmond Harmsworth, and Jim Boyd. This book has been a labor of love, and we have loved laboring together.

Foreword

Building a Better Culture

There are few issues with more significant impact on life in and out of organizations today than that of moral action. Crusades and jihads are moral righteousness taken to harmful and even evil extents—hurting others and demanding homogeneity of beliefs. The moral righteousness involved in trying to fix, save, or punish others has led to some of the most horrible episodes in human existence. Beyond the tragic loss of life, there is the subjugation of the human spirit. There is the loss of dreams and possibilities—the loss of spirit. Ironically, this travesty of moral imperialism comes at the same time as people worldwide are voicing the need for more spirituality and religion.

Most of us know right from wrong. In hundreds of studies of the characteristics that differentiate outstanding from average leaders from their less effective counterparts (both average and poor performers), integrity has never appeared to distinguish high performers. Is this evidence of a morally bankrupt system? No. It is that the moments of "out-tegrity" are so egregious and shocking that we become preoccupied with them. In the process, we miss the many tests of our morality and humanity that we face each day. For example, deciding how to promote a product or service is enacted in the context of one's values and an organizational culture that encourages consistency with a set of shared beliefs and norms.

The essential challenge of moral intelligence is not knowing right from wrong, but doing versus knowing. There are people who are suffering from mental illness and a small percentage of the population that are psychopaths or sociopaths. All of these people may not "know" right from wrong. But most of us are not in that category. So why don't we act appropriately more often? Most of us do—most of the time. Of the hundreds of decisions we make each day, most of us consider what is "right," what will be better and help our community, organization, and fellow humans. But we don't always agree on what is right.

Values and Operating Philosophy

This is where values and philosophy come into play. Our values are based on beliefs and determine our attitudes. A value typically includes an evaluation (i.e., good or bad designation) of an object or subject. Sets of values form proscriptions and prescriptions (i.e., statements of what *not* to do and what *to do*) that guide our daily life. Values also affect how we interpret and perceive things and events around us. But decades of research on values have shown little correlation to behavior.[1]

To understand people's actions, we have to look behind specific values to uncover how an individual determines value. This can be called a person's "operating philosophy." Research into typical operating philosophies has resulted in a test that allows us to measure a person's

1. Michael Hechter. "Values research in the social and behavioral sciences." In Michael Hechter, Lynn Nadel, and Richard E. Michod, (eds.). *The Origin of Values*. New York: Aldine de Gruyter, 1993.

relative dominance among three different ways to determine the value of a act, a project, a decision, how to spend your time, and so forth.[2] Our philosophy is the *way* we determine values.

For example, a consultant lists "family" as a dominant value, but still spends five days a week away from his wife and two children, traveling for his job. He says he's enacting his value by providing enough money for his family's needs. By contrast, a manufacturing manager who also lists "family" as his dominant value has turned down promotions so he can have dinner each night with his wife and children.

The difference between those two men might be in how aware they are of their true values, how aligned their actions are with those values, or in the way they *interpret* their values. Accordingly, they reveal deep differences in how each values people, organizations, and activities. Such differences may reflect disparate operating philosophies—the most common of which are pragmatic, intellectual, and humanistic.[3] And although no one philosophy is "better" than another, each drives people's actions, thoughts, and feelings in distinctive ways.

2. Gordon W. Allport, P.E.Vernon, and Garnder Lindzey, *Study of Values.* Boston: Houghton Mifflin, 1960.; Chris Argyris and Don Schon, *Theory in Practice Learning.* San Francisco, CA: Jossey-Bass, 1982.; Clyde Kluckhohn. "Values and Value-Orientations in the Theory of Action." In Talcott Parson and E.A. Shils, eds. *Toward a General Theory of Action.* Cambridge, MA: Harvard University Press, 1951. pp. 388-433.; Florence Kluckhohn and Fred Strodtbeck. *Variations in Value Orientations.* Evanston, IL: Row, Peterson & Co, 1961.; Milton Rokeach, *The Nature of Human Values.* New York: Free Press, 1973.; Shalom H. Schwartz, "Universals in the Content and Structure of Values: Theoretical Advances and Empirical Tests in 20 Countries," *Advances in Experimental Social Psychology,* volume 25. NY: Academic Press, 1992. pp. 1-65.; Michael Hechter, "Values Research in the Social and Behavioral Sciences," In Michael Hechter, Lynn Nadel, and Richard.E. Michod, eds. *The Origin of Values.* New York: Aldine de Gruyter, 1993. pp. 1-28.

3. "Assessing Your Operating Philosophy: The Philosophical Orientation Questionnaire" measures the relative dominance of each of these three for the person. Richard E. Boyatzis, Angela J. Murphy, and Jane V. Wheeler, "Philosophy as a Missing Link Between Values and Behavior," *Psychological Reports,* 86 (2000): pp. 47-64.

The central theme of a pragmatic philosophy is a belief that *usefulness* determines the worth of an idea, effort, person, or organization.[4] People with this philosophy often measure things to assess their value, and believe that they're largely responsible for the events of their lives. No surprise, then, that among the emotional intelligence competencies, pragmatics rank high in self-management. Unfortunately, their individualistic orientation often—but not always—pulls them into using an individual contribution approach to management.

The central theme of an intellectual philosophy[5] is the desire to understand people, things, and the world by constructing an image of how they work, thereby providing them some emotional security in predicting the future. People with this philosophy rely on logic in making decisions, and assess the worth of something against an underlying "code" or set of guidelines that stress reason. People with this outlook rely heavily on cognitive competencies, sometimes to the exclusion of social competencies. You might hear someone with an intellectual philosophy say, for example: "If you have an elegant solution, others will believe it. No need to try to convince them about its merits." They can use a visionary leadership style, if the vision describes a well-reasoned future.

4. The Pragmatic Operating Philosophy emerged from "pragmatism" (as reflected in the works of John Dewey, William James, Charles Sanders Peirce, and Richard Rorty,), "consequentialism" (as reflected in the works of C.D. Johnson, and P. Pettit), "instrumentalism" (as reflected in the works of John Dewey), and "utilitarianism" (as reflected in the works of Jeremy Bentham, and John Stuart Mill). See the Boyatzis, Murphy, and Wheeler article cited earlier for the full references.

5. The Intellectual Operating Philosophy emerged from "rationalism" (as reflected in the works of Rene Descartes, Gottfried Wilhelm Leibniz, Benedict de Spinoza), and the various philosophers claiming rationalism as their etiological root, such as Georg Wilhelm Friedrich Hegel and Jurgen Habermas, as well as the philosophical structuralists (Claude Levi-Strauss and Jean Piaget), and postmodernists (Friedrich Nietzsche). See the Boyatzis, Murphy, and Wheeler article cited earlier for the full references.

The central theme of a humanistic philosophy is that close, personal relationships give meaning to life[6]. People with this philosophy are committed to human values; family and close friends are seen as more important than other relationships. They assess the worth of an activity in terms of how it affects their close relations. Similarly, loyalty is valued over mastery of a job or skill. Where a pragmatist's philosophy might lead her to "sacrifice the few for the many," a humanistic leader would view each person's life as important, naturally cultivating the social awareness and relationship management competencies. Accordingly, they gravitate toward styles that emphasize interaction with others.

Each one of us believes in these three value orientations (i.e., pragmatic value, intellectual value, and human value). But most of us will prioritize three value orientations differently at different stages in our lives.

The point is that we have to be more aware both *of* our values and *how* we value—our philosophy. We need to be sensitive to those who have different values and different philosophies if we are to live together and make the world a better place. And we need to be sensitive to such differences if we are to have adaptive, resilient, and innovative organizations. Diversity brings us innovation, but only if we are open to it and respect it.

In this book, Doug Lennick and Fred Kiel define **moral intelligence** as, "the mental capacity to determine how universal human principles should be applied to our values, goals, and actions." They argue we are "hard wired" to be moral but often stray from the path. Within each of us are the values and basis for our moral compass. Each of us should pay attention to our moral compass often—more often than we do.

---

6. The Human Operating Philosophy emerged from "communitarianism" (W. F. Brundage), "hermeneutics" (Hans-Georg Gadamer), "humanism" (Francesco Petrarch and R.W. Sellars), and "collectivism" (R. Burlingame and W.H. Chamberlin).

Lennick and Kiel's exploration of this topic could not have come at a more important time.

Cultural Relativism and Moral Horizons of Significance

We are exposed to the vast differences in the world on the Internet, television, movies, and newspapers. We see it in our organizations and schools. We see it walking down the street of most cities of the world. Is every culture and subgroup within it assured that its values and philosophy are "OK" with the rest of us? Maybe not.

In his 1991 book, *The Ethics of Authenticity*, McGill University Professor and prominent philosopher, Charles Taylor, claimed that cultural relativism and postmodernism both violated basic ethical standards.[7] He claimed that cultural relativism ("everyone has their own morality based on their situation and culture") taken to its ultimate conclusion becomes moral anarchy. It breeds a form of egocentrism and selfishness. It suggests everyone is in their own world. Similar to the argument in *Moral Intelligence*, Taylor suggests that there are, among humans and society, "moral horizons of significance." These are the universals that Lennick and Kiel propose are so crucial to organizational success. We know it is wrong to kill another human. But we can be brought to that point by contingencies. Is it acceptable to kill someone to defend your family? To get food for yourself? To take their shirt or sneakers because you like them and cannot afford to buy them? Because they annoy you? Because they have insulted your faith? Taylor's concept is central to the application of the ideas in this book. How do we determine what exceptions to moral universals are justified and which show a lack of moral intelligence?

---

7. Charles Taylor. *The Ethics of Authenticity*. Cambridge: Harvard University Press, 1991.

But this brings us back to whose values and philosophy are right or more right than the others? Without a high degree of moral intelligence, Lennick and Kiel illustrate in their book with marvelous and moving stories, we fall back into fighting to defend our own views as best—and imposing them on others.

In deconstructing the components of moral intelligence, Lennick and Kiel show us how four clusters of skills integrate to form this capability: integrity, responsibility, compassion and forgiveness, and emotions. They offer many ideas as to how we can use our moral intelligence to evoke moral intelligence in others. Their combined effect will be more effective organizations. Why? First, we will be proud of where we work and for what it stands. Therefore, we will feel more committed to the organization, its culture, and vision. Third, we will access and utilize more of our own talent (and that of others around us) because we are free from guilt and shame. And fourth, it is the right thing to do!

Believing and Belonging

There is another crucial business impact from values, philosophy, and collective moral intelligence—they form the basis of our organizational vision, purpose, and culture. We want to believe in what we are doing. We want to feel that we are contributing and our work has some meaning. But looming labor pool demographics and skill shortages suggest that, as McKinsey and Company said, we are in a "war for talent."[8] This will become a battle for the hearts and minds (and even the spirit) of people your organization wishes to attract, keep, and motivate. Over the course of the next decades, an organization's vision, sense of purpose, and culture will become even more significant recruitment differentiators to discerning job applicants.

---

8. Elizabeth Chambers, Mark Foulon, Helen Hanfield-Jones, Steven Hankin, and Edward Michaels, III. *The War for Talent. The Mckinsey Quarterly*, #3, 1998.

Moral Intelligence

In the following pages, you will be provoked into reflecting on your own beliefs and style of using them. You will be inspired by reading about effective executives with high moral intelligence. You will be ashamed and embarrassed reading about ineffective executives who do not seem to be able to spell moral intelligence, nonetheless, live it. The apparent simplicity of their argument and smoothness of their writing style should not be misunderstood. This material is deep and significant. The impact of moral intelligence is much more than the long-term success of your organization. It is the preservation of our civilization and species.

> —Richard E. Boyatzis
> January 31, 2005

Introduction

George Kline was a venture capitalist. For those who knew him in the business world, he seemed to be a person of high integrity and truly "Minnesota nice." But in 2003, George was sentenced to six and a half years in federal prison and fined $5.25 million for insider trading. His two sons were also convicted of felonies. News reports at the time recounted how trading stock tips over coffee breaks at the IDS Center in downtown Minneapolis had mushroomed into a massive deception that engulfed George, his sons, and several business associates.

Contrast this to Craig Ueland's story. Craig is the CEO of the Russell Investment Group in Tacoma, Washington, a highly respected and admired international financial services company with over $125B in assets under management. It is owned by Northwestern Mutual in Milwaukee. Craig told us that when he was in college, it occurred to him that it would be useful for him to decide what principles and values he would honor as he entered his business career. He was an undergraduate at Stanford at the time and said he can still recall where he was walking on campus when he had this insight. Craig explained, "I decided that I would live by three principles. First, when faced with a major decision, I would try to do what was best for society, next what was best for the business and finally, I would consider my own needs. Secondly, I decided that until I was 30 (later he changed this to age 35), when faced with a career decision, I would choose the opportunity that allowed me to learn the most and secondarily would consider the money involved." Then Craig told us his third principle. "I vowed that I would take all my vacations!" This formula has obviously worked very well for Craig. He's at the peak of his career, is happily married, and is a very engaged father for his two small children.

When George and Craig were both young college students, we imagine it would have been difficult to see any major differences between them—both from good homes, both very ambitious, and both excited about moving into a business career. But Craig deliberately charted his life course in a way that George apparently neglected. One is now the CEO of a major global business and the other is participating in a government-sponsored residential program—a federal prison camp!

In the mid-1990s, well before the scandals of Enron and WorldCom and before the dot.com bubble burst, we had a conversation both authors vividly recall. Doug was then executive vice president, Advice and Retail Distribution for American Express Financial Advisors. Doug was well-known for developing a high performing sales force of approximately 10,000 financial advisors and was an early champion of emotional intelligence skills training at American Express. Fred, a pioneer in the field of executive coaching, was a psychologist and co-founder of a leading executive development company and then as now, actively engaged in helping senior executives improve their personal performance as leaders.

As we talked, we realized that we had some common ideas about the ingredients of high performance that we were both struggling to conceptualize. We agreed on the importance of emotional intelligence—the constellation of self-awareness, self-management, social awareness, and relationship management skills that are now commonly regarded as critical to success in the workplace.[1] We discovered, though, that neither of us thought emotional intelligence was sufficient to assure consistent, long-term performance.

In the course of nearly 30 years, we had collectively worked as business executives, entrepreneurs, and leadership consultants to chief executives and senior leaders of Fortune 500 companies, large privately held companies, and start-ups. We had each coached hundreds of leaders. The most successful of them all seemed to have something in common that went beyond insight, discipline, or interpersonal skill. We also spoke about noted public figures with masterful emotional intelligence skills who would sway like reeds in the wind when faced with morally loaded decisions. We hypothesized that there was something more basic than emotional intelligence skills—a kind of moral compass—that seemed to us to be at the heart of long-lasting business success. We decided to label this "something more" *moral intelligence.*

Moral intelligence is "the mental capacity to determine how universal human principles should be applied to our values, goals, and actions." In the simplest terms, *moral intelligence* is the ability to differentiate right from wrong as defined by universal principles. Universal principles are those beliefs about human conduct that are common to all cultures around the world. Thus, we believe they apply to all people, regardless of gender, ethnicity, religious belief, or location on the globe.

Our shared notion that moral intelligence was key to effective leadership led us to wonder: How do leaders get to be moral—or not? Are people born that way? Does our human "hardwiring" predispose us to be concerned for others? What accounts for the wide differences in moral behavior among leaders? Have we learned anything new about human nature over the past few decades that could help us understand the impact of moral sensibilities on leadership behavior? What do the

---

1. These skills were highlighted in Goleman, D. *Working with emotional intelligence.* New York: Bantam Books (1998).

fields of philosophy, social biology, developmental psychology, cultural anthropology, and the neurosciences have to say about these questions?

Before progressing to further develop our hypothesis, we hired crackerjack researcher, Orlo Otteson, to help us review the academic literature on the moral dimensions of human nature and experience. Orlo first reviewed over 1,800 article abstracts referencing *moral leadership* from the fields of business, religion, philosophy, anthropology, sociology, and political science but found few in-depth moral leadership discussions. Most articles focused on a specific kind of leadership (business, political, religious), on a specific leadership problem, or on the general need for honest and upright leadership. He then surveyed nearly 400 books and articles on morality from the disciplines of philosophy, psychology, biology, and neuroscience, distilling their insights as they applied to leadership and organizations.

Meanwhile, we began to organize our observations of the many hundreds of leaders we had encountered in our work. As our conviction about the importance of moral intelligence grew, we conducted in-depth interviews with 31 CEOs and 47 other senior executives to learn the precise ways that they deployed their moral intelligence to achieve important personal and business goals. We also discussed our ideas with many talented leaders and colleagues whose penetrating feedback helped us deepen and refine our approach to moral leadership.[2]

Scientific research supported our initial notions about the importance of moral intelligence for individuals, organizations, and societies. But it was our interviews and observations of leaders that taught us exactly how the best of them used their moral intelligence to overcome obstacles, consistently outperform their rivals, and quickly pick up the pieces when they occasionally missed the mark.

Having analyzed their experiences, we concluded that strong moral skills are not only an essential element of successful leadership, but are

2. List of those we interviewed and with whom we discussed book concepts appears at the end of the Introduction.

also a business advantage. Indeed, the most successful leaders in any company are likely to be trustworthy individuals who have a strong set of moral beliefs and the ability to put them into action. Furthermore, even in a world that occasionally rewards bad behavior, the fastest way to build a successful business is to hire those people with the highest moral and ethical skills you can find.

Business leaders have gotten a bad rap in the first years of this decade. Yes, of course, there are the "bad eggs," and they get a lot of press. But most business leaders are not like those in the newspapers. Consider, for example, a story we heard from Peter Georgescu, chairman emeritus of Young & Rubicam, who built a large advertising and marketing company and is widely known as an inspiring leader.

"Back in the 1980s, Warner Lambert approached us because they wanted to diversify their consumer products by selling sunglasses. They already had a celebrity spokesperson lined up, and they wanted us to advise them on how to roll out the new product. They told us we were competing with five other agencies to produce the best campaign. After we did the research, our group concluded that Warner Lambert wasn't going to be able to get enough market share to make the new product line successful. We had significant debate about whether to present a campaign anyway, but finally our group went to Warner Lambert and said, "We know this isn't what you want to hear, but we think the sunglasses line is a bad idea." We explained our reasoning. They looked a little surprised, said, "Thank you," and that was the end of the meeting—we had no idea what they thought.

Then a few weeks later, Warner Lambert called us and said, "You know, we agree with your analysis. No other agency was smart enough or honest enough to tell us, but you did. We have decided not to launch the line. Because of your honesty, though, we are going to give you some other business with us, and you won't have to compete for it."

Of all the executives we have queried about their beliefs and values, not one has hinted that they are driven to get to the top at all costs or that diddling with the books is a reasonable tactic for achieving results.

Likewise, none have stated that their work is only about increasing shareholder value. True, we might have been hearing politically correct answers, but with only a little bit of further questioning, we discovered all the leaders we interviewed have a *moral compass*—a set of deeply held beliefs and values—that drives their personal and professional lives. They revealed beliefs such as being honest no matter what; standing up for what is right; being responsible and accountable for their actions; caring about the welfare of those who work for them; and owning up to mistakes and failures. They told us vivid stories about how such beliefs played into the choices they made and the way they behaved. For some, it was the first time they had spoken out loud about their moral compass and its contribution to their business performance because many of those we interviewed think they shouldn't wear their beliefs on their sleeves and that discussions of moral values don't belong at work. We think work is exactly where moral values should be—and be discussed.

Why? All the leaders we interviewed recognize the importance of values to their business success. But the courageous ones who routinely communicate about their core beliefs and values—personal values as well as universal human principles they endorse—have discovered a great source of organizational energy. When a leader is explicit about what he or she believes and values, it becomes much easier for others to hold him or her accountable. Furthermore, it allows others who share those beliefs and values to say to themselves, "Hey, I agree with that. This is why *I* come to work, too! This is a place I can be myself and really be inspired to produce results." When a leader is explicit about what he or she believes and values, creates a vision, strategy and goals aligned with those values, and then *behaves* in alignment with all of that—followers respond with deep trust of their leader.

Four years into our research and experimentation with moral intelligence tools, the new century began and with it the corporate accounting scandals that dominated its headlines. We realized it was time to go public with our findings about the relationship between morality and business performance. While business practitioners were now defensively eager to discuss compliance-based ethics, no one we knew was focusing on the personal character, principles, and moral skills that must be baked into every leader and every organization that wants to ensure long-term sustainable results. The research that forms the basis of this book is largely observational and case study-based. Over the next several years, we plan to conduct quantitative research in partnership with academic and business institutions. We will be studying the relationship between leaders' moral intelligence and the long-term financial performance of their companies. But leaders who face today's urgent business challenges can't afford to wait for further research to confirm the importance of moral intelligence to their success. Countless leaders we have coached and trained in the last few years have told us that our methods for enhancing moral intelligence are making a difference in their own performance, helping them inspire higher performance in their workforces, and contributing to better financial results.

We offer this book as a roadmap for leaders to find and follow their moral compasses. Although we believe that doing the right thing is right for its own sake, we are convinced that leaders who follow their moral compasses will find that it is the right thing for their businesses as well. This book is *not* about telling you what is right or wrong. It's not about helping you try to become a moral paragon. We are all imperfect, none more so than your authors. Though we all want to be our best, most ideal selves, we face daily obstacles and temptations that threaten our performance as leaders and our integrity as human beings. In this book, we hope you will find the tools to become the best leader you can be. You—and your organization—deserve nothing less.

Leaders Interviewed

We are deeply indebted to the large group of leaders who contributed to our thinking and research. Our interview subjects were especially generous with their time and candid in their self-assessments.

Douglas Baker	CEO, Ecolab Inc.
Dan Brettler	CEO and Chairman, Car Toys, Inc.
Kenneth Chenault	CEO and Chairman, American Express Company
Paul Clayton	CEO Jamba Juice
Michael Connolly	Former CEO, Heartland Juice; former CEO, Great Clips, Regional Companies, A Great Clips Franchisee
Stan Dardis	CEO and President, Bremer Financial Corporation
Lynn Fantom	CEO, ID Media
Paul Fribourg	CEO and Chairman, Conti-Group Companies
Peter Georgescu	Chairman Emeritus, Young & Rubicam
Harvey Golub	Chairman of the Board of Directors, Campbell's Soup Company and Chairman and CEO (retired), American Express Company
Brian Hall	CEO, Thomson Legal & Regulatory Group
Don Hall, Jr.	CEO and Vice Chairman, Hallmark Cards
Dick Harrington	CEO, The Thomson Corporation
David Hubers	CEO (retired), American Express Financial Advisors
Ken Kaess	CEO, DDB Worldwide
David Kenny	CEO and Chairman, Digitas, Inc.
Mike McGavick	CEO and Chairman, Safeco Corporation
Rowland Moriarty, Ph.D.	CEO and Chairman, Cubex Corporation; Founding Director, Staples; Founding Director, PetsMart
Mark Oja	CEO ACTIVEAID
Larry Pinnt	Chairman, Cascade Natural Gas
Michael Phillips	Chairman, The Russell Investment Group

Keith Reinhard	Chairman, DDB Worldwide
Spenser Segal	CEO, ActiFi
Dale Sperling	CEO, Unico Real Estate Company
Jay Sleiter	CEO and Chairman, BWBR Architects
Mayo Shattuck	CEO and Chairman, Constellation Energy
Lynn Sontag	CEO, MENTTIUM Corporation
Craig Ueland	CEO and President, The Russell Investment Group
Charlie Zelle	CEO and Chairman, Jefferson Bus Lines
Ed Zore	CEO and President, Northwestern Mutual
Jim Berrien	President, *Forbes* Magazine
Brenda Blake	Senior Vice President, Global Leadership Marketing, American Express
Walt Bradley	Financial Advisor, Thrivent Financial for Lutherans
Sam Bronfman	Former Senior Vice President, Seagrams, Inc.
George Brushaber	President, Bethel University
Mike Campbell	President, Safeco Financial Institution Solutions
Cindy Carlson	Former President, Capital Professional Advisors
Kevin Carter	Vice President, Diversity Iniatives, Safeco Corporation
Rick Clevett	Vice President of Human Resources, The Carlson Companies
Eric Drummond-Hay	Vice President, Chief Actuary, SBI, Safeco Corporation
Dave Edwards	Senior Vice President, International Information Management, American Express
Patrick Grace	Former Senior Vice President, The Grace Corporation
Jim Greenawalt	Senior Vice President Executive Development, Thomson Legal & Regulatory Group
Kim Garland	Vice President, National SPI Auto, Safeco Corporation

Jim Swegle	Vice President, National SPI Property, Safeco Corporation
Maurice Hebert	Senior Vice President and Controller, Safeco Corporation
Brian Heath	Senior Vice President and General Manager, American Express Financial Advisors
Lori Kaiser	Former Senior Vice President, Cray Computer Co.
M'Lynn Hoefer	Senior Vice President, MENTTIUM Corporation.
Mike Hughes	Senior Vice President, SBI Regular , Safeco Corporation
Gary Kessler	Senior Vice President of Human Resources Honda America
Diane Kozlak	Vice President, MENTTIUM Corporation
Ken Krei	President, Wealth Management Group, M&I Bank
Jeanne Lind	Director of Automation (SBI), Safeco Corporation
Karen Lane	Former Governor's Staff, State of Washington
Mike LaRocco	Co-President, Product, Underwriting and Claims, Safeco Corporation
Dale Lauer	Executive Vice President, Claims, Large Commercial, SFIS and Surety Safeco Insurance
Harvey Leuning	Associate Pastor, Gloria Dei Lutheran Church, St. Paul, MN
Ann Levinson	Deputy Director, Seattle Monorail Authority
Don MacPherson	Co-President, Modern Survey
Christine Mead	Co-President, Service, Technology and Finance and Chief Financial Officer, Safeco Corporation
Pam Moret	EVP of Products and Marketing, Thrivent Financial for Lutherans
Eric Morgan	Former Senior Vice President, Lawson Software
Allie Mysliwy	EVP of Human Resources and Operations, Safeco Corporation
Gary O'Hagan	President of Coaches Division, IMG
Carla Paulson	Senior Vice President of Human Resources, Bremer Financial Group

Tom Perrine	Vice President, Cardinal Health
David Risher	Former Senior Vice President, Amazon.com
Pat Roraback	Vice President, M&I Bank
Jim Ruddy	EVP and General Counsel, Safeco Insurance
Joe Schlidt	Vice President, M&I Bank
John Schlifske	Senior Vice President, Northwestern Mutual
Tom Schinke	Managing Division Vice President, Thrivent Financial for Lutherans
Jim Thomsen	Senior Vice President of Distribution, Thrivent Financial for Lutherans
Kim Vappie	President and Chief Operating Officer, MENTTIUM Corporation
Mike Woodward	Senior Vice President, American Express Financial Advisors

Thought Partners

We greatly appreciate our many colleagues and mentors whose input has helped sharpen our thinking about the moral dimensions of leadership. They include

Rick Aberman, Ph.D.	Psychologist, emotional intelligence expert and coauthor of *Why Good Coaches Quit—and How You Can Stay in the Game*
Reuven Bar-On, Ph.D.	University of Texas Medical Branch, in the Department of Psychiatry and Behavioral Sciences, where he directs research in emotional and social intelligence
Richard Boyatzis, Ph.D.	Professor and Chair of the Department of Organizational Behavior at the Weatherhead School of Management at Case Western Reserve University, and co-author of *Primal Leadership: Realizing the Power of Emotional Intelligence*

Kate Cannon	President, Kate Cannon and Associates
Robert Caplan, Ph.D.	Director, Beach Cities Health District, an organization charged with promoting mental and physical wellness in three adjacent communities in Southern California
Cary Cherniss, Ph.D.	Director of the Rutgers University Organizational Psychology Program, professor of Applied Psychology and coauthor of *The Emotionally Intelligent Workplace*
Stephen Covey, Ph.D.	Author of *The 7 Habits of Highly Effective People* whose conversations with Doug in the early 1990s reinforced early versions of our alignment model
Vanessa Druskat	Associate Professor, University of New Hampshire,Whittemore School of Business and Economics
Robert Emmerling, Ph.D.	Consultant and researcher specializing in the application of emotional intelligence concepts in the workplace
Jim Garrison	President and co-founder (with Mikail Gorbalhev) of the State of the World Forum and author of *America as Empire*
Roy Geer, Ph.D.	Psychologist, consultant, and co-author (with Doug Lennick) of *How to Get What You Want and Remain True to Yourself*
Daniel Goleman, Ph.D.	Co-director of the Consortium for Research on Emotional Intelligence in Organizations at Rutgers University, author of *Emotional Intelligence*, *Working with Emotional Intelligence*, and co-author of *Primal Leadership: Realizing the Power of Emotional Intelligence*
Marilyn Gowing, Ph.D.	Vice President for Public Sector Consulting and Services with the Washington office of AON Consulting
Darryl Grigg, Ph.D.	Psycholgist
Dorothy Hutcheson	Head of School, Nightingale-Bamford School for Girls

Jennifer Hugstad-Vaa, Ph.D.	Professor, St. Mary's University Minnesota
Ruth Jacobs	Director of Research and Technology at McClelland Center for Research and Initiatives, The Hay Group
Stuart Kantor, Ph.D.	Co-founder and principal of Red Oak Consulting, an executive development firm
Carol Keers	Co-founder, Change Masters Inc
Kathy Kram,	Ph.D. Professor of Organizational Behavior at the Boston University School of Management
Richard Leider	Founding partner of The Inventure Group and author of *Repacking Your Bags*, *the Power of Purpose*, and *Life Skills*
Jim Loehr, Ph.D.	Performance psychologist and co-author of *The Power of Full Engagement: Managing Energy, Not Time, Is the Key to High Performance and Personal Renewal* and author of *Stress for Success*
Fred Luskin, Ph.D.	Senior Fellow at the Stanford Center on Conflict and Negotiation, co-founder of the Stanford University Forgiveness Project, and author of *Forgive for Good*
Stephen Kelner, Jr.	Global Knowledge Manager, Egon Zehnder International, Inc.
David Kidd	Partner, Egon Zehnder International, Inc.
Matthew Mangino	Consultant Director, Johnson & Johnson
Jim Mitchell	Executive Fellow, Leadership at the Center for Ethical Business Cultures in Minneapolis
Tom Mungavan	President and co-founder, Change Masters, Inc.
John Nicolay, MBA	MBA instructor, University of Minnesota
Hy Pomerance, Ph.D.	Co-founder and principal of Red Oak Consulting, an executive development firm
Richard Price, Ph.D.	Professor of Psychology and Business Administration at the University of Michigan, and Senior Research Scientist at the Institute for Social Research

Fabio Sala, Ph.D.   Associate Director, Learning and Development,
                                 Millennium Pharmaceuticals, Inc.

Tony Schwartz   Co-author of *The Art of the Deal* and *The Power
                                 of Full Engagement: Managing Energy, Not Time,
                                 Is the Key to High Performance and Personal
                                 Renewal* and author of *What Really Matters:
                                 Searching for Wisdom in America*

Hersh Shefrin, Ph.D.   Professor of Finance at the Leavey School of
                                 Business, Santa Clara University, and author of
                                 Beyond Greed and Fear

Judy Skoglund   Partner, Lennick Aberman Group

Lyle Spencer, Ph.D.   President, Spencer Research and Technology,
                                 co-founder of Competency International,
                                 Cybertroncis Research Fellows, Director, Human
                                 Resource Technologies, author and independent

Therèse Jacobs Stewart,   Master Psychologist
Ph.D.

Jeff Stiefler   CEO, Digital Insights

Redford Williams, Ph.D.   Professor of Psychiatry and Behavioral Sciences,
                                 Professor of Medicine, and Director of the
                                 Behavioral Medicine Research Center at Duke
                                 University Medical Center

Larry Wilson   Founder of Wilson Learning and Pecos River
                                 Learning Center, author of *The One Minute Sales
                                 Person* and *Changing the Game: The New Way to
                                 Sell* and co-author of *Stop Selling, Start
                                 Partnering*

PART ONE

MORAL INTELLIGENCE

1 ──────────

Good Business

Gary O'Hagan is a division president of International Management Group, the world's largest sports marketing and talent representation agency. Gary is an intense, competitive, and imposing man who looks like the football player he once was. As a young man, he was drafted and then cut by the San Francisco 49ers, then picked up and cut by the New York Jets. Gary was devastated but determined to find another route to high achievement. He got a job as a financial trader with Solomon Brothers and attended law-school classes every weekday night. When his grandfather died, Gary was expected to attend the wake, the funeral, and a host of other family gatherings. Gary was anxious about falling behind at work and school, so he thought he could attend the funeral, make a quick appearance at the after-funeral lunch, after which he'd head back to work. But when he got to the restaurant, the significance of his family's loss finally registered, and Gary realized that his priorities were out of whack. He called his boss and told him he wasn't coming in to work. His boss was concerned and upset, but Gary stayed. He knew that if he didn't have the compassion to help his family in that moment, he would never amount to much either personally or professionally.

Gary O'Hagan is only one of the many leaders we know with high moral intelligence, those who do their best to follow their moral compass. They do it because they believe it's the right thing to do. A funny thing happens when leaders consistently act in alignment with their principles and values: They typically produce consistently high performance almost any way you can measure it—gross sales, profits, talent retention, company reputation, and customer satisfaction. We think this is no accident. The successful leaders we know always attribute their accomplishments to a combination of their business savvy *and* their adherence to a moral code. Doug Baker, CEO of Ecolab, a $4 billion dollar cleaning-products manufacturer, tells us that "living by my personal moral code is one of the key reasons I have this job." Ed Zore, CEO of Northwestern Mutual, says, "Being moral—which to me means being fair, predictable, up-front and not devious—all of this has been very important in my career. Everybody knows what I stand for. People know that we will never, ever be deceitful. We won't leave a nickel on the table, but in the end our word is our bond, and this is a real advantage in business because people want to deal with us and want to deal with me." Gary Kessler, a vice president with the Honda Motor Company, credits his principles and values for his career success. "I was VP of a business unit at Bausch and Lomb when I was 36 and at Honda when I was 45. I think I had the good fortune of working with people who recognized that I had sincerity and a conviction to do the right thing along the way."

A Special Kind of Intelligence. Each of these leaders and others you will meet throughout this book are morally gifted. They are high in moral intelligence. Most of us are familiar with other kinds of intelligence, such as our cognitive intelligence (IQ) and our technical intelligence. IQ and technical intelligence are undeniably important to a leader's success. Leaders need to be good learners (IQ) who have expertise about their particular business (technical) areas. We call cognitive and technical intelligence *threshold competencies* because they are the price of admission to the leadership ranks. They are necessary but not sufficient for exceptional performance. They don't help you stand out from the competitive crowd because your rivals' leadership teams have as much basic intelligence and business savvy as you do.

Intelligence that Makes the Difference. To outpace your competition, you need to cultivate different kinds of intelligence we call *differentiating competencies. Moral intelligence* and *emotional intelligence* are two types of intelligence that are difficult for your competition to copy. Many corporate leaders ignore these differentiating competencies because they are soft skills that are difficult to measure. In recent years, however, an increasing number of organizations have realized the performance benefits of emotional intelligence. Daniel Goleman deserves enormous credit for bringing emotional intelligence out of the academic closet and into the tough-minded halls of commerce. His books on emotional intelligence provide a rich and compelling case for the importance of emotional skills to corporate leaders.[1]

Although emotional intelligence is widely recognized as a business tool, its definition is still evolving. In 1990, Professors Peter Salovey of Yale University and John Mayer of the University of New Hampshire first coined the term. Their original definition of emotional intelligence

---

1. For example, Daniel Goleman. *Emotional Intelligence: Why It Can Matter More Than IQ*. New York: Bantam, 1995, and *Working with Emotional Intelligence*. New York: Bantam, 1998.

was "the ability to monitor one's own and others' feelings, to discriminate among them, and to use this information to guide one's thinking and action." They identified the components of emotional intelligence:

- Appraising emotions in self and others

- Regulating emotions in self and others

- Using emotions adaptively

Salovey later expanded those into five domains, which Dan Goleman adapted in 1995 in *Emotional Intelligence: Why It Can Matter More Than IQ*:[2]

- Knowing one's emotions (self-awareness)

- Managing emotions

- Motivating oneself

- Recognizing emotions in others

- Handling relationships

In 1997, Salovey and Mayer recharacterized emotional intelligence as "the ability to perceive, appraise, and express emotion accurately and adaptively; the ability to understand emotion and emotional knowledge; the ability to access and/or generate feelings when they facilitate thought; and the ability to regulate emotions in ways that assist thought." The revised components became

- Perceiving and expressing emotion

- Using emotion in cognitive activities

- Understanding emotions

- Regulation of emotions

2. Ibid.

Other experts in the field of emotional intelligence offer slightly different twists, but the definitions are consistent with those of Salovey, Mayer, and Goleman.

Moral intelligence is new to the playing field. Just as emotional intelligence and cognitive intelligence are different from one another, moral intelligence is another distinct intelligence. Moral intelligence is our mental capacity to determine how universal human principles—like those embodied by the "golden rule"— should be applied to our personal values, goals, and actions. This book focuses on four principles that are vital for sustained personal and organizational success:

- Integrity

- Responsibility

- Compassion

- Forgiveness

Integrity is the hallmark of the morally intelligent person. When we act with integrity, we harmonize our behavior to conform to universal human principles. We do what we know is right; we act in line with our principles and beliefs. If we lack integrity, by definition, we lack moral intelligence.

Responsibility is another key attribute of the morally intelligent person. Only a person willing to take responsibility for her actions— and the consequences of those actions—will be able to ensure that her actions conform to universal human principles. Compassion is vital because caring about others not only communicates our respect for others, but creates a climate in which others will be compassionate toward us when we need it most. Forgiveness is a crucial principle, because without a tolerance for mistakes and the knowledge of our own imperfection, we are likely to be rigid, inflexible, and unable to engage with others in ways that promote our mutual good.

Compassion and forgiveness operate on two levels: first in how we relate to ourselves and second, in how we relate to others. Since we have yet to meet a person with *perfect* moral intelligence, putting principles into action requires that when we make inevitable mistakes, when our behavior fails to conform to universal human principles, we need to be able to treat ourselves with compassion and forgiveness. If we are not gentle and forgiving of ourselves, we will not have the energy to move forward to build our moral capacity. Similarly, to inspire others to enhance their moral intelligence, we need to treat others with compassion and forgiveness.

Research tells us that emotional intelligence contributes more to life success than intellectual or technical competence. Emotional intelligence can help you behave with great self-control and interpersonal savvy. But emotional intelligence alone won't keep you from doing the wrong thing. Moral incompetence surfaces in moments when personal or business goals conflict with core values. Just about everyone has worked with someone who had great interpersonal skills but dropped the ball on a moral issue—perhaps an employee who let a colleague take the blame for something that was undeserved or a manager who gave an inflated performance rating to the boss' nephew. But until now, no one has paid much attention to systematically developing moral intelligence—even though the best leaders know it's their secret weapon for lasting personal and organizational performance.

Some competencies that appear on lists of emotional competencies have a definite moral flavor, such as the ones listed here (from Daniel Goleman's *Working with Emotional Intelligence*):

- Have a guiding awareness of (personal) values and goals

- Voice views that are unpopular and go out on a limb for what is right

- Act ethically and are above reproach

- Build trust through their reliability and authenticity

- Admit their own mistakes and confront unethical actions in others

- Take tough principle stands even if they are unpopular

We believe it is more accurate to describe them as moral competencies. They are aspects of the four principles we describe and, in this book, we explore these attributes as well as the other competencies we see present in integrity, responsibility, compassion, and forgiveness. Perhaps it has been safer to think of these clearly moral competencies as emotional competencies because the culture of business in the last half century has discouraged all of us from talking about the "m" word. If there is a silver lining to the recent corporate scandals, it is that moral lessons are inescapable. The time has come to openly acknowledge the contribution of moral intelligence to effective leadership and sustainability.

Although both emotional intelligence and moral intelligence come into play when moral decisions are at stake, they are not the same. Emotional intelligence is values free. Moral intelligence is not. Emotional skills can be applied for good or evil. Moral skills, by definition, are directed toward doing good.

Emotional intelligence and moral intelligence, though distinct, are partners. Neither works in a truly effective way without the other. In *Primal Leadership: Realizing the Power of Emotional Intelligence*, Goleman and his co-authors, Richard Boyatzis and Annie McKee, tackle the boundary between emotional and moral intelligence when they discuss how good and bad leaders can use the same emotional competencies:

> **Given that adept leaders move followers to their emotional rhythm, we face the disturbing fact that, throughout history, demagogues and dictators have used this same ability for deplorable ends. The Hitlers and Pol Pots of the world have all rallied angry mobs around a moving—but destructive—message. And therein lies the crucial difference between resonance and demagoguery...**

Demagoguery casts its spell via destructive emotions, a range that squelches hope and optimism as well as true innovation and creative imagination (as opposed to cruel cunning). By contrast, resonant leadership grounded in a shared set of constructive values (our emphasis) keeps emotions resounding in the positive register. It invites people to take a leap of faith through a word picture of what's possible, creating a collective aspiration.[3]

Without a moral anchor, leaders can be charismatic and influential in a profoundly destructive way. As *Primal Leadership* emphasizes, truly effective leadership is "grounded in a shared set of constructive values."[4] Without knowledge of those values— in other words, moral intelligence—the skills of emotional intelligence are ultimately ineffective in promoting high performance.

Moral intelligence is not just important to effective leadership—it is the "central intelligence" for all humans. Why? It's because moral intelligence directs our other forms of intelligence to do something worthwhile. Moral intelligence gives our life purpose. Without moral intelligence, we would be able to do things and experience events, but they would lack meaning. Without moral intelligence, we wouldn't know why we do what we do—or even what difference our existence makes in the great cosmic scheme of things.

A Renewable Asset. The more you develop your moral intelligence, the more positive changes you will notice, not only in your work but in your personal well-being. Staying true to your moral compass will not eliminate life's inevitable conflicts. Will you have to compromise sometimes between your beliefs and the demands of your work environment?

---

3. Daniel Goleman, Richard Boyatzis, Annie McKee, *Primal Leadership: Realizing the Power of Emotional Intelligence*, Harvard Business School Press, 2002.

4. Ibid.

Yes! Will you make mistakes? Will you sometimes say the wrong thing out of jealousy or greed? Definitely! But staying the moral course will give you singular personal satisfaction and professional rewards.

Your "Moral Positioning System." Think of moral intelligence as a "moral positioning system" for your life's journey, analogous to the global positioning system used in some cars as a navigational tool. You can be a great driver, and your car can have a powerful engine and four-wheel drive, but when it's dark and you've never been in this neck of the woods before, you have directions that were given you by someone who doesn't know street names, and you cannot see the map you got from AAA, you are lost. Despite all your tools and resources, you have no idea if you are headed in the right direction. But if your car had a global positioning system, it would be virtually impossible for you to get lost. Like having a GPS for your car, your moral intelligence allows you to better harness all your resources, your emotional intelligence, your technical intelligence, and your cognitive intelligence, to achieve the goals that are most important to you—whether on the job or in the rest of your life. Unlike today's GPSs, moral intelligence is not optional equipment. It is basic equipment for individuals who want to reach their best creative potential and business leaders who want to capture the best efforts of their workforce.

What Does Moral Intelligence Look Like? Most successful leaders are morally gifted, but very few of them are moral geniuses. They all make mistakes from time to time and, earlier in their careers, they typically made moral mistakes more often. But because of their high moral intelligence, they were quick studies. They held themselves accountable for their moral lapses, learned from them, and moved on. Consider Jay Coughlan's story. Today, Coughlan is the CEO of Lawson Software, but no one would have predicted his rise to that top spot back in 1998 after he fell asleep while driving intoxicated, causing a devastating accident that left him seriously injured and his father dead. The accident was the beginning of a remarkable personal transformation marked by a reawakening of his religious faith, a stronger relationship with his family and involvement in the community, and an intensive commitment to Lawson. Coughlan pleaded guilty to vehicular homicide and was sentenced to one month in jail, five months of house arrest, and 10 years of probation. But because of Coughlan's honesty and the support of the community, the judge reduced his offense to a misdemeanor after he had served over three months of his sentence. Meanwhile, during his absence from Lawson, the health care division that Coughlan had launched was flourishing. "That's when I learned I actually was successful as a leader," he told *The Wall Street Journal*, "when you can pull yourself out of the machine and it can still run."[5] His financial results were impressive and likely were the most significant factor in his subsequent promotions. The accident would have been a career-ending event for most people in Coughlan's shoes, but his response to the accident was extraordinary. "Jay, to his credit, stood right up and took responsibility; there was no hesitation," says Richard Lawson, the company's chairman and former CEO. "To me that is what counts. It's not the mistakes you make, it's how you react to those mistakes."

Lynn Fantom, CEO of ID Media, the largest direct response media service company in the U.S., is another morally gifted leader. It is late in the afternoon one cool spring day when Lynn walks back to her corner office in a New York City skyscraper. The Empire State Building is visible out one window, the Met Life and Flat Iron building out the other. Lynn barely notices the spectacular view. She goes straight to her desk and opens an e-mail from a Human Resources manager at her parent company, Interpublic. HR, it seems, is worried about how overloaded she is. They wonder if it is the best use of her time to respond to the employee comments and questions she gets on the "Ask Lynn" column on the company's intranet. Her public relations folks are also concerned about her schedule. They've recommended that she stop

---

5. Reported in Marcelo Prince, "Manager Discovers Leadership in an Accident's Aftermath," *The Wall Street Journal*, April 5, 2002.

spending precious time posting her thoughts on media and marketing trends on the intranet. But Lynn thinks her personal responses to employees are an important part of the ID Media culture. She thinks that "Ask Lynn" gives her an opportunity to demonstrate that she cares about her workforce. She thinks that she has a responsibility to her workforce to share her business insights. To her, it's time well spent. Lynn is certain that employees like knowing they can ask her about anything and that she will give them an honest response. They also like knowing that she understands market trends and shares her understanding with them. "In exchange," says Lynn, "I really get their commitment to help us succeed." Lynn is sticking to her principles. She won't be giving up her intranet contributions anytime soon.

Moral Intelligence and Business Success. Though leaders may attribute their companies' success to their commitment to moral principles, their evidence is based only on their personal experiences. So far, there has been no quantitative research that specifically studied the business impact of moral intelligence. But there are objective indications that moral intelligence is critical to the financial performance of your business. One measure of the influence of moral intelligence on business results comes from American Express Financial Advisors, an American Express company that implemented a highly effective emotional competence training program. American Express defined *emotional competence* as "the capacity to create alignment between goals, actions, and values." The program emphasized development of self-leadership and interpersonal effectiveness and demonstrated how those emotional skills led to business and personal success. The bottom line impact of the program was impressive, with participants in a pilot group producing sales that were 18 percent higher than a control group that didn't have the benefit of the training—no small change in a company that managed or owned assets in excess of $232 billion at the time. At the heart of the program was a special subset of skills that helped people to discover their principles and values and then create goals and action steps that flowed from those deeply held principles and values. American Express Financial Advisors' leaders came to realize that it was this overriding moral framework, that is, the emphasis on *principles* and *values*, that accounted for much of the success of the program. American Express had already found from internal studies that the most successful advisors were highly confident, resilient under adverse circumstances, and, most importantly, acted from a strong core of principles and values. To form trusting partnerships with clients, advisors needed to be genuinely trustworthy. To be seen as trustworthy, advisors had to act in accordance with worthwhile personal values. If advisors practiced the self-management and social skills they learned in the training, but failed to operate from moral principles and values, they would fall short of sustainable success.

While American Express' data demonstrates the importance of an individual advisor's moral intelligence to financial performance, other businesses have discovered that they produce the best results when their company overall is known for its moral intelligence. Market research tells us that consumers judge a company's reputation mainly on the basis of its perceived values. A company's reputation translates straight to the bottom line: Consumers prefer to make purchases from companies who are known for their ethical practices.[6]

The business case for moral intelligence gets another boost from a study done at DePaul University in Chicago. Researchers from the School of Accountancy and MIS compared the financial performance of 100 companies selected by *Business Ethics* magazine as "Best Corporate Citizens" with the performance of the rest of the S&P 500. Corporate citizenship rankings were based on quantitative measures of corporate service to seven stakeholder groups: stockholders, employees, customers, the community, the environment, overseas stakeholders, and women and minorities. The study found that overall financial performance of the 2001 Best Corporate Citizen companies was significantly

6. Cone/Roper Cause Related Trends Report, 1999.

better than the rest of the S&P 500. The average performance of the Best Citizens, as measured by the 2001 *Business Week* rankings of total financial performance, was more than 10 percentile points higher than the mean rankings of the rest of the S&P 500. According to *Strategic Finance* magazine, which reported the study, "It casts doubt on the persistent myth that good citizenship tends to lead to additional costs and thus negatively impacts a firm's financial results."[7]

Moral Intelligence and the War for Talent. Everyone agrees that talent is a key corporate asset, no matter what the state of the economy. A company's best employees can walk out the door at any time. They are much more likely to take their expertise and potential elsewhere if they don't like the ethical or moral tenor of their workplace.[8] Sometimes, this manifests itself as a reaction to an organization that fails to embrace universal human principles; at other times, the talent walks simply because their immediate supervisor or boss is lacking in moral intelligence. Several years ago, a young man we know abruptly quit a job that he had been thrilled to get only a few months before. He loved the work and loved the product—selling sports hospitality pack-ages of high-profile sports events to large corporations—but couldn't tolerate the moral climate. Some years before beginning his job, his company had run afoul of a major sports association for using mislead-ing and unethical tactics to get people to buy tickets for a major golfing competition and was now under a court order that prevented them from lying to get people to buy tickets. The company's solution was to create two sales scripts for the golfing competitions—an "official" sales script for marketers to keep by the phone and show to the CEO if he stopped by. The actual sales script used by the marketers was the same kind of misleading pitch that had gotten the company into hot water in the first place. The final straw for this young man came when he was asked to start selling tickets for a major tennis event. There was a huge surplus of

7. *Strategic Finance*, Vol. 83, No. 7, p. 20, January 2002.
8. National Business Ethics Survey 2000, www.ethics.org/2000survey.html.

tickets for this event because the company's usual big-spending corporate clients were not buying, no doubt in the wake of a weak economy and the public furor over corporate accounting irregularities. The sales script he was told to use was essentially this: "WorldCom originally signed up for a block of tickets and had already made their first payment of 50%. They have now backed out, for obvious reasons. So you can get the full deal by paying only half of the original cost." In fact, the company never had a deal with WorldCom, but was fabricating a plausible story to avoid embarrassment and encourage sales.

It's not just your current employees who expect a morally intelligent workplace. First-time job seekers increasingly rate the ethical character of prospective employees as a consideration in their decisions about where to work.[9] Patrick Gnazzo, vice president of business practices for the manufacturer, United Technologies Corp. in Hartford, Connecticut, reported in a *The Wall Street Journal* article that a growing number of their job candidates apply for positions with UTC based on the job seekers' research into the company's ethics program.[10]

Moral Stupidity. The business advantages of moral intelligence may be hard to quantify, but the business costs of moral ignorance are undeniable. We have all seen more than enough images of corporate executives being carted off in handcuffs. But by now, it's clear that the corporate accounting scandals of 2001–2002 were more than blips on the business radar screen. At the time of this writing midway through 2004…

- Mitsubishi Motors' former president and 10 other senior leaders are in jail on charges related to systematic suppression of widespread vehicle defects. Five of those were charged with negligence related to a fatal accident caused by a known defect in one of its automobile models.

9. Reported in Kris Maher, "Wanted: Ethical Employer: Job Hunters, Seeking to Avoid an Enron or an Andersen, Find It Isn't Always Easy," *The Wall Street Journal,* July 9, 2002.

10. Ibid.

- Former Adelphia Communications CEO, John Rigas, and his son Timothy were convicted of hiding more than $2 billion in debt while embezzling cash for numerous extravagances.

- The Securities and Exchange Commission has charged Lucent Technologies with "fraudulently and improperly" recognizing more than $1 billion in revenues and $470 million in pre-tax income during fiscal 2000.

- After a two-year investigation, former Enron CEO Ken Lay has been indicted on several counts of fraud.

- Richard Scrushy, former chairman and CEO of health-care services provider, HealthSouth Corporation, faces trial in 2005 for $2.5 billion in accounting frauds. More than a dozen HealthSouth executives have already pleaded guilty in the case.

Corporate moral dysfunction does more than hurt stock performance. Remember those consumers who like to purchase from ethical companies? They also hesitate to buy from unethical ones, and they don't hesitate to make their displeasure known. More than 70 percent of American consumers have, at some point, punished companies they view as unethical either by avoiding a company's products or speaking negatively about the company to others.[11] Mitsubishi is feeling the effects of consumer punishment: It expects its Japanese sales to drop 40 percent in fiscal year 2005 in the wake of its recent scandal.

The evidence is clear—moral intelligence plays a big part in corporate success. Without it, your organization risks devastating financial failure. The implications for your leadership effectiveness? If you pay attention to your own moral intelligence and encourage development of moral intelligence throughout your organization, you inspire the best efforts of everyone—and your performance will outpace your rivals'. It is possible to get ahead without moral intelligence—everyone knows of

11. Millennium Poll on Corporate Social Responsibility, *Environics International Ltd.*, May 1999.

powerful executives who have done well despite notable moral lapses. But they could do even better if they tapped into their moral smarts. Without moral intelligence, long-term business success is ultimately not sustainable. *Fortune* magazine rated Enron one of its "globally most admired" companies the year before its infamous collapse, and Arthur Andersen, arguably once the gold standard in accounting firms, is defunct.

Of course, moral intelligence isn't the only determinant of sustainable business performance. You also need solid business skills, and you need a product or service that people want to buy. What's more, moral intelligence won't immunize your company from the financial ups and downs of doing business in a volatile economy. But you need it to *stay* in business over the long haul.

Take your leadership to the next level—go beyond the usual formulas for leadership success and become the kind of leader who inspires the very best efforts of everyone who works with you. But how do you begin? Exactly how does moral intelligence produce better business performance? What are the specific moral skills you need to inspire the best efforts of your workforce? How can your organization—whether large or small—use moral intelligence to create high-performing work environments? You find answers to these questions in the pages that follow.

Born to Be Moral

What makes a leader effective? Turns out, the best leaders are not the charismatic or heroic types lionized in years past. According to the latest research, they are "quiet leaders" who accomplish great things modestly and without fanfare.[1] Leaders at the helm of the perennially great companies all share a common trait—humility.[2] They inspire high performance in others through their sensitivity to their followers' needs.[3] The best leaders think "we," not "I."[4] They are, quite simply, good people who consistently tap into their inborn disposition to be moral. They follow a moral compass—even when it's tempting not to.

1. Joseph Badaracco, Jr. *Leading Quietly*, Boston: Harvard Business School Press, 2002.
2. Jim Collins. *Good to Great: Why Some Companies Make the Leap…and Others Don't,* New York: Harper Collins, 2001.
3. Dan Goleman, Richard Boyatzis, Annie McKee. *Primal Leadership: Realizing the Power of Emotional Intelligence*, Boston: Harvard Business School Press, 2002.
4. Peter Drucker. "What Makes an Effective Executive," *Harvard Business Review*, June 2004.

They make hard choices between right and wrong, or even between two different "rights." Great people—and great leaders—share common moral values. They believe in honesty and in being responsible for themselves and others. They show compassion for their fellow humans and know how to forgive others—and just as important—themselves.

What the Best Leaders Believe

The most effective leaders hold to a common set of principles and consistently use those principles to guide their day-to-day actions. The principles business leaders follow *are the same set of principles that all human societies throughout time have believed to be "right."* These fundamental beliefs have been embedded in human society for so long that they are now widely recognized as *universal.*

It's no coincidence that good leaders, no matter what their style or personality, all seem to follow the beat of the same drum. They don't make up their values as they go along; they listen carefully to the call of moral values that already lie within all of us.

Universal Principles. Noted anthropologist Donald E. Brown found in his research that the moral codes of all cultures include recognition of responsibility, reciprocity, and ability to empathize.[5] Other studies have confirmed his findings.[6] The major world religions preach common values: commitment to something greater than self, responsibility, respect, and caring for others. Genuine differences in behavior in different cultures may distract us from what we have in common with all people— *a universal moral compass.* Consider a study that compared children

---

5. Donald E. Brown. *Human Universals*, Philadelphia: Temple University Press, 1991.
6. R.T. Kinnier, J.L. Kernes, and T.M. Dautheribes. "A Short List of Universal Moral Principles," *Counseling and Values*, October 1, 2000.

in India with American children.[7] The differences in values were predictable: Indian children displayed more deference to elders and acceptance of tradition, while American children valued personal autonomy and freedom. But their moral codes were virtually identical. Both groups of children believed that it was wrong to lie, cheat, or steal, and both thought that it was important to treat the sick or unfortunate with kindness.

Stephen Covey, author of *The Seven Habits of Highly Effective People*, offers more evidence of universal principles. "From my experiences in working with different people and cultures," he says, "I find that if certain conditions are present when people are challenged to develop a value system, they will identify essentially the same values. Each culture may express those values differently, but the underlying moral sense is always the same."[8]

Good leadership is not a function of some rare talent for inspiring others. Each one of us can be a good person and a great leader because we are all "hard-wired" to be moral. We were born that way. A glance at the news headlines might make that hard to believe, but here's why we think it is so.

A Visit to the Nursery

Walk into a hospital nursery, and you enter another world. It's bright and bustling, and its residents—most not more than a day or two old—are amazingly social. In the nursery, there is no such thing as one crying infant. When one begins to cry, the others join in. Psychologists who study newborn behavior call this "neonate responsive crying." The newborn is crying in reaction to another person's distress. How can a baby only a few hours old respond to someone else's pain? Researchers

---

7. Reported in Damon W. "The Moral Development of Children," *Scientific American*, August 1999.
8. Covey SR. "Universal Principles," *Executive Excellence,* May 1, 2000.

aren't sure how, but they have ruled out other explanations for the infant's response. It seems newborns don't cry when they hear a recording of their own crying—so it can't be the noise itself that's bothering them. Many psychologists believe that neonate responsive crying is the first indication of an inborn capacity for empathy. To become compassionate moral beings, we first need the ability to see the world through others' eyes (or hear their world through their cries!). Empathy is a key step in which infants appreciate that others exist independently of them and that others have their own separate needs. Yet the simple appreciation that others have emotions and physical needs and are completely separate from us is not sufficient to make us moral beings. We can still, as many children (and adults) do, decide that the search for our own pleasures justifies our causing others pain.

Nature Versus Nurture

The explanation? Moral hard-wiring is not enough. We also need *moral software*, the programming that our moral hardware relies on to make moral choices. Like any other human capacity, morality is a combination of our biology (our nature) and our experiences (our nurture). Take language, for example. You speak at least one language fluently. But you couldn't speak a word when you were born. You had to learn to speak. We know that speech is a learned proficiency because children invariably speak the language of their caregivers. But we also know that language requires an inborn capacity to speak and comprehend. Development of our morality follows a similar path. No one could teach us right and wrong unless we were wired to acquire, and act on, a moral compass. But just as we don't come out of the womb spouting Shakespeare, we are not born with a fully operational moral compass. It takes time—and the right set of experiences—to become fully moral.

Growing Up Moral

Let's pick up the story of our moral development as we leave the nursery. Our newborn crying response sets the stage for a more mature empathy that emerges gradually during our early childhood. By the time we are two or three months old, we begin to respond to the emotional expressions of our primary caregiver. We play with our parents by making faces and exchanging excited noises with each other. By five months of age, we can tell that there is a difference among different emotional expressions of others. By the time we are one year old, we can tell that facial expressions or changes of voice intonation have particular emotional meanings. We then know that other people have feelings that are distinct from our own. If you have been around one-year olds, you may have seen them checking out other people's reactions to figure out how they themselves should respond to a situation. Parents often take advantage of this habit to prevent a child from getting upset over a minor tumble. If a child falls down, she will look to her parent to see how that parent is reacting. If the parent stays calm, it is likely that the child will also. Empathy development continues at a rapid clip throughout the second year. By 15 to 18 months of age, we share, cooperate, and give care, as long as the situation is not too stressful. Think of the 16 month-old who tries to pat someone who is crying. By two years of age, we are very empathic people. We try to comfort people in distress. We express sympathy. We make suggestions. We bring a tissue to someone who is crying.

Learning to Be Responsible

But more than empathy is developing. By age two, we begin to show some grasp of justice, responsibility, and blame. We have all heard children as young as three or four respond to real or imagined injustice with an emphatic, "That's not fair!" Many of us begin at an early age to do

things we know will be upsetting to others. Being negative is an important part of learning to be moral. If we didn't do bad things once in a
while, it would be difficult to understand the difference between right
and wrong behavior. Think of the earliest time you can remember doing
something wrong. How old were you? What did you do? How did you
know it was the wrong thing to do? Most of us can recall getting in trouble with our parents for some early childhood infraction. They used
those incidents to teach us some version of the "golden rule"— treat
others as you would wish to be treated. *Think of others. Don't take
something that belongs to someone else. Tell the truth.* We learn to be
moral, not just from being scolded for bad behavior, but by being loved
unconditionally for who we are. We grow morally through the interplay
between our biological disposition to be empathetic and through our
loving relationship with our parents. Because they love us, we love
them, and because we love them, we work to please them. Eventually,
we adopt our parents' values because we want to be like them.
Throughout our preschool years, we grow in empathy and in our moral
sense. By the time we are six or seven years of age, we can tell right
from wrong and feel guilty if we do something we know we shouldn't.[9]

When Things Go Wrong

We tend to take the natural process of moral development for granted
until we see a situation where it doesn't happen. It can't happen, for
instance, if we are born with certain neurological problems. Moral
development also goes off course if our caregivers are not willing or
able to provide the right kind of early nurturing. Our parents don't need
to be perfect. They do need to be "good enough" to treat us well most of
the time.[10] They need to be consistently affectionate and dependable.

---

9. Jerome Kagan and Sharon Lamb (eds.). *The Emergence of Morality in Young
   Children*, Chicago: University of Chicago Press, 1987.

They must show us how to be empathetic, and they must help us develop positive beliefs about ourselves.

If our parents don't provide that kind of support, we won't be able to develop into those amazingly empathetic two year-olds and, later on, into morally competent adults. Again, moral development is much like language development. If you happened to be raised by wolves for the first five years of your life (as a rare number of people have been), you'll learn how to howl, but you'll probably never learn to speak normally. No amount of inborn ability to develop language can help you if you weren't also exposed to the right set of experiences at the right time.

Inside Your (Moral) Brain

In the previous section, we looked at our moral development from the outside in. We saw that our moral development, like language development, depends on both biology and learning. We saw that our relationship with our parents is key to our growing moral understanding. But we can't learn positive values and altruistic motivation before we are neurologically ready to acquire them.

Let's recall once again the crying babies in the hospital nursery. The empathic response of newborns happens so immediately that it is most likely genetically based rather than learned.[11] Think about the biological priorities involved: Before we can crawl or speak, we can respond empathically to our peers. Empathy must be incredibly important.

---

10. English Pediatrician D.W. Winnicott's concept of "good enough" parenting as described in Robert Cole's *The Moral Intelligence of Children*, New York: Random House, 1997.
11. Interpretation of Martin Hoffman's work on empathy by author William A. Rottschaefer in *The Biology and Psychology of Moral Agency*, Cambridge, UK: Cambridge University Press, 1998.

We also learned that by age two, those of us who have been exposed to "good enough" parenting spontaneously demonstrate helping behavior. What is going on in our brains at age two? The brain of a normal two year old who has had "good enough" parenting also happens to have a normal limbic system—the part of the brain that is involved in emotional processing. But if we haven't had "good enough" parenting, our brains do not grow normally. When a child has been abused or neglected, the cortical and subcortical areas of the brain are roughly *20 to 30 percent smaller* than normal. In addition, the brain "wiring" isn't as dense or complex so that abused or neglected children are lacking some brain organization that would allow them to make strong connections to other human beings.[12] Without those connections, no empathy is realized, and without empathy, you have impaired morality.

It's All in Your Head

Scientists who study the relationship between brain function and behavior are beginning to chart the "moral anatomy" of the brain. They've learned how the brain affects moral behavior by studying both normal and brain-injured individuals. Perhaps the most famous case of moral impairment caused by brain damage happened over 150 years ago. Phineas Gage headed up a group of men who were laying track for a new rail route across Vermont. Admired by family and friends, Gage also had a great reputation as a strong, intelligent, and efficient worker. But something went wrong one hot summer day in 1848, when the group was preparing to blast through rock to pave the way for the new track. The explosive went off prematurely, propelling a 13-pound iron rod through the prefrontal cortex of Gage's brain. Miraculously, Gage survived with his faculties intact—or so the doctors thought. He

12. Bruce Perry and Ronnie Pollard. "Altered brain development following global neglect in early childhood." *Society For Neuroscience: Proceedings from Annual Meeting*, New Orleans, 1997.

remained conscious, was able to speak and walk immediately after the injury, and survived a serious infection around the wound. Within two months, the doctors considered him cured. Gage looked the same as he always had, but his personality was completely altered, and his family and friends soon realized that the man they had known was gone. No longer able to work as a railway foreman, Gage began a downward spiral of impulsive, aggressive, and socially disconnected behavior that ended with his death from severe epileptic seizures in 1861.

Gage's chroniclers don't tell us whether his value system was destroyed by his prefrontal injury or whether he was simply unable to act on a value system that survived his injury. For practical purposes, it did not matter—either way, Gage could no longer function as a moral being. But there is a big practical distinction between *moral intelligence* (our internal moral compass) and *moral competence* (our ability to act in alignment with what we know is right). Most of us know what's right. Sometimes, though, it's a struggle to do what we know is right— when we lack the moral competence to act in alignment with our moral compass. Researchers have discovered that our brain makes the same distinction. When neuroscientists compared the behavior of two adults who had suffered prefrontal brain injuries as infants with patients who had suffered similar injuries as adults, they found a striking difference in their post-injury capacities.[13]

One patient, a woman, was run over by a car when she was 15-months old. Although she recovered from her physical injuries, her parents were dismayed to discover that by the time she was three-years old, she simply did not respond to verbal instructions or even physical punishment. Although her intelligence was normal, her behavior became increasingly disruptive, and she could not function in a regular school.

13. Steven W. Anderson, Antoine Bechara, Hanna Damasio, Daniel Tranel, Antonio R. Damasio. "Impairment of Social and Moral Behavior Related to Early Damage in Human Prefrontal Cortex," *Nature Neuroscience*, Vol. 2 No. 11, November 1999.

As a teenager, she shoplifted, stole, lied, and was verbally and physically abusive. She showed no remorse for her behavior, blamed her misdeeds on others, and seemed incapable of empathy. The second patient, a man, had surgery for a brain tumor when he was three-months old. He seemed to recover fully from his surgery, and his parents were relieved that his physical development was normal, given that he began to walk and talk on a typical timetable. He seemed a little behind academically in early elementary school, and by age nine, his overall behavior was becoming cause for concern. He was generally unmotivated, had few social contacts with peers, and lacked normal expressiveness, although occasionally he would lose his temper. He got through high school, but after graduation, his behavior deteriorated. He sat around watching TV or listening to music, ate his way into obesity, and neglected his personal hygiene. He could not keep a job and he committed numerous petty crimes. Like the first patient, he showed no guilt or remorse for his bad behavior and seemed incapable of empathy for others.

What actually caused the behavioral problems of the two brain-injured individuals? Both came from middle-class homes with attentive, college-educated parents, so we can assume they had "good enough" parenting. Neurological testing showed that both were normal on tests of basic mental ability. But when they were tested on tasks that required them to use reasoning to guide social behavior, they had trouble. Their moral capabilities were severely impaired. On moral reasoning tasks, they were only able to think about moral situations from the perspective of avoiding punishment, much like that of children before 9 years of age. They lacked any capacity for moral reasoning based on the "golden rule" or any ability to consider what is fair from an empathetic perspective.

Because the two suffered their brain injuries so early in life, their moral capabilities were more severely affected than those of people who suffer brain injuries later in life. People whose brains are injured as adults show different levels of moral impairment. People with adult-onset injuries have already acquired their moral reasoning ability as part of normal childhood development. They may have had years of experience in applying moral judgments in actual life situations before becoming injured. If you ask people who have suffered an adult-onset brain injury to respond to a hypothetical moral reasoning scenario, for example, *should someone steal a drug to save someone's life*, they are quite able to tell you what the morally correct decision should be. In real life, however, they don't seem able to put their abstract moral sense into practice. Researchers speculate that the part of the brain that holds emotionally related knowledge essential for good moral decision making has been disabled or disconnected by the adult-onset brain injury, even though the individual retains factual knowledge of moral rules. Young children who suffer a prefrontal brain injury apparently never get the chance to learn the moral rules because the part of their brains that would have allowed them to develop moral reasoning has been unalterably damaged. The impact of the time of injury is considerable. Adult-onset brain injury patients suffer impairments in their social and moral behavior but generally do not display the kind of anti-social or criminal behavior characteristic of people who suffered prefrontal brain damage in infancy.[14]

The Moral Map of Your Brain

Studies of brain-damaged individuals tell us what general area of the brain is involved in moral reasoning and decision-making. They don't tell us exactly how our brains typically function when confronted with a moral decision. To find out, scientists have been studying the brains of normal individuals (if you can call college students who are the most common research subjects "normal") using a technique called "functional magnetic resonance imaging (fMRI)." Functional MRIs resemble

14. Ibid.

the MRI procedures that you might have undergone to diagnose an injury or illness. Regular MRIs produce "snapshots" of thin slices of body tissue, while functional MRIs use an advanced scanner that detects changes in blood flow to areas of the brain. When a particular part of the brain is involved in a certain activity, the fMRI image of that area "lights up." For example, if you were put under an fMRI scanner and you heard a loud noise, the area of your brain that processes sound would show a lot more activity. fMRI technology is now being used to chart the unique parts of the brain involved in our moral intelligence. One study, for example, found that viewing pictures with moral content (such as physical assaults, poor children abandoned in the streets, war scenes) *activated distinct areas of the brain that were not activated by any of the other types of pictures,* including those with strong emotional content.[15]

Why We're Good and Why We're Bad

It's clear we are programmed to be moral. But why? Though many philosophers and psychologists believe that truly moral emotions are uniquely human, anthropologists have found evidence of altruism, fairness, and empathy in other species. A whale, for instance, might go to the aid of a sick member of the pod, or a squirrel might risk its own safety by giving a warning call about a nearby predator. Perhaps the reason we are programmed to be moral comes not from our uniqueness as a species, but from what we have in common with other species such as whales, squirrels, or chimpanzees—we all live in social groups. As members of social societies, we need others to help us survive and prosper.

---

15. Fabio Sala. "Do Programs Designed to Increase Emotional Intelligence at Work- Work?" *Research Report, Hay/McBer Group and Consortium for Research on Emotional Intelligence in Organizations* (http://www.eiconsortium.org/research/ do_ei_programs_work.htm).

Most of us are familiar with Charles Darwin's theory of natural selection, the idea of "survival of the fittest." Darwin believed that plants and animals with physical characteristics that help them survive are more likely to reproduce—carrying their survival-friendly genes forward into future generations. Similarly, it is likely that altruistic and cooperative behavior is part of basic human behavior today because it was crucial to the survival of our early human ancestors.[16] People who banded together were better able to master the elements, fight off predators, and acquire food. Individuals who cooperated and helped others tended to live longer. They were more likely to procreate and thereby get their traits into the gene pool. As an example, the tendency to provide care for helpless infants would be an advantage to our species, protecting us from extinction. Because early humans lived in small groups of related individuals, we would expect to see in our own behavior today a tendency to care for our relatives. Given the complexity of contemporary society, it's likely that evolution has favored the genes of those who extended their cooperation beyond their immediate kin. What would have guided those cooperative relationships of our earliest ancestors? It's not hard to see how the Golden Rule might have evolved—*treat others as you would like to be treated*—is a practical principle for living harmoniously and working for the common good.

So What Went Wrong?

If it is true that we have been wired over eons to follow the Golden Rule, how then can we explain all of its flagrant violations? We could try to write off crime and cruelty as mutations of normal human nature. Most of us, however, realize that there is a dark side to our own nature. There are times when selfishness prevails, when other needs overtake us and we will not, or think we cannot, do what we know is right.

---

16. E.O. Wilson, author of *Sociobiology: The New Synthesis*. Cambridge, MA: Belknap Press, 1975, a pioneer of sociobiological theory.

According to Harvard Business School professors Paul Lawrence and Nitin Nohria, we all have four basic human drives created by evolution to improve survival.[17] Our drives can sometimes conflict. For example, the competitiveness generated by our drive to acquire will often act at odds with our desire to cooperate, driven by our desire to bond. We see the conflict play out in young children who want exclusive use of a new toy at the same time that they want to play with their friends. We see it in corporations where senior managers rake in salaries that are 100 or 1,000 times greater than that of some employees, while preaching to their employees—and honestly believing—that "we're all in this together." In the battle between competing drives, selfishness often wins out. We may want to live by the Golden Rule, but in some cases, the drive to acquire or defend overtakes our drive to bond. Lawrence and Nohria also point out that there is a "dark side" to each drive. Even the drive to bond, arguably the foundation of human morality, has a dark side, setting us up to define an "in group" and an "out group." We bond with our "in group." It is a series of short steps from connecting with our own group to demonizing an "out group." Early humans flourished by expanding their definitions of their "in group." At this time in history, our survival may depend on expanding our "in group" to include all the people of the earth. With the inevitable march of globalization, in which economic trouble in one country reverberates throughout the global economy, the need to recognize the importance of interdependence is even clearer. Radioactive material from nuclear warfare or HIV and SARS viruses do not recognize cultural or governmental boundaries. Balancing competing drives and managing the dark side of our human nature is the essence of moral intelligence. Choosing among competing desires is the essence of morality. There is no morality without choice. Making decisions between our sometimes competing drives requires us to make moral choices. It is our moral intelligence, the ability to balance competing drives, that makes us truly human.

17. Paul Lawrence and Nitin Nohria. *Driven: How Human Nature Shapes our Choices.* San Francisco: Jossey-Bass, October 2001.

Moral Software

By now, you should have a flavor for the compelling evidence that we are biologically wired to be moral. We have used the analogy that our innate moral disposition is our "moral hardware." We come into the world with rudimentary skills, such as empathy, which are the building blocks for our moral intelligence. Before we are two years of age, we seem naturally to help others in distress, and by the time we are four or five, have a good idea of what our parents and caretakers think is right and wrong. Our moral hardware is preinstalled, and the upgrades come online surprisingly quickly. We turn now to our "moral software," the content of our moral compass that we use to make moral decisions. If you and I were to compare our moral software, we would find that some of our software is identical, while other aspects of our software are specific to the culture or family we grew up in. We live in an age where cultural diversity is increasingly respected. There has been a great deal of academic research documenting the customs and rules of conduct of different ethnic groups and societies, as well as concern about the homogenization of cultures as a result of the enormous economic influence of the United States across the globe. It has been far less fashionable lately to look for the principles all people share in common. But we think it is important to pay attention to the moral principles we all hold in common. It is not that we think everyone should have identical moral beliefs. But we do think that the existence of universal moral principles offers yet more proof that we are wired to be moral. Beyond the biological implications, the existence of universal principles may be our best hope for surviving and thriving in an inescapably intertwined global community. If all people of the earth share a small list of critical principles in common, together we will be better able to make decisions that could determine the survival of the planet.

What are the universal principles, and how do we know that they are indeed universal? Anthropologist Donald E. Brown is one of the most reliable sources for information about the human activities that are found in all societies and cultures. Human universals, he says, "comprise those features of culture, society, language, behavior, and psyche for which there are no known exception." In his book, *Human Universals*,[18] Brown provides an exhaustive list of universals, including the ability to distinguish right from wrong, and notes that universally peoples' morality includes recognition of responsibility, reciprocity, and ability to empathize. In another study, researchers Richard T Kinnier, Jerry L Kernes, and Therese M Dautheribes identified a short list of universal principles by analyzing earlier lists and examining the official tenets of major world religions.[19] Their rationale was that the principles held in common by major world religions are the ones most likely to be universal and enduring. They found the following principles espoused in common by all or most religions, as well as by secular organizations including American Atheists, Inc., the American Humanist Association, and the United Nations Declaration of Rights:

- Commitment to something greater than oneself
- Self-respect, but with humility, self-discipline, and acceptance of personal responsibility
- Respect and caring for others (that is, the Golden Rule)
- Caring for other living things and the environment

Finally, noted psychologist Martin Seligman and his colleagues in the field of "positive psychology" have conducted research that led them to identify six "universal virtues" honored in all cultures in the world: wisdom, courage, humanity, justice, temperance, and transcendence.[20] Although the labels might vary slightly and though each culture may

---

18. Donald E. Brown. *Human Universals,* New York: McGraw-Hill, 1991.
19. R.T. Kinnier, J.L. Kernes, and T.M. Dautheribes. "A Short List of Universal Moral Principles," *Counseling and Values,* October 1, 2000.
20. Christopher Peterson and Martin E.P. Seligman. *Character Strengths and Virtues: A Handbook and Classification,* Oxford, UK: Oxford University Press, 2004.

express these principles differently, the underlying moral sense is always the same. We believe that these universal principles exist, even though we know they are not universally applied. We believe that living in alignment with these principles is crucial to our individual and organizational survival and success.

Libraries are crowded with hundreds of books offering detailed explanations for the emergence of moral intelligence in the human species. They lend weight to the notion that it is as important to be moral as it is to drink, eat, breathe, or be active. How we exercise our moral intelligence is as critical to our health and happiness as eating well and staying physically fit. In the next chapter, consider a concrete framework for understanding your personal moral compass and the role it plays in your effectiveness as a leader.

3

Your Moral Compass

As we've just seen, nearly all of us have an inborn "talent" to be moral. But talent is never enough. Think of the major league baseball teams who spend fortunes on rookies and then send them off to farm teams for a few years to hone their skills. Professional ball players begin with *baseball intelligence*, but they must train hard to turn their baseball intelligence into on-the-field *baseball competence*. So they practice technical skills such as batting or pitching, along with non-technical skills such strategy, judgment, and emotional composure. Why do they work so hard? Because they want to satisfy their goals and desires. Maybe they like winning, or money, or adulation, or they love playing the game. Successful ball players know that getting what they want means doing whatever it takes to reach their goals. In other words, the best ball players make sure that their talents, skills, and actions are *aligned* with their goals.

Reaching our own personal goals also requires alignment. When we decide to start a daily exercise program but never get on the treadmill, we feel uneasy because our actions are inconsistent with our goals. If we want to go on vacation, we feel good when we book the flight because we're doing something to reach our goal. Similarly, most of us want to be moral because we crave that experience of consistency between our moral values, our goals, and our actions. We call that state of moral consistency "living in alignment."

Think of living in alignment as the interconnection of three frames:

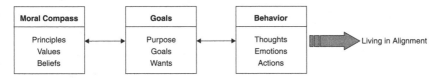

FIGURE 3.1   Living in Alignment

The first frame contains your moral compass—basic moral principles, personal values, and beliefs. The second frame holds your goals. Your goals range from the lofty (your life's purpose) to the ordinary (a new house). The third frame contains your behavior, including inward thoughts, emotions, and external actions. Living in alignment means that your behavior is consistent with your goals and that your goals are consistent with your moral compass. Living in alignment keeps you on course to accomplish your life purpose and achieve the best possible performance in all your life roles.

Dale Lauer is an executive vice president with Safeco Insurance Company. Living in alignment is key to his success and longevity with his company. "The fact that I work for Safeco," says Dale, "and that I've been here for a long time is because the company aligns well personally with my own moral code. You need to work for a company that you're aligned with or you'll have stress every day." Dale believes that alignment was at the heart of Safeco's heralded turnaround. According to Dale, "The turnaround at Safeco is a clear financial result of practicing values of trust, honesty, loyalty, and responsibility. People on the front line, who really make the company what it is, responded because the leadership exhibited those values." But living in alignment isn't always easy, especially when personal values conflict. Dale had to lay off a number of people he'd worked with for years, including a close friend and weekly golf partner. Balancing personal loyalty with his responsibility to his company was painful. It meant doing the right thing for Safeco's future and, at the same time, doing whatever he could to ease laid-off employees' transition to other employment.

Living in alignment may sometimes be difficult, but it doesn't require superhuman acts. It is about the day-to-day steps we take to do what we need to do to reach our goals. One of our colleagues used to avoid speaking engagements before large audiences, preferring to work with people one on one or in small groups. Eventually, he realized that he could not effectively communicate his values and beliefs if he limited himself to small group presentations. So he joined Toastmasters, the worldwide organization that helps people develop their public-speaking abilities. Our friend's desire to have a positive impact on the world led him to work on overcoming the anxiety of large group presentations.

Living in alignment is not accidental. It requires doing things on purpose and for a purpose. How to begin? Living in alignment is a two-part process: First, build your own personal alignment model:

- **Moral Compass**—What do you value, and what are your most important beliefs?

- **Goals**—What do you want to accomplish personally and professionally?

- **Behavior**—What actions will allow you to achieve your goals?

Then, after you've built your own alignment model and know what ideally should be in each frame, you do your best to maintain alignment among your frames.

Your Moral Compass. Your moral compass consists of principles, values, and beliefs that guide your aspirations and your actions. Everyone has one. Suppose we asked you to tell us about your moral compass. What would you say? What is the set of values that anchors you? How would you want others to think of you? Our guess is that you would describe an interesting and accomplished person, one whose actions are guided by a set of admirable values, not unlike the ones we heard earlier.

Everyone is predisposed to be moral. That doesn't mean that we always act in accordance with our values, just that it is very difficult to find someone who doesn't have positive values, even where you would least expect to find them—behind prison walls. Consider this dialogue from a personal effectiveness seminar conducted for inmates in a work/study program at a maximum security prison in Minnesota:

> *Seminar Leader*: "How many of you know people in here that you would describe as having praiseworthy values?"
>
> *Inmates*: All raise their hands.
>
> *Seminar Leader:* "What do you suppose it was that you found in each other that caused you to feel this way?"
>
> *An Inmate*: "I think what we found was the little boy in each other."

This exchange is touching but not surprising if you factor in what psychologists tell us about the formation of values. Most people, assuming their brains are intact, have developed good core values by the time they reach the age of four. Nearly everyone, no matter how they actually behave, wants to be a good person. As we saw earlier, everyone with a normally functioning brain has one, and nearly everyone's moral compass bears a striking resemblance to everyone else's. That's because our moral compass is based largely on universal principles.

Embracing Universal Principles

Moral Compass:
Principles
Values
Beliefs

As we discussed in the last chapter, researchers have identified several overlapping principles that they judge to be universal. You might want to use the following worksheet to chose the words that describe universal principles that you embrace.

WORKSHEET 1   Embracing Universal Principles

Please look at the list and identify the principles that you embrace—the ones that clearly resonate with you as being very important or even the most important to you in your daily life. If you feel important values are missing, feel free to add your own at the bottom of the list. Select a total of four. Then, rank the four you selected in the box to the right.

1.	Integrity	
2.	Responsibility	
3.	Compassion	
4.	Forgiveness	
5.	Generosity	
6.	Commitment to a transcending power	
7.	Justice	
8.	Temperance/Self-Discipline	
9.	Humility	
10.	Care for living things and the environment	
11	Wisdom	
12.	Courage	

Now, list your chosen principles in rank order:

1. _____

2. _____

3. _____

4. _____

After you list the principles, check out your understanding of the principles with a trusted colleague, friend, or family member. Most of us don't make a habit of discussing universal principles in the course of a normal day, but if you do, you will discover the similarities in your and others' lists. You will validate the universal quality of the principles and will likely forge deeper connections with the people around you.

Universal Principles. When you wrote down your guiding principles, how many of these did you include in your top four—*integrity, responsibility, compassion, forgiveness?* The leaders studied and interviewed for this book consistently demonstrated the importance of these principles. They were at their most effective when acting in alignment with principles. When they ignored them, business results suffered. Integrity and responsibility are essential minimum requirements for effective leadership. Ed Zore, CEO of Northwestern Mutual , for example, attributes his personal success to his decision to work in a business that he thought added value to society.

Compassion and *forgiveness* may not be absolutely necessary, but they make the difference between a good leader who is essentially moral and a great leader who inspires exceptional performance in others. Consider the following examples of the business value of compassion.

Don MacPherson, co-president of the measurement company, Modern Survey, tells this story:

> **We lost a big client and went through some difficult times. One of my partners was getting married, and we were cutting salaries, including his. I knew he was facing a lot of stress. I left a note on his desk for him and his fiancée, along with a cash loan to help with the wedding expenses. They were both elated. He could have left the company during that difficult time, but he chose not to. Our business got healthy again. His salary was restored. He's a valuable part of our company to this day, and he has repaid the loan!**

Lynn Sontag, CEO of MENTTIUM Corporation, which helps companies nationwide coordinate mentoring programs for women with high potential, recalls:

> **Everyone here knows we walk our talk. We are both passionate and compassionate and that comes through. One of our women employees has had some health problems. She is a single parent with no extended family nearby. Other employees take her to medical appointments and we all chip in to make sure her work gets done when she can't be here. Another employee's husband had cancer requiring a bone marrow transplant. We agreed to and supported her working from home for six months. We've gained tremendous loyalty from our employees because of our approach. Our workforce is fully engaged, which contributes significantly to our company's performance.**

Discovering Your Values

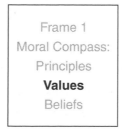

When we grew up, we learned a set of values, those qualities or standards that parents or caregivers considered important to our well-being and that of others. Over time, we came to adopt those values as guides to our own behavior. Families vary in the weight they place on certain values. Lori Kaiser, former VP for supercomputer maker Cray, Inc., came from a large family where grandparents, great aunts and uncles, and even older siblings all got involved in teaching moral lessons. They emphasized that telling the truth was not about avoiding getting caught in a lie and that the most important persons she had to answer to were herself and her higher power. When Lori was young, her mother once caught her telling a lie. Instead of punishing her like many parents might, Lori's mother simply told her, "That's your issue, not mine! Now what are you going to do about it?" Like Lori, most of us were raised to value honesty. Families often emphasize a variety of values, such as helping others, creativity, knowledge, or wealth accumulation. We may begin by adopting our families' values, and as we mature, we often add our own. By selecting, interweaving, and prioritizing our values, we define who we are—or at least who we want to be. Just as we recognize people by their physical characteristics such as hair color, height, or the way they laugh, we also come to know people by the values they embody. As we get to know friends or colleagues, we begin to recognize what means the most to them. Do they crave excitement, care about the environment, or seek status? We evaluate others based on how well our values mesh. You might value personal time for creative work more than social activities, while I might value relationships and family time more than professional recognition. We feel comfortable around people who share our most important values and often avoid those who don't.

Unlike universal principles, which by definition apply to everyone, values are individual. They are personal. There is an especially urgent reason for identifying your most important values. Life is finite. Values help us to be selective about how we spend our precious time. Without values, how would we decide what goals are worth having? From all the opportunities that life presents us, which are most important to us? While values can help us tell right from wrong, they can also help us to decide right from right by guiding our choice from among more than one attractive option. Suppose you had a choice between a job with a high salary and a lower paying overseas assignment that offered con-siderable opportunities for adventure and growth. How would you decide? Now suppose that both jobs would require that you spend a considerable amount of time away from your family. What would your decision be? Neither option is necessarily right or wrong in itself. To make the right decision, you would have to weigh the relative importance of personal values such as wealth, personal development, adventure, and family.

The Morality of Values

Not all values are created equal, as in the previous example. Without some context, values are neither moral nor immoral. It is only when we need to make decisions that have moral consequences that values take on moral significance. Being moral means more than honoring your personal value system. Because we choose our values, it is possible that personal values may be out of alignment with the principles. Try to imagine the contents of Osama bin Laden's moral compass. No one would deny that bin Laden has a strong value system, one that probably includes some admirable beliefs. But his willingness to harm innocent victims, including members of his own Islamic faith, in pursuit of his values, violates the universal principle of compassion. Osama bin Laden "walks his talk;" that is, his goals and actions are consistent with his values, but some of his values violate our universal moral compass. We don't have to travel half-way around the world for examples of values misalignment, as demonstrated in 2004 when several bankrupt U.S. airline companies used Chapter 11 to skip mandatory pension contributions, putting retirees' livelihoods in jeopardy.

When we make a decision that does not have any particular moral significance, as in deciding where to go on vacation, we might indulge our desire for adventure without a second thought. But when we are making a decision that involves others, as is the case when considering a career move that would affect family members, the priorities we assign to our values must be consistent with universal principles. In that instance, we must honor the principle of responsibility. We may realize that our desire for adventure, growth, or more money would come at the cost of our responsibility to family.

Identifying Your Values. As with every element of effective leadership, good decision-making requires clarity about your personal values. You can use the following worksheet to better understand your values and their relative importance in your life.

WORKSHEET 2:   Identifying Your Core Values

Please circle the number at the left of each personal value you believe to be one of your core values. If you feel important values are missing, feel free to add your own at the bottom of the list.

1.	Achievement	21.	Curiosity
2.	Power	22.	Spirituality
3.	Affiliation	23.	Altruism
4.	Thriftiness	24.	Perseverance
5.	Creativity	25.	Order
6.	Wealth	26.	Inner Peace
7.	Autonomy	27.	Gratitude
8.	Status	28.	Open-Mindedness
9.	Comfort	29.	Meaningful Work
10.	Safety	30.	Competence
11.	Wisdom	31.	Influencing Others
12.	Enjoyment	32.	Stability
13.	Friendship	33.	Challenges
14.	Health	34.	Competition
15.	Security	35.	Economic Security
16.	Service	36.	Cooperation
17.	Community	37.	
18.	Independence	38.	
19.	Loyalty	39.	
20.	Growth	40.	

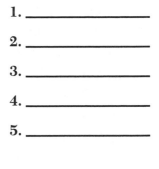

Now, select five you believe to be your most important core values and list them here:

1. _____

2. _____

3. _____

4. _____

5. _____

This short list of five most important values probably represents the aspects of life you hold most dear. That does not mean you will always behave in ways that are consistent with your ideal values. But if you consistently behave in ways that are in conflict with what you say you value, it may be useful to reexamine your values statement. Do you espouse a value because it is politically correct in your organization or because you were brought up to believe in it?

What Your Decisions Reveal About Your Values. Sometimes, we don't actually value what we say we do. If, over time, you find yourself behaving inconsistently with your espoused values, you have a choice. You can learn to better align your behavior with your values by developing your moral and emotional competencies, or you may simply accept that you value some things that you did not realize were important to you. Either path is fine, as long as your actions don't violate the universal principles.

To find out what your outward behavior can tell you about your values, keep a running log of all your decisions over the course of a few weeks. For each decision:

- Write down the values that influenced your decision.

- Ask yourself, "If people who did not know my inner motivations saw the outcome of this decision, what value or values would they think this decision reflected?

SAMPLE VALUES LOG

Problem and Decision	What Values Drove Your Decision	What Values Others Might Think Drove the Decision
Example: Financial shortfall in division led to laying off the three newest employees.	Responsibility to preserve jobs for the most by stabilizing the division. Loyalty to longer term employees.	Power—being seen as a take-charge leader. Financial gain—for company and for manager's bonus.
Example: A senior employee with many years of loyal service but a mixed reputation for competence is promoted to a new position.	Responsibility to reward and promote loyalty to organization. Compassion.	Friendship—in this case was more important than merit in promotion decisions. Order—making promotions predictable.

This exercise can give you some insight into personal motivations that you might not have admitted to yourself before. Consider whether the values others might attribute to your decision may actually have some bearing on your choices.

Uncovering Values Conflicts. After you identify what you value, ideally and really—look at your list of values and compare it with the universal principles. To ensure that your values are consistent with principles, ponder questions like these:

- Is my desire to achieve financial results so strong that I behave as if the end justifies the means?

- Does my desire for high achievement lead me to lack compassion for an employee whose family crisis takes him away from work at a critical time?

- Does my need for economic security discourage me from speaking out with integrity about an unethical corporate practice?

If you accept that universal principles universally apply, you must—as a morally intelligent leader—reprioritize your values in line with the principles. We are not saying that you should not value what you value. But in some cases, it will be important to find a way to honor your values while upholding principles. You can honor both principles and personal values when you look for answers to questions such as, *"How can I arrange my financial affairs so that I am protected if my ethical position gets me fired?* Or, *"How can I creatively allocate resources to preserve or improve group productivity while an employee is out on leave?"*

It should be clear by now that values can be applied in a morally bad, neutral, or positive way. We are not encouraging you to abandon your values in favor of certain values that may have a more obvious moral veneer.

Power's Value

Power often gets a bad rap. Power has the potential to be seductive, intoxicating, or lead to abuse. When power is abused, individuals and organization suffer. But like most other values, power can be leveraged for good or ill. Power that is used to promote universal principles is a tremendous force for organizational success and global advancement.

"The problem of power is how to achieve its responsible use rather than its irresponsible and indulgent use—of how to get men of power to live for the public rather than off the public."

—Robert F. Kennedy (1925–1968), "I Remember, I Believe,"
The Pursuit of Justice, 1964

Beliefs

Moral Compass:
Principles
Values
Beliefs

Beliefs are the third component of our guidance system. For each of us, our beliefs are the "executive summary" of our individual world view. Beliefs represent our self-understanding about what we think is important and how we think of ourselves in relation to the outer world. They are the condensed version of our moral compass. Beliefs capture our larger list of principles and values in a streamlined form that is easier to communicate. Beliefs are the language we use to describe our values and our understanding of principles to ourselves and others. They connect our understanding of principles with our choice of values. You can't really know what your values are unless you can make a statement about what you believe.

Notable Beliefs

Kites rise highest against the wind—not with it.

—Sir Winston Churchill (1874–1965)

I am a strong believer in luck and I find the harder I work the more I have of it.

—Benjamin Franklin (1706–1790)

I really do believe I can accomplish a great deal with a big grin, I know some people find that disconcerting, but that doesn't matter.

—Beverly Sills (1929–)

I believe in God, only I spell it Nature.

—Frank Lloyd Wright (1869–1959)

The probability that we may fail in the struggle ought not to deter us from the support of a cause we believe to be just.

—Abraham Lincoln (1809–1865)

There are admirable potentialities in every human being. Believe in your strength and your youth. Learn to repeat endlessly to yourself, "It all depends on me."

—Andre Gide (1869–1951)

Life is not easy for any of us. But what of that? We must have perseverance and above all confidence in ourselves. We must believe that we are gifted for something and that this thing must be attained.

—Marie Curie (1867–1934), two-time Nobel prize winner in Chemistry

I was brought up to believe that how I saw myself was more important than how others saw me.

—*Anwar el-Sadat (1918–1981)*

Believe me! The secret of reaping the greatest fruitfulness and the greatest enjoyment from life is to live dangerously!

—*Friedrich Nietzsche (1844–1900)*

I believe that unarmed truth and unconditional love will have the final word in reality. That is why right, temporarily defeated, is stronger than evil triumphant.

—*Martin Luther King Jr. (1929–1968), Accepting Nobel Peace Prize, Dec. 10, 1964*

Identifying Your Beliefs

You probably have 10,000 beliefs about yourself, your world, and human nature. But most people have a relatively short list of beliefs that they hold as their "convictions"—beliefs they use to guide decision-making when the going gets rough. Many of these might even operate at an unconscious level most of the time, but with a little thought, most people can bring them up to the surface. What do you believe? You can use Worksheet 3 to record your "top ten" beliefs.

WORKSHEET 3   My Top Ten Beliefs

Please take a few minutes to record your "top ten" beliefs in the following spaces. Remember…try to focus on your beliefs about yourself, your world, and human nature.

1. I believe...	6. I believe...
2. I believe...	7. I believe...
3. I believe...	8. I believe...
4. I believe...	9. I believe...
5. I believe...	10. I believe...

By this point, you have identified the key elements of your moral compass. You have chosen the universal principles you embrace, you have articulated your values, and you have summarized your beliefs. Understanding your moral compass is essential to effective decision-making. Living in alignment means that you hold yourself accountable for decisions consistent with your moral compass. But before you take action, you need to understand your goals and wants.

Goals

Goals:

Purpose

Goals

Wants

Scientists who study behavior tell us that humans have an innate need to make sense out of our lives. We constantly develop theories to explain why things happen as they do.

Say you see a cloud-like substance billowing out of a window. Maybe you hypothesize that something is on fire. If you're an astute observer, you might notice that the substance is pale and there is no smell of smoke and realize that it's actually steam. Whether you're right or wrong about the nature and origin of the billowy substance, in both cases you are trying to create meaning out of your observations. We have a similar need to attribute meaning to our lives. How do our day-to-day events combine to create a coherent whole? What is the point of doing what we do? If we can begin to answer those questions, we have the beginning of our highest goal—our life's purpose. Not everyone develops and follows a life purpose. People who were injured or severely neglected or abused might lack the capacity to formulate a meaningful purpose. But most of us are hungry to make sense out of our lives, so we create goals. Everyone's life purpose is distinctively theirs, but each must be consistent with universal principles of integrity, responsibility, compassion, and forgiveness. Albert Schweitzer once said, "I don't know what your destiny will be, but one thing I do know: the only ones among you who will be really happy are those who have sought and found how to serve." Oprah Winfrey, who created one of the wealthiest entertainment empires in the United States, says this about purpose: "I've come to believe that each of us has a personal calling that's as unique as a fingerprint—and that the best way to succeed is to discover what you love and then find a way to offer it to others in the form of service, working hard, and also allowing the energy of the universe to lead you."[1] So take a few minutes to reflect on your life purpose using the following worksheet.

WORKSHEET 4   My Purpose[2]

Be patient. The discovery of purpose can take some time. But when you come to "feel it," you'll know it was worth the wait.

These questions might help:

1. What are my talents?

2. What am I passionate about?

3. What do I obsess about, daydream about?

4. What do I wish I had more time to put energy into?

5. What needs doing in the world that I'd like to put my talents to work on?

6. What are the main areas in which I'd like to invest my talents?

7. What environments or settings feel most natural to me?

8. In what work and life situations am I most comfortable expressing my talents?

1. Oprah Winfrey, *O* Magazine, September 2002.

2. This worksheet is based on material from Richard J. Leider. *Repacking Your Bags: Lighten Your Load for the Rest of Your Life,* San Francisco: Berrett-Koehler Publishers, 1995).

Now, draft your purpose statement:

My purpose in life is…

What Do You Want for Yourself? *WDYWFY* (pronounced "widdy wiffy") is a process developed to help people clarify their goals.[3] *WDYWFY* is an acronym for "What Do You Want for Yourself?" First, let us dispose of a myth. Wanting is ok. Being moral does not mean that you must be an anti-materialistic saint. Wanting is part of human nature. Being human means that you are a wanting being. In their book, *Driven*, Harvard Business School professors Paul Lawrence and Nitin Nohria argue that fulfillment in life depends on finding ways to satisfy our inborn instinctual drives.[4] It's the way we satisfy our instinctual drives that makes the difference between being morally intelligent and morally impaired. For example, as humans, our sex drive is instinctual, but there's a big difference between consensual love-making and date rape.

---

3. Doug Lennick and Roy Geer. *How to Get What You Want and Remain True to Yourself,* Minneapolis, Minnesota: Lerner Publications Company, 1989.

4. Lawrence and Nohria, ibid.

Getting what we want is good. But if we don't channel our instinctual drives, we get in trouble. That is why goal-setting is vital to living in alignment. Without goals, it's hard to create meaning out of our actions. Without goals, our ability to fulfill our life's purpose would be a matter of chance. Setting deliberate goals allows us to satisfy our wants in a way that is aligned with our moral compass.

Not only does your goal frame help you satisfy your wants within a moral framework, paying attention to goals also increases the odds that you will actually accomplish what you desire. If you don't work on your goal frame, there is a random occurrence of achieving your goals. Career expert David Campbell made that point famously in his book *If You Don't Know where You're Going, You'll Probably End Up Somewhere Else.*[5] Apparently, it's not enough to have a set of goals in your head. You will boost your ability to achieve your goals when you write down your goals and your plans to achieve them. Why do written goals have such a positive impact? The most basic reason is that we tend to forget things. The physical process of writing helps our brain retain and recall the things we want to accomplish. When we write down goals, we have an opportunity to reflect carefully on what we really want and consider the best ways to accomplish them. When we record our goals, we can use our list as a reminder to stay on track. The process of writing down goals enhances our commitment and capacity to be responsible for the choices we make. We have all known of highly intelligent individuals who never lived up to their potential. Similarly, moral intelligence is wasted unless you use it in service of positive results, and goal setting will help you leverage the power of your moral intelligence to have a positive impact on your organization and the world.

5. David Campbell. *If You Don't Know Where You're Going, You'll Probably End Up Somewhere Else.* Notre Dame, Indiana: Ave Maria Press, 1990.

Why Leaders Love Goals

Every effective leader we know has crystal clear goals. Goals are crucial to effective leadership because they move you beyond awareness or good intentions to specific actions. Effective leaders accept responsibility for their choices by "getting on the record" with their goals. Effective leaders have goals that they really care about. They also encourage their followers to develop personally satisfying goals. One of the most powerful motivational tools of a good leader is to show that you care about the wants and goals of the people who work with you.

Employees with that rare boss who shows genuine interest in their goals—and who spends time helping them chart a course to reach those goals—respond with loyalty and commitment. Brian Heath, General Sales Manager of American Express Financial Advisors, is a body builder who does a mean impression of Arnold Schwarzenegger. Brian's sheer size and dominating demeanor fool some people into thinking he's nothing more than a tough guy. But Brian is also a people builder. When Brian was a regional vice president, he spent a lot of time listening to his employees. He learned that they wanted to be very successful but that many of them lacked confidence that they could achieve their goals. He learned a lot about what bothered them and how their fears got in the way of their performance. Brian decided that his employees needed him to help them overcome their insecurities and demonstrate confidence in their ability to accomplish their goals. So he decided on a regional goal that would reflect the ambitions the advisors had for themselves: They would set a goal that would require above average performance from everybody. Going forward, they would expect the average performance of all the division's advisors to equal the current level of performance of the top five percent. Brian presented it to his group in a speech titled, "Our Ridiculous Goal"—ridiculous because the bar was set so high. But Brian knew that all his advisors wanted to be top performers, and in the end they achieved their ridiculous goal.

Your Goals

What exactly do you want for yourself? What are your goals? The majority of us want to play the roles we have in life well. Most people who are parents want to be good at it. Even terrible parents want to be good at it. There are very few of us who don't care about how we perform. How many of you want to be part of a family that you are proud of? How many of you want to be part of an organization that you are proud of? What do you have to do to accomplish that?

Put It in Writing

Whether you are developing new goals or reinforcing long-standing goals, writing your goals down here will make them more real. Keep in mind that there are two kinds of goals. Some goals are a *state of being goal*, such as "I have three children. I want to be a good father now." Another type of goal is a *future based goal*, for example, "I want to retire within five years" or "I want to lose weight." We recommend that you include goals of both types.

WDYWFY (What Do You Want For Yourself?) Follow these steps to decide on the goals that are most important to you:

Step 1: Goal Identification. Decide what your top three to five life goals are and record them on Worksheet 5.

WORKSHEET 5   My Most Important Life Goals

1. _____

2. _____

3. _____

4. _____

5. _____

Step 2: Goal Alignment. Think about your top long-term goals. How well do your goals fit with your principles, values, and beliefs?

GOAL ALIGNMENT TEST

My Beliefs	My Goals	Consistencies	Inconsistencies
Sample: Caring for others	Buying a vacation home	Between my belief in caring for others and my goal of buying a vacation home that my family would enjoy	If the vacation home is too expensive, it might mean that I would have to reduce my usual charitable contributions

You don't need to abandon any goal that would make you wildly happy. But you will find that your overall happiness and effectiveness will be enhanced if each of your goals is strongly aligned with your moral compass.

Behavior

Behavior:
Thoughts
Emotions
Actions

The *behavior frame* puts the "living" in "living in alignment." Your behavior frame represents what you actually do, including your thoughts, emotions, and outward actions. Your behavior frame is what inspires people to follow you as a leader. People will not know you as a moral leader unless you communicate what you stand for—and act accordingly. When we act stupid, we give ourselves the benefit of the doubt, but others might not. So keeping your behavior in alignment with your moral compass and goals is essential for effective leadership.

Thoughts. What makes thoughts part of our behavior frame? Psychologists recognize thoughts as a form of *cognitive behavior*. They can't be seen by the outside observer, but like outward actions, they are within our control. We can act on them—we can change what we think. Most important, thoughts profoundly affect your emotions and your outward behavior. In a later chapter you will explore in greater detail about how to manage thoughts in ways that keep you in alignment.

Emotions. Everyone has them, even the most rational and composed of us. Emotions are neither good nor bad. They are simply emotions. But because strong emotions, whether positive or painful, can get in the way of effective behavior, emotions must be managed. The most effective leaders know how to regulate their own and others' emotional responses in a way that promotes a positive and high-performing work environment. If leaders lack emotional control or insight into the emotional needs of their followers, the work environment suffers. Earlier in her career, when MENTIUM CEO Lynn Sontag was a senior leader in executive development at a Fortune 100 company, she once made the mistake of transferring a call from an irate executive spouse to her boss. The caller, who had considerable clout, was having a temper tantrum about something that the organization wouldn't as a matter of policy give her. Lynn realized too late that she should have prepared her boss for the call so he wouldn't get stuck in a political bind. She still has vivid memories of his reaction and the impact on her subsequent performance:

> **I can visualize the whole thing. My office was kitty corner from the executive director, and I could see his expressions as he talked to her, and it was pretty visual. His door was closed, but I could see him through his window, and I knew where he was heading as soon as he opened the door. He blew up in front of me and everyone else around. The next**

day he calmed down, and we walked through it and processed it so that it wouldn't happen again. We got through it, but I was derailed on a personal level for a long time. I still had to work with the woman for another year and a half. It took me more than a couple months to let go. It hit me right where my confidence was. I didn't trust my own judgment, and I became unwilling to make decisions without checking with a lot of people first.

Actions. We all know they speak louder than words. Having a moral compass and admirable goals is worthless unless we do what it takes to make them real. In fact, failure to act in concert with our values and goals is worse than worthless. It does us harm. It makes us untrustworthy. Whom do we trust? People who do what they say they will do. People we can count on to behave with integrity and compassion.

In Search of Alignment. Now that you see the canvas inside each of your frames, how do you keep your frames aligned? In the next chapter, we turn to the skills that connect our frames and the obstacles that interfere with living in alignment.

4

Staying True to Your Moral Compass

Knowing who you want to be—an honest, responsible, and compassionate leader—is one thing. Knowing *how* to become your best self is another. Actually *doing* what you know you should is still another matter. That is the essence of *alignment,* a shorthand term that means "your goals and your behaviors are consistent with your moral compass." We need three qualities to help us keep us in alignment:

- **Moral intelligence**—Part of us that shapes our moral compass and ensures that our goals are consistent with our moral compass

- **Moral competence**—Ability to act on our moral principles

- **Emotional competence**—Ability to manage our and others' emotions in morally charged situations

Moral Intelligence. Can you interpret this formula?

$$\frac{\mathrm{d}}{\mathrm{d}x} \int_a^x f(s)\mathrm{d}s = f(x)$$

Here's a hint: The equation here represents the "fundamental theorem of calculus." It expresses the fact that differentiation and integration are inverse operations of each other. Now do you understand? If you're like most people, that explanation helps a little, but not much. You can tell that the diagram is a mathematical equation, and you've heard of calculus, but you might not understand or remember the distinction between differentiation and integration. For people who are mathematically inclined, the fundamental theorem of calculus probably looks as simple to them as 2+2=4 does to the rest of us. A complicated equation makes sense to the mathematician because she has two qualities—mathematical intelligence (basic aptitude) and mathematical competence (learned skills). Mathematical intelligence isn't sufficient to be good at math, but no amount of practice will make you a good mathematician if you don't have an underlying aptitude. Moral intelligence is another kind of aptitude. Without it, no amount of training will turn us into moral leaders. Recall the brain-injured toddlers. No matter how hard their parents tried to instill positive values, they simply lacked the basic neurological equipment to distinguish between right and wrong.

Moral intelligence is our basic aptitude for moral thought and action. We call on it to make sense out of moral principles (the "fundamental theorems" of morality). Moral intelligence allows us to develop moral values and beliefs and to integrate those values and beliefs into a coherent moral compass. Because it's the part of us that knows what's right, we use it to ensure that our goals and behavior are in alignment with our moral compass. Like a smoke detector, our moral intelligence sounds the alarms when our goals or actions move out of synch with our moral compass.

When Charlie Zelle was a young New York investment banker, his family's Midwestern transportation and real-estate business went into a financial tailspin. After he returned home to help save the business, company lawyers called a meeting of management and key family shareholders to decide the firm's fate. When lawyers and family members began to talk, Charlie was astonished at how glib they all seemed. It was clear that they had already decided to throw in the towel and no one seemed all that upset about it. Charlie got angry—his moral intelligence alarms were deafening. He thought shutting down the company was unfair and a selfish move on the part of his family. If the company folded, 500 employees would lose their jobs, and people in the community would lose access to the public transportation they provided.

Moral Competence. While moral intelligence involves *knowing* what to do, moral competence is the skill of actually *doing* the right thing. How do we do what we know is right? How do we do the right thing even when we are scared or pressured? For that, we need moral competence. We need it to understand what goals will allow us to be true to our principles, and we need moral competence to act in alignment with our values and beliefs. Charlie Zelle's moral intelligence told him that it was selfish for his family to simply cut their losses at the cost of fairness to employees and the community. But it took moral competence for Charlie to act on that awareness. He was just a kid, but fueled by his anger and encouraged by a mentor, Charlie found his voice. He found some investors, formed a new company, bought the buses back from bankruptcy court, and rehired all the employees from his family's old company. The odds of success were low, but with the help of a senior vice president who knew and loved the business, they survived. Fifteen years later, Charlie's company, Jefferson Bus Lines, is a thriving regional bus operator.

Emotional Competence. To live in alignment, we also need to be emotionally competent. Emotional competence helps us manage our emotions and the emotional quality of our relationships with others. It's almost impossible to be morally competent without being emotionally competent as well. For example, most of us value honesty and most of us have the moral competence to be truthful. After all, we've told the truth countless times. But if we're such experts at telling the truth, why then do many of us lie so often? A UK women's magazine survey, for instance, found that 94% of women admitted that they tell lies, half of them lying on a daily basis. Emotional competence helps us answer questions like these:

- What makes it hard to tell the truth in a particular situation?

- How will others act if I tell the truth or fail to tell the truth?

- How can I tell the truth in a way that will preserve my relationships with others?

Emotional competence allows us to understand our own emotions, especially those that can get in the way of doing the right thing. Emotional competence also helps us understand and respond intelligently to the emotions of others. That ability to respond to others' emotional needs in turn creates a positive work environment in which people feel safe enough to do what is morally right—and not incidentally, perform at their best.

When leaders lack emotional competence, they create a negative climate that encourages self-protection rather than integrity. Lori Kaiser, former vice president at supercomputer maker Cray, Inc., ran into an emotionally incompetent manager at a previous company where she had worked early in her career. He was a foul-mouthed senior manager who routinely harassed his juniors. Everyone knew he was obnoxious, but no one called him on it. Lori tolerated it for years. Then while on maternity leave, she realized how great it felt to be away from him.

When she returned from leave, she took advantage of her newfound status as the company's most senior woman to draw a line in the sand. Lori told her superiors she would only return if she did not have to work with the obnoxious manager. Her superiors agreed, but did nothing to correct his behavior. Other employees, in part weary of dealing with him, began to leave the company. Only then did management begin to pay attention to his behavior, but by then, they had lost some valuable people— largely because of the negative environment created by one emotionally incompetent leader.

Lori faults herself for failing to act sooner. She tolerated his negative behavior for a long time because the company paid her well to do the kind of work she wanted to do. Though she was not the source of a negative environment, she believes she was partially responsible for allowing it to continue. "Even though I may be able to tolerate difficult people," says Lori, "the people who follow me need someone who can speak up. If I condone bad behavior in front of junior men or women, it's unacceptable. Now I speak up for all of the people who are junior to me and can't speak up, even if it makes me look like I'm not one of the gang."

Staying Aligned. When you consistently use your moral intelligence, moral competence, and emotional competence, you will find that you are spending more and more time living in alignment with your moral compass. When your three frames are in synch, you feel as though you are "in the zone," and your creativity and performance are at their best. When you are in a leadership role, your state of alignment is palpable and appealing to followers. Your state of alignment contributes to an emotionally positive and high-performing work environment for others.

Think of the leaders who have inspired you the most. They are almost invariably those who consistently demonstrate their commitment to principles that you also believe in. Lynn Fantom, CEO of ID Media, says of her boss, David Bell, who heads parent company Interpublic, "I would do anything for him because he shows respect to me and everyone in the company by doing simple things like sending short e-mail messages of appreciation."

Moral Misalignment. The most successful leaders spend the majority of their time in alignment. But all of us experience times when it is hard to stay in alignment, times when our moral intelligence doesn't seem to be having an impact on what we want or what we actually do. Instead of being connected to our ideal selves—who we would like to be at our best—we disconnect from our moral compass. Misalignments don't usually happen because we lack moral or emotional skills. Typically, they occur because **moral viruses** or **destructive emotions** are interfering with our ability to use moral and emotional competencies that we have successfully used in the past.

Moral viruses are disabling and inaccurate negative beliefs that interfere with alignment. Moral viruses infect our moral compass and lead us to adopt goals that are inconsistent with our moral compass.

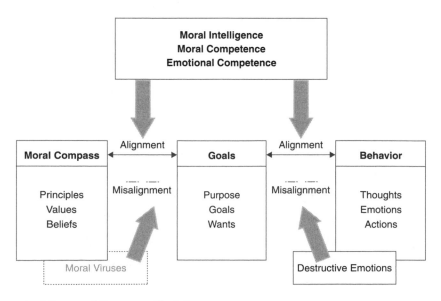

FIGURE 4.1   Alignment Model

Diagnosing a Moral Virus. Moral viruses are unfounded negative beliefs that are in conflict with universal principles. Like computer viruses that infect a computer's operating system, moral viruses invade your moral compass and often lead to breakdown. Moral viruses remind us of computer "adware," the insidious advertising software programs that are installed on your computer via the Internet without your consent. Suddenly, your computer desktop is overwhelmed by pop-up ads, and when you try to find and delete the adware program, you find it's very difficult. Your antivirus software probably will not work. The unwanted program has the ability to hide its files and to resist attempts to remove it. Like adware, moral viruses sneak into your moral operating system. They hide themselves well: At a conscious level, you may articulate a set of principles, values, and beliefs that are admirable, without realizing that you are secretly harboring an unsavory belief that affects the quality of your goals. Your "official" goals are in alignment with your moral compass. But without your awareness, you have adopted some "unofficial" goals that are at odds with your moral compass. The end result is that you do things that are inconsistent with your moral compass, and you are probably pretty confused about the reasons why.

Consider the experience of John Simmons (pseudonym), founding partner in a growing professional services firm. He was attending a partner's meeting for his firm. Compensation was on the agenda, and during the discussion, John found himself insisting that his fellow owners adopt a lot of legalistic provisions that he thought necessary to ensure he would be compensated fairly for all his efforts. During the discussion, John became increasingly rigid, frustrating his partners. Finally, they told him he was acting as if they were his enemies rather than people who shared his goals. John knew instantly they were right, but it took a few hours of reflection to figure out why he had behaved with such suspicion.

John explains, "When I was about four years old, I got into an argument with my older brother and I bit him! My father insisted that I apologize. I refused. Before I realized the stakes of the game I was playing, my father said, "If you don't apologize, you can't be a part of this family." He proceeded to take me about a half a mile away from our farmhouse and dump me off in the pasture. I recall running back home, crying as I ran. My false conclusion was that when it comes to basic needs like personal safety you really can't trust anyone, even those close to you. Even people who have never actually taken advantage of you might still turn on you in unpredictable ways. Always be on guard!"

Once John uncovered his "moral virus," he went back to his fellow owners to own up to the negative beliefs that had infected his moral compass and disrupted their meeting.

Common Moral Viruses

- Most people can't be trusted.

- I'm not worth much.

- I'm better than most other people.

- Might makes right.

- If it feels good, do it.

- My needs are more important than anyone else's.

- Most people care more about themselves than anyone else.

- People of other (races, religions, nationalities) are not as good as people of my (race, religion, nationality).

Dealing with Moral Viruses. A good way to manage moral viruses is to scan for them in your thoughts. To figure out what you are thinking, tune in to your "self talk"—the continuous internal conversation that you have with yourself. Like computer antivirus software that periodically scans for new viruses, you should regularly scan your self talk to stay aware of the internal beliefs that are influencing your daily actions. In addition to regular moral virus scans, we recommend that you scan your self talk for possible moral viruses whenever you are experiencing strong emotion, either positive or negative. Because thoughts and emotions mutually influence each other, it is especially important to understand the beliefs that may be the root cause of uncomfortable emotions.

Disabling a Moral Virus. When you have detected a moral virus in your thoughts, you have the opportunity to replace it with a thought or belief that is consistent with your moral compass. Countering a moral virus is effective in the moment, but it is not a permanent fix. Moral viruses sometimes act like certain biological viruses that lurk indefinitely within us. For example, the virus that causes shingles, a relative of the chicken pox virus, is a chronic virus. After an outbreak of shingles, the virus doesn't die. It retreats to the base of a bundle of nerves, where it lies dormant unless the affected person's immune system is weakened by another illness, allowing the old virus' symptoms to reappear. Similarly, when we are under stress, the symptoms of a moral virus can once again resurface. In the example just described, John Simmons figured out how he had been infected by a moral virus, but he knows he may run into the same virus in the future. John is not "cured," but his awareness will help him to recognize moral virus symptoms and move quickly to minimize its negative affects in the future.

Because none of us had a perfect upbringing, most of us will have at least one moral virus lying in wait to overtake us in a difficult moment. That is why it is important to scan our thoughts regularly and why it is necessary to actively remind ourselves of our more desirable frame one beliefs. A good rule of thumb is this: When you find yourself doing something that is puzzling to you—when you say to yourself, "I don't know *why* I behaved that way…," you are likely dealing with some sort of moral virus. That is a good signal to talk it out with a good friend or trusted advisor. Like a virus that thrives in the dark, moral viruses brought out into the light often wither and die.

Destructive Emotions. Destructive emotions are the most common culprits in keeping us from acting consistently with our goals. Emotions such as greed, hate, or jealousy are powerful and can overwhelm our normal ability to act in a morally and emotionally competent manner. It is human nature to experience periodic emotional "breakdowns"—not usually the kind that sends us off for a long rest cure, but the more commonplace stresses that can lead us to become emotionally overwhelmed. Our moral compass is intact, and our goals are clear, but in the heat of the moment, we act in a way that is completely inconsistent with what we say we want. We lose control and allow destructive emotions to take hold. Greed is an especially destructive emotion, one that likely lies at the heart of the ongoing corporate scandals. It's hard to imagine that any of the executives prosecuted for accounting or securities fraud in the last four years needed more money than they already had. For an executive in the throes of greed, however, enough is never enough. We're all too familiar with the impact of greed-driven schemes —employees deprived of jobs and retirement funds, shareholders betrayed, and companies bankrupt. Ironically, giving into greed hurts ourselves as much as others, as Dennis Kozlowski, Ken Lay, and numerous others have discovered.

Managing Destructive Emotions. There will always be occasions when you feel negative emotions. Your goal should not be to eliminate all traces of negative feelings from your experience, but rather to develop the emotional control to manage destructive emotions so they don't derail you. Managing destructive emotions is vital to a successful leadership career because left unchecked, they are a frequent cause of career derailment among executives. A senior manufacturing executive interviewed for this book notes the importance of managing potentially destructive emotions: "Someone will renege on something or not do something they promised, or they'll misrepresent things and I just want to get even. I've had to develop a lot of self-control. I don't often lose my temper and if I do, I try to do it behind closed doors with my team. So the challenge is treating people the way I'd like to be treated versus the way I'd like to treat them because they screwed me. I don't feel like I've had to be extremely sensitive so much as I've needed to control my revenge motive and be professional."

A powerful antidote to negative emotions is the deliberate cultivation of a positive emotional state. Controlling emotions must come from within. No one having a temper tantrum—child or adult—wants to be told by others to "calm down." Fortunately, we can learn how to short-circuit highly charged negative emotions. Deep breathing exercises, deep muscle relaxation exercises, and meditation, are just a few of the scientifically documented ways to produce more positive emotional states.[1] Depending on your personal preferences, activities as varied as hobbies, community service, spending time in nature or with family members, even washing the dishes can trigger a positive mental state. They work because you cannot have two incompatible physiological states at the same time. You cannot be angry when you are happy. You cannot be anxious when you are calm. Regular practice of your preferred technique is key to your ability to manage your emotions. Through practice, you can create a calm and peaceful internal state that automatically kicks in when you need it. When you deliberately cultivate a positive and relaxed emotional state, you will be better able to call upon that positive state whenever a destructive emotion is beginning to take hold.

---

1. Many techniques for inducing positive emotional states can be found in Herbert Benson, M.D. and William Proctor's *The Break-Out Principle*, New York: Scribner, 2003.

The Experiential Triangle. We each operate within an *experiential triangle* of *thoughts, emotions*, and *behavior,* all of which mutually influence one another. Although we discussed moral viruses and destructive emotions as though they were separate phenomena, in reality, they are typically found together and often reinforce the negative effects of each. Emotions are usually the product of our thoughts. When we admire someone, for example, our happiness in seeing that person stems not from their physical existence, but because of the *ideas* we have about them. Similarly, when we are in the throes of a destructive emotion, we have a reason. Our negative feeling is prompted by some thoughts or beliefs we have about the situation we are in. You think, "I knew I couldn't trust them," or "I should have gotten more," and you feel terrible. The worse you feel, the more likely it is that a moral virus has invaded your belief system. Destructive emotions such as anger and jealousy are the "fever" that often accompanies a moral virus. But emotions also stimulate thought processes. When a destructive emotion overcomes you, it can negatively influence the way you think about yourself or others, thereby causing a moral virus. Finally, our thoughts and emotions affect our behavior. The behavioral impact of moral viruses and destructive emotions is widespread and obvious. For a leader, the effects of moral viruses and destructive emotions can be career-ending. At the very least, your performance suffers along with that of your co-workers.

Consider these contrasting experiential triangles:

A Case of Alignment

The Situation: My boss is hiding the extent of a new product line's manufacturing problems from the senior management group until performance reviews are completed.

Thought: I know that my boss's actions are violating the principle of integrity and I have a responsibility to get involved.

> *Emotions*: Some apprehension about challenging my boss's decision, mixed with confidence and determination.
>
> *Behavior:* I confront my boss about her actions and urge her to provide accurate information about production problems.

Suppose, on the other hand, that you found yourself unable to confront your boss. Would it be because you were unaware that what she was doing was wrong, or because you did not know how to raise the issue? Probably not. More likely, your failure to act would be the result of your beliefs about the situation. Your beliefs create a context, or framework, for deciding how to respond to your boss's actions. You might then be operating in an experiential triangle that operates something like this:

A Case of Misalignment

> *Thoughts*: What other people do is none of my business. Human nature being what it is, I will probably be punished for standing up for what is right. If I do get involved, my boss might retaliate and I could lose my bonus or even my job.
>
> *Emotions:* Fear and anxiety.
>
> *Behaviors:* I look the other way or I help my boss conceal the extent of the production line problems.

In this example, we can detect a moral virus in the belief that one should "mind one's own business," coupled with the belief that others will do you harm if you challenge their negative behavior. This moral virus is likely contaminating more positive beliefs about human nature and our responsibility to do what is right. But a moral virus can deactivate positive beliefs in a difficult moment, replacing them with negative beliefs about other's motives and our own responsibility. In this example, we can also see the destructive power of emotions such as fear and anxiety that further reinforce negative beliefs and the misguided actions that result.

Preventive Maintenance. Staying in alignment requires regular tune-ups to monitor and prevent damaging effects of moral viruses and destructive emotions. But most important, alignment depends on continuously developing our moral and emotional competence. But how? What are the practical day-to-day actions we must take to stay in alignment? For that, we need to be proficient in a group of specific moral and emotional skills—as we will see in the next several chapters of this book.

PART TWO

DEVELOPING MORAL SKILLS

Universal principles show up everywhere. They turn up in speeches and sermons and scoldings; they are chiseled into monuments. We know they sound good, but what do they really require of us? Exactly what are we supposed to do to live in alignment with principles? Fortunately, we "know it when we see it,"—we recognize when someone is acting in concert with an important principle. A colleague follows up with us when she said she would. A team member owns up to a costly mistake. A boss gives us some well-deserved "constructive" feedback and then goes on to treat us as cordially and respectfully as before. But it's a challenge to bring those lofty principles down to the level of day-to-day life. It's our moral competence that makes our principles concrete. Moral competence, as we've said, is actually a collection of competencies. Each is related to one of the four universal principles that we have found are key to effective leadership—integrity, responsibility, compassion, and forgiveness (see Table PII.1). In this section, we explore the competencies associated with each principle. We also discuss another kind of moral skill—the emotional competencies that help us in our efforts to maintain alignment. Though we will discuss each competency in turn, keep in mind that in the real world, individual moral competencies and emotional competencies are interwoven. Like a master artist who simultaneously uses all his talents—including brush technique, composition, color perception—to create a work of art, the best leaders seamlessly blend all of their competencies to create their personal and organizational masterpieces.

Principles	Related Moral Competencies
Integrity	• Acting consistently with principles, values, and beliefs • Telling the truth • Standing up for what is right • Keeping promises
Responsibility	• Taking responsibility for personal choices • Admitting mistakes and failures • Embracing responsibility for serving others
Compassion	• Actively caring about others
Forgiveness	• Letting go of one's own mistakes • Letting go of others' mistakes

5

Integrity

Every individual, like a statue, develops in his life the laws of harmony, integrity, and freedom; or those of deformity, immorality, and bondage. Whether we wish to or not, we are all drawing our own pictures in the lives we are living...

—Harriot K. Hunt (1805–1875) U.S. Physician and Feminist

To starve to death is a small thing, but to lose one's integrity is a great one.

—Chinese Proverb

The Integrity Competencies	• Acting consistently with principles, values, and beliefs • Telling the truth • Standing up for what is right • Keeping promises

Acting Consistently with Principles, Values, and Beliefs

This is the primary moral competency that encompasses the others. Acting consistently with principles, values, and beliefs means being purposeful in everything you do and say. Integrity is authenticity. It is saying what you stand for and standing for what you say. Awareness is the first step to being able to act with consistent integrity. That's why it's so important to be clear about what's in your moral compass. Acting consistently with your moral compass also means letting others know the principles that are most important to you, as well as holding yourself accountable for decisions and behaviors consistent with that.

Before becoming an advisor with financial services company Thrivent Financial for Lutherans, Walt Bradley spent 20 years selling cars. One day, a young woman came on the used car lot to buy her first car. The only car she could afford had a lot of miles, a few dents, and a leaky exhaust. Walt told her that if she bought the car, they would check out the leak and fix it. "When we inspected it, the pipe was shot," says Walt. "My boss said to just patch it. I argued with him, but he said, 'I don't give a shit. Just get it out of the building. There's no warranty.' Right in front of my boss, I told the mechanic not to do that—to fix the car right. My boss and I got into a shouting match about it, but the mechanic fixed it." Asked how hard was it to stand up to his boss, Walt replies, "I hate confrontation, but the woman trusted me, and I know that if my word isn't any good, then my product isn't any good."

The High Cost of Inconsistency. Leaders who blatantly ignore universal principles do great harm to their constituencies and ultimately to their bottom line. But just as bad are leaders who pay lip service to integrity while ignoring it in practice. Take this example of Kevin Reynolds (pseudonym), CEO of a $400 million dollar consumer products company. Kevin talked a lot about integrity in his speeches to shareholders, employees, and his board. But Kevin's direct reports didn't trust him at all, and each could cite numerous examples of betrayal or deception on Kevin's part. None of Kevin's direct reports was willing to go out on a limb for their company in the environment that he had created. Some of them spent a lot of time planning how to protect themselves from his treachery, while a few braver souls openly threatened to leave if the board did not fire him. The final straw came when, at the end of a financially troubled year, Kevin manipulated the bonus pool to get his maximum year-end bonus, leaving his team with unfairly low payouts. For a time, Kevin managed to conceal his bonus scheme by withholding information and presenting confusing data, but eventually, his mishandling of the bonus money leaked out. The board asked for his resignation. No one mourned Kevin's departure. His reputation for dishonesty dogged him in the industry, barring him from landing a top executive post anywhere else.

In corporate settings, a lack of integrity usually signals a lack of moral competence, as was the case with Kevin. But at times, a lack of integrity stems from a deeper lack of moral intelligence. There are some people whose moral compass is badly dented, like Jeff Walsh (pseudonym), who applied for a job as regional sales manager for a large Fortune 500 company. On paper, Jeff had a great track record in sales and management and an MBA from a prestigious university. The vice president of Sales was so impressed after interviewing Jeff that he was ready to hire him on the spot. "Don't let that one get out the door," he told the recruiter. But when the recruiter checked his credentials, he discovered that Jeff had no undergraduate college degree, let alone an MBA. In fact, he had never taken a single college course. When the recruiter confronted him, Jeff broke into a sweat and admitted that he had faked his resume. You might think that the sweat on Jeff's forehead was evidence that he knew right from wrong. But Jeff recovered his composure quickly and promptly talked his way back into the VP of Sales' office to try to convince him that it really wouldn't matter that he did not have his MBA. Without a functioning moral compass, Jeff completely missed the notion that lying about his credentials was a big deal. He might sweat because he was caught—but not because he had a guilty conscience.

Telling the Truth

Susan Desimone (ficitious name) was chief financial officer for a major division of a huge financial services firm. Her CEO, a demanding and explosive character (in actuality a high-profile top executive), was determined to meet Wall Street's expectations for the quarter's profits— no matter what it took. The financial analysts who worked for Susan were stressed. "The CEO is badgering us to make these numbers work," they complained. "If we show him the results we have right now, he will blow his fuse." Susan knew they weren't exaggerating, but she also knew she could handle her CEO's tantrum without letting it unhinge her. "What is the worst thing he can do to us?," she replied. "He'll yell at us for sure, but he's yelled at us before, and we are going to tell the truth."

Susan's moral stance did more than keep her company out of the scandal section of *The Wall Street Journal.* She provided "cover" for the people in her finance unit and by her actions made it safer for them to do what they knew was right. Her truthful response to the CEO's pressure was both morally skilled and fiscally smart. She motivated her people to keep working for the company during an economic boom when their skills were highly marketable and corporate attrition was at record high levels.

Leading with the Truth. In organizational settings, telling the truth often means defining reality under challenging circumstances. When times are tough, leaders need to be able to tell the truth while providing people with real reasons for hope and optimism.

Imagine that you are captain on a sailboat that is cruising through the Caribbean. When you left dock a few hours ago, it was warm and sunny with a gentle breeze pushing the boat forward. Then the weather turns suddenly ugly. Before long, the wind is fierce, the waves are pounding, and your passengers are afraid. What should you do? You tell them the truth. You say, "This is a dangerous storm. Something bad could happen. You need to keep your life jackets on and stay below deck while I get us through this. I have been through storms like this before, and I am very optimistic that we are going to weather the storm."

Cindy Carlson, former president of Capital Professional Advisors (CPA), a financial services firm, faced her own storm. Her company was only in its second year and it wasn't likely to see its third. Breadwinners would lose their jobs, and she felt responsible. She had recruited top people by convincing them that they were signing on for a great opportunity. She promised them that the owners had the resources and the commitment to ride a rocky start up. But the owners had a short attention span—they were already itching to sell or, failing that, close up shop. It didn't matter much to them how they got out of the deal as long as they did.

On a frigid winter morning in 2002, Cindy called her seven senior managers into the boardroom of their Minneapolis offices. She recalls the scene vividly. "I told them that if we didn't have a solid buy-out offer in the next two months, we were history. I also told them that I believed in them and what they were doing. I said I hoped they would stay, but I wouldn't blame them if they left." It was frightening to be that upfront with them. Cindy worried that they might bolt, lowering the company's market value and making it that much harder to sell. But she went ahead and told the rest of the organization what was happening. Much to Cindy's relief, no one on the management team left, and that encouraged the other employees to stay as well.

Cindy admits that she was afraid to tell her staff what was going on with the company, but she knew it was the right thing to do. She had promised to always be truthful about the state of the company. Though Cindy was honest as a matter of principle, she believes it paid off for her business. Her employees stayed—and stayed engaged—because they trusted her. She says, "I felt like I had failed them, but they stayed with me because I was both candid about the status of our business and optimistic about what could still happen if we found a buyer." In a characteristic stroke of modesty, Cindy adds, "It wasn't because of me. Everyone believed in what we were doing." CPA owners soon found a buyer, and within six months the sale was complete. Right on cue, the company began to perform better. In 2004, Capital Professional Advisors celebrated its fourth anniversary and it now is well on the road to profitability and success.

Telling the Truth about Performance. Many of us are afraid to discuss poor performance with a subordinate. We imagine that people will be upset, and we don't want to be responsible for causing them pain. Paul Clayton, former president of Burger King North America and current CEO of Jamba Juice, is not known for pulling his punches. The only time he can recall when he has withheld the truth was when he had to sit down with someone and talk about his or her performance. "I have made mistakes in not being direct enough. I had to give a negative performance review and circled around the issues, and I've had that happen to me as well. I've always been critical of my communication skills, but for a long time, no one said a word to me. I knew that if someone had the courage to tell me sooner that I needed work, it would have helped me."

We have all heard horror stories about co-workers who got a glowing performance review coupled with a bonus, only to be fired a month later. When that happens, it is usually because the manager has not been honest about the employee's performance problems over some period of time. Some managers are so non-assertive that employees who are being given negative feedback have no idea that they are being criticized. We know of several extreme examples when an employee who was fired on a Friday showed up for work as usual on Monday because she didn't realize she had been terminated.

Exceptions to the Rule of Honesty. A seemingly contradictory aspect of the competency of telling the truth is that it includes knowing when *not to* tell the truth. Consider an example posed by eighteenth century philosopher, Immanuel Kant. Imagine that a murderer comes to your door, wanting to know where your friend is—so that he can kill her. Your friend is, in fact, hiding in your bedroom closet. Most people would probably agree that your obligation to your friend overrides your general obligation to tell the truth. For some brave World War II Europeans, this scenario was not hypothetical—they risked their lives sheltering Jews from the Nazis. *The Diary of Anne Frank* is a famous telling of the story of a Dutch Jewish family hidden by a former employee of Ann Frank's father. When the Nazis made their regular sweeps of their Amsterdam neighborhood in search of Jews, the family protecting the Franks would have failed in moral competence if they had told the truth about what they were doing.

Honesty is often complicated for business leaders as well. At times, a leader has information that cannot be divulged. This is common in situations involving downsizings, initial public offerings, and mergers and acquisitions. When planning workforce reductions, for example, leaders know that employees would find it helpful to get advance warning that their job could be at risk. On the other hand, leaders have a responsibility to owners not to divulge information that could be harmful to the market value of their companies. To tell the truth prematurely would be a disservice to the business, yet to say when asked that no reorganization is looming would be dishonest. If there are legal requirements to withhold information, the leader should simply acknowledge that. A leader can still be truthful by saying something like, "We do have plans but we cannot discuss them at this time. Please know that we will implement the plan with high regard for our employees, our customers, and the people who own the company."

Withholding information is also justified to protect the privacy of employees. Consider computer programmer, Jeanetta Shaw (pseudonym) who discovered that her husband and his family were all involved in criminal activity that was about to hit the newspaper headlines. Her distress was obvious to her co-workers, and they began to ask their manager what was going on. The manager decided to tell the truth, but not the whole truth. He told Jeanetta's colleagues that there were personal circumstances beyond her control that were causing her a great deal of stress. He expressed his commitment to help her get through a rough time and asked others to do the same.

The Painful Truth? Telling the truth and tact are not incompatible. Some of us pride ourselves on being honest to a fault. We might say things others would be afraid to say, but it doesn't necessarily add up to more truth. Some of us use "honesty" as an excuse to vent our hostility. We might make very cruel, competitive, or aggressive comments under the guise of "calling it like you see it" and then excuse ourselves by claiming, "I'm only being truthful." According to Jefferson Bus Line's CEO, Charlie Zelle, the disclaimer "'I'm just being honest' is a classic Minnesota passive-aggressive way of being hurtful." When we go out of our way to communicate a hurtful truth, we are usually not being honest with ourselves. So, when we feel obligated to tell another something "for his own good," we need first to examine our own motivations. Are we competitive? Are we jealous? Are we trying to even up an old score?

Good Intentions. Truth telling works best when paired with the emotional competency of self-awareness. We need self-awareness to understand how our own goals and desires influence what we say to others. Leaders who limit information about pending changes should rigorously examine their motivations. Although it is important to protect their companies, leaders who withhold information because they put personal stock option considerations over employee well being, clearly violate principle of integrity.

We also need emotional competencies to understand other's emotions and be able to discuss the truth in ways that people can accept and use productively. Employees sense when their leaders make self-serving decisions or shade the truth about pending changes. The resulting negative impact on morale and performance can undermine the implementation of any change effort.

How Truth Fuels Performance. Truth telling has a huge impact on leadership effectiveness and workforce engagement. When people work for a dishonest leader, they censor information to protect themselves from a negative or unpredictable reaction. The dishonest boss creates a climate dominated by political intrigue. Instead of working productively, people who work for dishonest superiors spend a lot of time wondering about their manager's agenda, trying to gather information, trying to jockey for power, and doing only those things they think will keep them out of harm's way. In contrast, leaders who are known for being honest generate a powerful climate of trust. People who work for honest superiors relax because they know there will be no hidden surprises coming out of the organizational woodwork. People accomplish more and are able to work with great creativity when they don't have to waste energy watching their back.

Standing Up for What Is Right

Leaders who live the principle of integrity inevitably must take principled stands. David Risher recalls this incident during his tenure as a Microsoft executive:

> **One day, we were in the middle of a meeting, and my strong-willed boss started to beat up on a young new employee of mine, asking her questions she couldn't possibly have answered because she was so new. My boss was a hard person to stand up to, but in this case, I did. I**

remember that it caused a bit of a commotion in the room because people couldn't believe I was standing up to her— she was just that strong. When I later went to Amazon.com, my former boss ended up working for me. She ended up being a supporter of mine, and I think it was because she respected me for having been willing to stand up for people.

Honda Motors VP, Gary Kessler, recalls a time 20 years ago when he took a quiet but vital stand. He discovered that a member of his team who was also a personal friend had fabricated his academic background. Gary knew that he could forgive his friend, and he knew he could keep anyone else from finding out what his friend had done. But Gary believed that to ignore his friend's deception would be deceptive on his part. It would devalue the efforts of others who were expected to have a certain level of academic training. So he steeled his courage and fired his friend.

Unlike Gary's admirable private stand, most principled stands must be taken in the face of stiff resistance. Don Hall, Jr. is the CEO of Hallmark Cards. Early in his career, Don headed product development. Don had a fine-tuned sense of what customers expected from Hallmark. He steadfastly resisted proposals to save on production costs by cheapening their product. To maintain customer loyalty, Don insisted that quality, rather than cost, be the company's primary focus.

Defying conventional wisdom to make a principled stand can be challenging. In most organizations, there is a lot of pressure to agree with popular positions. People who take unpopular stands can put their career advancement or their livelihoods at risk. Acting with integrity means that you accept the risks that come with taking a principled stand because the moral consequences of looking the other way are unacceptable. Think of the hazards that have resulted when no one stood up for what was right—buildings that collapse because of poor construction, bankruptcies caused by predatory lending practices in low-income neighborhoods, the explosion of the space shuttle *Challenger* after NASA executives ignored engineers' concerns about faulty O-rings.

Keeping Promises

Keeping promises is a hallmark of integrity because it demonstrates that we can be trusted to do what we say we will do. Keeping promises is a competency highly valued in organizational settings, but in our wired 24/7 world, it's a competency many of us have a hard time practicing consistently. We have good intentions but may let our ever-expanding "to do" list overtake our earlier promises. This was the case with Kari Wang (pseudonym), a senior executive in a professional services firm, whose career was in jeopardy and whose team was delivering inferior results. Kari had lost the respect of her colleagues because of her poor track record in keeping her commitments to them. When a high-profile project came her way, Kari dug in and took over all the detailed work herself, saddling herself with more work than even an overachiever like Kari could handle. Kari resisted delegating, rationalizing that she'd be happy to delegate if only she could find someone who could do a good enough job. When Kari did reluctantly delegate, she routinely forgot to provide all the information needed for the work to be done successfully. She changed her mind about priorities seemingly every hour and then failed to communicate those changes to her staff. Kari was incapable of saying "no"—she agreed to do so many things that she inevitably dropped the ball on some important commitments. People who knew Kari well did their best to work around her bad habits, believing that though her execution was poor, her motives were good. People who did not know Kari personally saw only her lapses. They mistrusted her and labeled her a liar. Her harshest critics viewed her missteps as deliberate efforts to advance her own career by sabotaging others. Fortunately, Kari's boss proposed that she use a leadership coach to help her make the transition from high-powered individual performer to leader of others. As a result, Kari came to recognize the costs of her actions and was able to develop the disciplined work habits that would eventually allow her to rebuild her credibility with her team.

Keeping promises usually requires assistance from a few emotional competencies—the self-awareness to recognize the inconsistency between our intentions and actions and the self-control to adopt disciplined work habits that allow us to keep our promises.

Honoring Confidences. One of the most frequent promises leaders are asked to keep is to preserve the privacy of others. A common complaint about low-integrity leaders is that they have failed to keep confidences. Some leaders betray confidences with good intentions because they believe that sharing the information with someone else will help the person who revealed private information. Others wrongly believe that it is acceptable to share confidential information about a third party that they trust will not pass the confidential information on to others. It's ironic that some of us expect a third party to keep a confidence that we ourselves have betrayed. When you discuss private information about another person with anyone, you can assume that it will become public—*and* that the person whose confidence you betrayed will know that you were the source.

When leaders betray confidences, they lose more than the respect of their work associates. They also dry up valuable sources of information because their employees and colleagues learn to withhold sensitive information from a loose-lipped leader.

Leaders who pass on confidential personal information do not suffer as much career damage as those who lack other dimensions of integrity. If the leader has an otherwise good reputation, people may try to compensate by emphasizing forcefully to the leader that certain information *must* be held in confidence. When a well-intentioned leader hears the urgency of the request, he will usually get the message.

Acting on Confidences without Betraying Them

If you hear something in confidence that you strongly believe needs to be shared with others, ask for permission to share the confidence, or work with the person who disclosed the information to find a way to communicate about the issue in a protective way.

Integrity competencies are clearly central to your effectiveness as a leader. Recall Cindy Carlson, who kept Capital Professional Partners afloat and secured her employees' trust in large measure because they knew she would always tell them the unvarnished truth about the company's condition. Mike Hughes, a senior VP with the insurance company Safeco Corporation, is convinced that leadership integrity is his most powerful retention tool. Mike says, "People see my leadership and they want to be part of a team where moral leadership is shown."

6

Responsibility

I think of a hero as someone who understands the degree of responsibility that comes with his freedom.

—Bob Dylan

We've gotten to the point where everybody's got a right and nobody's got a responsibility.

—Newton Minow, former Chairman of the FCC

The Responsibility Competencies	• Taking responsibility for personal choices
	• Admitting mistakes and failures
	• Embracing responsibility for serving others

The Buck Stops Here. That was the saying on the plaque on President Harry Truman's desk in the Oval Office. He referred to it on several occasions to underscore the idea that an American president didn't have the luxury of passing off accountability for decisions to anyone else. That the expression has survived for over half a century is testament to the importance of the responsibility principle. The fact that we need the reminder is an indication of how difficult it can be to live in alignment with the responsibility principle.

Irresponsibility is nothing new. In biblical lore, the first human excuse followed close on the heels of God's creation of the species: When God caught Adam eating the forbidden fruit, Adam promptly claimed, "Eve made me do it." We live in a culture that tolerates a high degree of daily responsibility-dodging, but when it gets to the level of, say, widespread corporate scandals, it's the failures of responsibility that upset us most. We know that executives of Enron, WorldComm, and others involved in corporate scandals, lacked integrity. But the question we heard the most after the collapse of those enterprises was this, "How could they have done that to their employees? How could they leave their workers stranded with no jobs and no retirement funds?" Three years after the Enron debacle, former CEO Ken Lay claims that he had no idea former CFO Andrew Fastow was manipulating the accounting ledger. That may be so, but it also seems that Lay never heard about the sign on Truman's desk. Leaders are responsible. It comes with the job. We can shirk it, and we can make excuses when things get tough, but we do so at our peril. We suffer and so does our business. But as challenging as it may be to accept responsibility, the rewards of accepting responsibly are great. As with every other moral competency, we do it because it's morally right and then discover that it's right for our business as well.

Taking Responsibility for Personal Choices

The hallmark of personal responsibility is our willingness to accept that we are accountable for the results of the choices we make. Everything we do follows the law of cause and effect. When we cause something to happen, there is an effect, usually more than one effect. Some of the consequences of our actions are planned; other consequences come as a surprise. Owning personal choice entails that we take responsibility for all consequences of our behavior, both anticipated effects and unintended consequences.

Middle managers frequently struggle with the responsibility competency because they often feel caught between their responsibility for the people they lead and the demands of their senior managers. Frustrated middle managers often complain that they have all the responsibility and none of the authority. That complaint may be code for "I am not really responsible for my actions because my boss made me do it."

Responsibility is a radical competency because it requires that we accept personal responsibility for everything that we do, even though we each live in a complicated world where bosses, family members, and friends all exert pressure on us to act in certain ways. Responsibility means no excuses, even though none of us is perfect and all of us have good explanations for failing to do what we know is right.

No Excuses. Mike Manning (pseudonym) loves golf. Ironically, his passion for golf led him to a moral crossroads early in his career. Mike's goals at one time were to be successful in business, be a great golfer, and be a good father. Mike was very clear about what he needed to do to be successful in his work. He knew what he had to do to become a better golfer—he had to get in a certain number of rounds per week to improve his game. "The trouble is," Mike said, "I don't have time to be

a good father if I want to do well in business and excel in golf."
Someone suggested he kill two birds with one stone by golfing with his
kids. Mike was scornful. "That wouldn't work at all," he complained.
"It wouldn't be fun, and it certainly wouldn't help my game." But on
reflection, Mike came to this realization: "Saying I don't have time to
be a good father makes it sound like it's not my responsibility, as though
time is at fault. Being a good father is a more important goal than being
a good golfer. If I want to be a good father, I have to make choices about
how I spend my time." At first, Mike thought he would have to give up
golf, and then he realized that the idea about golfing with his kids was a
good one. He could enjoy playing golf and let go of the need to aggressively improve his game. Mike admitted responsibility for his choice to
put other goals above his desire to be a good parent. Only when he realized that the choice was his was he able to take steps to be a more
responsible father.

Accepting responsibility for personal choice does not mean mindlessly holding to decisions no matter how unproductive they turn out to
be. But neither does it mean that we have to be sure we have made the
perfect choice. Responsibility is not about making the perfect choice.
Instead, it is about making the choice you have made the perfect choice
for you. Some leaders make it a priority to find work that is consistent
with their moral compass, even if it involves declining promotions or
passing up tempting external job offers. Jim Thomsen, SVP of
Distribution with Thrivent Financial for Lutherans, says, "What has
kept me with this organization is that I can make a difference while honoring my values. It's not about the money. I've had opportunities to
make more money, and I've had opportunities that would give me more
prestige. But values have played a central role in my decision to work
where I work." Other leaders who have been seduced by jobs, with
attractive compensation and perks, come to feel trapped in roles that
might not reflect their most deeply held values. They may sense a need
for change, but out of a misguided notion of responsibility cling to their
current position. "I took this job, so I need to see it through." A leader

who senses he or she is in the wrong job can demonstrate responsibility in one of two ways—help reshape the organization so it is worth remaining, or have the courage to make a values-driven career change.

Admitting Mistakes and Failures

Another important aspect of responsibility includes the willingness to take responsibility when things go wrong. Many of us grew up naively assuming that when we turned 21, graduated from college, got married, or got our first job, we would then be perfect finished products. Others have found that career success has allowed them the illusion that they are indeed perfect. The higher you go in an organization, the less likely it is that people around you will give you accurate feedback, so it becomes easy to forget that you are as flawed as the most junior staffer. What's more, the higher you go in an organization, the easier it is for you to confuse power with perfection. So the best advice to senior managers is, "Don't believe your PR." The more elevated your organizational status, the more important it is for you to actively solicit feedback on your weaknesses.

Even if you know you are not perfect and even if you realize that you make mistakes, it may be frightening to admit it. Some organizational cultures are punitive, and the cost of failure can be very high. You may worry about losing a raise, a promotion, or even a job if your mistake is discovered. The irony is that punishing mistakes dampens the risk-taking and experimentation so crucial to sustainable business performance.

If you really do work in an organization that does not tolerate mistakes, our advice is to get out as soon as you can.

Fortunately, most of us work in organizations that tolerate our mistakes, even if they aren't happy about them. Even more fortunately, admitting mistakes and failures will enhance our leadership reputation more often than it damages it. Don MacPherson of Modern Survey Company can attest to the positive effects of admitting mistakes. "One time, we had prepared a report for the SVPs of a Fortune 500 company. We made a mistake in some top line data. We inadvertently didn't include all the survey responses in the results, and it seriously distorted the picture. Of course, we realized that if we didn't tell them about our mistake, they would have no way of knowing that the report was inaccurate. But we didn't want them to make decisions based on faulty data, so we never debated whether or not to tell them, only how we should go about it. I called my client contact, let her know the extent of the problem, and shared what I thought we should do to fix the problem. Her reputation was important to her and to us, and it was essential that we take 100% of the responsibility for the error. We redid the report—of course, at no cost—and we submitted a signed memo taking the blame. They are now our best client, and our client contact is the same woman, and she is fiercely loyal to us."

Admitting personal mistakes helps an organization be healthier in several ways. First, admitting that you have screwed up prevents someone else from being blamed for your mistake. It's common in organizational hierarchies for junior staff to take the fall for their senior managers, and few things are more demoralizing to employees than unfair criticism. Second, admitting mistakes creates a bond with other employees who feel that you are more approachable by virtue of your admission of fallibility. Finally, admitting mistakes communicates a strong message of tolerance to the organization at large. It says, "We all make mistakes. We know that mistakes and failures are a part of the road to success. We want you to learn from your mistakes, and we hope in the future you will make new mistakes and not repeat old ones." By admitting mistakes and failures, you can help create a more risk-tolerant climate that leads to innovation and financial success.

Rick Clevette, now at the Carlson Companies, tells a story from his days as an executive in a large Fortune 500 company. One of the firm's top business heads was a pillar of a leader, long on integrity but a bit short on patience. He had a reputation for being very hard on people. The training department had brought in Ken Blanchard of "The One Minute Manager" fame to talk to hundreds of top and mid-level managers. Ken gave his usual entertaining and enlightening stump speech about the importance of looking for opportunities to give employees "one minute" of praise. Not long after, this leader blew up at a junior manager who was making a presentation. The leader soon realized his mistake. He apologized—in writing. He sent a memo to the manager and a copy to the training people, asking them to contact Ken Blanchard about adding another principle to the "One Minute Manager,"— suggesting the need for a "one minute apology." By apologizing in such a public way, this leader not only admitted his own error, but modeled the value of admitting mistakes to his whole organization.

Admitting mistakes makes sense, not only as a moral imperative, but a practical one. Covering up mistakes takes a lot of time and energy and often makes a situation far worse than it need be. Martha Stewart's conviction and prison sentence is a famous example. Stewart was not convicted of insider trading, but of obstructing justice. When the FBI interviewed her in connection with their investigation of insider trading, they concluded she lied about why she had sold her ImClone stock. Had she admitted that she sold her stock when she heard that ImClone's CEO was dumping his, she would probably never have been charged with a serious crime.

As important as it is to admit mistakes, it is not a "free pass." It does not absolve you of responsibility for the situation you created or magically undo the harm you may have caused. Though most people would understandably prefer to avoid mistakes that hurt others, there are times when admitting a mistake creates opportunities that would not have existed otherwise. Consider this example of a mistake that transformed a contentious work relationship. Faith Shanley (pseudonym) was a bright, up and coming executive who was frequently on the opposite side of issues from her colleague Louis Draper (pseudonym), a seasoned executive who had been with their company since its inception.

At a management meeting both attended, Faith decided she needed to make a stand about a proposal she viewed as unethical. She made her point forcefully and, in the process, became sarcastic and confrontational with Louis. Faith felt great after the meeting, proud that she had said something important and confident that her views were well-founded. Shortly after, Louis walked into Faith's office and told her he was very upset about what she had done in the meeting. In a flash, Faith realized that she had been so caught up in standing up for what she thought was right, that she was oblivious to the impact of her confrontational style on Louis and the rest of the group. Faith promptly apologized to Louis. She admitted that she should have come to him privately before the meeting to explain her point of view because she knew in advance that there would be a conflict with his ideas. Faith was grateful that Louis came directly to her to discuss her behavior instead of gossiping behind her back. Louis was impressed with Faith's willingness to admit her mistake. Instead of avoiding each other as they had done in the past, Faith and Louis began to meet regularly on the issues that affected them, and over time, their once distant relationship became closer and more productive.

Embracing Responsibility for Serving Others

We are all responsible for contributing to the well-being of others. Why is serving others an essential moral competence? Think back to the biological origins of morality. We come into the world programmed to be interdependent. We wouldn't be around today if our earliest human ancestors hadn't huddled together to help their fellow tribes people survive. If we do not work to serve others, we fail to act as morally intelligent leaders. Serving others is, in fact, a great way to show integrity and to encourage others to model it—in other words, to lead by example.

When Charlie Zelle bought out his family's troubled transportation business, much of his motivation was to be of service to his employees and the community. Explaining his distress at the family's plans to close up shop, he added, "I just felt that some kind of moral boundary was being violated—perhaps it is the idea that you should consider everyone, not just yourself, in any decision."

Suppose you don't buy the idea that interdependence is innate. It still makes sense to actively care about the well-being of others. Here's why: We all value personal happiness. We want to be happy even though we know it is a self-centered motivation. For most of us, the happiness we seek doesn't happen in a vacuum. Happiness is hard to come by without help from others. Most of us need others to help us be happy.

Gary O'Hagan agrees that service is important, but he thinks that serving others serves himself at least as much. "Every time I've done something for others, it's given me a better feeling about myself. When I help family or friends or even charities, I actually have stopped and asked myself if I'm really serving others or if I'm just being selfish."

Ignoring the needs of others keeps us from experiencing the genuine pleasure that Gary experienced in helping others. The mentality expressed by the 1990s bumper sticker, "Whoever dies with the most toys wins," describes fleeting pleasure but not true happiness. For most people, lasting happiness comes from activities that give us a sense of meaning and purpose—such as serving others. Recent studies on longevity have found that serving as a volunteer with some worthwhile organization adds years to our lives (not to mention life to our years).

Accepting responsibility for serving others is also a secret weapon for leaders who want to promote high performance among their workforce. To make their businesses successful, leaders need committed employees. One of the best ways to encourage people to unleash their creative energy in service to their company is for their leaders to serve *them*. Employees don't need to be coerced into doing their best work for your organization. People have an inherent and insatiable appetite for

personal growth. Left to their own devices, employees will spontaneously contribute to your organization as their way of growing and
succeeding in life. That is why leaders don't need to impose goals from
on high. Much of the time and effort companies devote to complicated
performance management systems is unnecessary. The most efficient
way to elicit strong financial results is for leaders to serve their employees. When we serve our employees, we send them this message:

> **I know that what you are capable of producing is far
> greater than what our company needs in order to succeed.
> So my opportunity as your leader is to serve you as you do
> what you want to do, which I already know goes beyond
> what I need from you. My goal is to serve your needs and
> help each of you be as successful as you want to be and help
> you get out of life what you want. If I can help you accom-
> plish what you want to do, then I know our company will
> do very well. I don't have to focus on the numbers. I have to
> focus on you and all our people. Then the numbers will be
> fine. Because together our people will perform better than
> our financial targets require. I know that serving you serves
> the bottom line.**

The Retention Value of Servant Leadership. Imagine how your
employees will respond if you consistently demonstrate that your primary leadership job is to help employees accomplish their own goals.
They will stay. Because most businesses yield more value from experienced employees than new recruits, your decision to serve employees
will translate into higher levels of knowledge and performance. Because
you respect your employees' goals, they will be highly motivated to
give their best efforts to you and your organization.

At American Express Financial Advisors, managers are encouraged
to spend considerable time helping financial advisors to develop life
goals that include business goals *and* important personal goals.

Managers are also expected to find ways to support their advisors as they reach for their goals. This approach has resulted in excellent retention and bottom-line performance. Because the company is able to keep a high percentage of financial advisors, it generates revenue it would have otherwise lost—while at the same time lowering expenses through reduced turnover costs.

7

Compassion and Forgiveness

If you want others to be happy, practice compassion. If you want to be happy, practice compassion.

—The Dalai Lama

Forgiveness is almost a selfish act because of its immense benefits to the one who forgives.

—Lawana Blackwell, The Dowry of Miss Lydia Clark

The Compassion Competency	• Actively caring about others

Actively Caring About Others

When you are a leader, embracing your responsibility to serve others flows into compassion. Actively caring about others means that you do things that actively support the personal choices of others. Sometimes, it means you care about others' goals as much as they do. At times, you might find yourself taking others' goals more seriously than they feel able to. Mike Woodward, SVP of American Express Financial Advisors, is a conscientious and productive leader, but also a very private person who, early in his career, was reluctant to share his personal goals with his manager. After some nudging from his boss, Mike confided, "I really want to spend more time with my daughters. I have done a lot of hunting and fishing with my sons, but I haven't spent as much time with my girls, and I'm missing that." Then, soccer season rolled around for one of his daughters who was a strong athlete. Mike had arranged his schedule to attend her soccer games. Then, Mike was called to a meeting of the top national sales managers to be held in Minneapolis. The meeting was running late, and Mike's boss realized Mike would need to leave before the meeting ended if he wanted to see his daughter's soccer game. But Mike wasn't moving. Mike's boss interrupted the meeting. "Mike, don't you have a flight to catch?" he asked. "Yeah," Mike answered, "but the meeting is going long." His boss then demonstrated his support for Mike's personal goals, saying, "Leave now. Go to the airport. Go home and see your daughter's game."

AEFA's Brian Heath, the body-building executive with the bouncer's physique, doesn't look like a compassionate type. Appearances to the contrary, he is deeply compassionate. In Brian's mind, compassion isn't just about taking pity on the helpless. It is about taking people's hopes and dreams seriously and doing what he can to help them achieve their aspirations. He sets ambitious goals, but only after he is sure he understands what his people hope to accomplish.

IMG President Gary O'Hagan also subscribes to the notion that compassion means challenging people to do their best, believing that they can accomplish their goals, and providing the tools they need to succeed. There was a time right after Gary was cut by the New York Jets when he coached junior varsity high-school football. There were only 25 teens on his team, and 4 of them were handicapped. He wasn't sure what to do. He was afraid his handicapped players would get hurt, but they wanted to play badly, so he decided that they were going to play. Gary explains, "The handicapped kids were offside all the time, but we decided to work on that. With the help of the non-handicapped kids—who were phenomenal—we instituted a special series of concentration drills—that by the way had nothing specifically to do with football. We put in some penalties for not doing the drills right. We were very nurturing, and the coaching staff and the whole team were very compassionate, and we converted the handicapped kids' weakness into a strength. We never went offside during a game that whole season. Their progress was incredible. The solution was unique, and it allowed everyone to contribute."

Jefferson Bus Line's CEO, Charlie Zelle, points out that compassion doesn't mean ignoring bad behavior—that sometimes the most compassionate thing a leader can do is hold an employee accountable for unacceptable behavior. A number of years ago, Charlie had a senior manager who began to act like a loose cannon. It was a stressful time because the company had to close down a division. In a misguided attempt to show compassion for an employee he was letting go, the manager started badmouthing the company's decision during his termination discussion with her. Every employee he laid off got a different explanation for the layoff. Then, the manager began an affair with someone in the corporate office. Other people tried to ignore the manager's missteps, but Charlie knew he had to let him go. If Charlie ignored the manager's bad behavior, it would wreak havoc with the trust other employees had in him and the company.

Three years later, the manager he had fired came back and asked for a half hour with Charlie. Turns out, he came to thank Charlie. He had been drinking heavily during those last few months with Charlie's company and getting fired had been the wake-up call that prompted his entry into a treatment program. If Charlie had kept the manager on board out of misplaced compassion, it might have taken a lot longer for him to get the help he needed. Charlie's reaction? "This said to me, you've got to do the right thing even if at the moment it feels like the person will really hate you."

ID Media's Lynn Fantom has an unusual appreciation for compassion. She considers it central to her leadership approach. "I take my model for management from my mother. To me, the behavioral model of a mother is perfect for management. A mother is very compassionate and encouraging and forgiving. Think about how a mother behaves when she is helping a young child learn to walk. When I became a mother, I became a much better manager."

Jay Sleiter, CEO of BWBR Architects, discovered that compassion can open the door to unexpected business opportunities. In the early 1990s, due to some federal legislative decisions, the bottom had dropped out of their specialty market designing healthcare facilities. However, many opportunities existed in the international market, so they decided to pursue markets in Southeast Asia. They knew that these countries were revamping their health-care systems and didn't have enough regional capacity to build the required facilities. Quickly, BWBR found that there was plenty of work if they were willing to go along with some very corrupt business practices characteristic in the region at that time. But they finally found a firm of Chinese and Malay architects operating in Malaysia, whose business values were remarkably consistent with those of BWBR. Jay said, "So we partnered with them. Then the Southeast Asian economy tanked. This proud Malaysian company was now faced with laying off many of their staff. Meanwhile, BWBR's domestic business had come back full steam, so Jay's company sent the Malaysian architects enough work to help them stay in business.

Today, that relationship has grown so that the Malaysian has become more and more a part of BWBR's business. Because of compassion, what began as an opportunistic alliance has become a genuine partnership.

The Forgiveness Competencies	• Letting go of one's own mistakes • Letting go of others' mistakes

The two forgiveness competencies are "mirror competencies," clearly very closely related. It is hard to talk about one without the other, but they are not the same skill. Some of us are much better at forgiving ourselves than others and vice versa. Many of us are hard on ourselves because of perfectionism. We can let go of other's mistakes but hold on to our own. Sometimes, we are our own worst critics. Others of us have an easier time forgiving ourselves because we know our own underlying good intentions, while we may resist forgiving others because we distrust their motives. Effective leaders know that letting go of mistakes—their own and others—clears the way for better future performance.

Letting Go of Your Own Mistakes

The founders of Modern Survey were riding high. They knew they had developed a unique technology for providing survey-based business information. Right out of the gate, they landed a big contract with a Fortune 500 client and had several projects going on at the same time, each with a different contact person. They worked hard on the various projects and were sure the results had impressed their clients. They geared up to bid on another project for this company. Then co-founder, Don MacPherson, got an unwelcome call from a key contact in the company. They were taking all their business to a competitor and wouldn't even let Modern Survey submit a bid. The problem? Don and his partners had assumed that their superior technology was the only thing they needed to be successful. Don was responsible for managing the account, and he hadn't spent any time cultivating high-quality relationships with his client contacts. They wanted more attentive service, and when they didn't get it from Modern Survey, they went elsewhere. Don says, "My mistake was not taking good care of that relationship. We expected the business. We felt entitled to the business rather than understanding we have to continually work for the business. We've never gotten the client back."

Don's partners were upset about the situation, but they didn't blame Don. Don, however, blamed himself. He dwelled on his mistake for almost six months. Three years later, he still thinks about it occasionally and gets upset. But only by letting go were Don and his partners able to think more clearly about how to change their business practices, and those changes have helped the company with their other clients. "Now," says Don, "I make sure I give all my clients the kind of service and nurturing that I failed to give the one we lost."

Letting go of our mistakes doesn't mean we have to excuse or explain away unacceptable behavior. It is important, after all, to accept responsibility for what you did and commit to do better going forward. But we do have to give up the negative self-talk that can crowd our brain when we have disappointed ourselves. Why? When we are busy talking to ourselves about our frustration, anxiety, and guilt, there is no mental space for learning the lessons of our mistakes. If we can't forgive ourselves, we stay stuck; we hold ourselves back from fresh experiences and opportunities.

Brian Heath discovered that the hardest part of letting go of a mistake is first to admit that you have made one (the responsibility competency of admitting mistakes). When Brian was promoted from a regional VP to the newly created Group VP job, he had a stellar track record for developing high performing sales teams. Several months into his new role, his group's performance had slid below the national average. For someone who had never been in that territory, the experience was shocking and debilitating. It took him a while to figure out what was going wrong. He was frustrated in his job and missed the direct contact he used to have with his field sales force. Now, instead of concentrating on developing his field team, he was spending a lot of energy developing a new piece of the bureaucracy—a mandated coordinating team intended to link him to the regional market groups. Finally, Brian had an epiphany, "I was focusing more on a method than an outcome. The evidence was there for several months, but I couldn't or wouldn't see it. It was hard to let go because I was vested in my own decision how to go about my new job. Finally, I realized I needed to be more courageous at helping advisors and helping clients."

In some professions, constant self-forgiveness is the only way to survive. When Gary O'Hagan was a young bond trader with Solomon Brothers, he found that if he didn't quickly let go of trading mistakes, he would be immobilized. When he made a mistake, he had to let it go, so he'd have the courage to trade another day. Gary reminisces, "I recall one day when I was managing the municipal bonds trading desk. For some reason, the municipal market was lagging in spite of other bond markets doing pretty well. I decided to take more risk and add to our position. I didn't find out until the day was over that Congress was considering removing tax exempt status from municipal bonds. I could have and should have paused and dug in to find out why the municipals' prices were dropping. Another bond house had done its homework, but I didn't, and it cost the firm a lot of money." Asked what happened after that, Gary responds, "Although we lost a lot of money that day because of my mistake, I was able to let it go the next day, and we went on to have a very good year!"

Letting Go of Others' Mistakes

There is an apocryphal story about legendary IBM CEO, Thomas Watson. A high-potential junior manager reputedly made a mistake that cost IBM $5 million dollars. Devastated by his error, the junior executive offered his resignation, but Watson would not accept it. The young man was confused. "I don't understand," he told Watson, "I made a terrible mistake. Why on earth would you want to keep me?" Watson replied, "I just invested $5 million on your learning curve. Why would I want to waste that kind of money?"

The Forgiving Leader's Perspective. Imagine that I have made a mistake that affects you or causes you harm. Forgiving you does not mean that I endorse what you have done. In the case of serious harm, it does not mean giving up my claim for justice. You are still accountable for what you did. When I forgive you, what remains is a belief in your probable good intentions (unless you are a *very* bad person). But when I forgive you, I allow my resentment and anger to recede, along with my negative judgments about you that would prevent me from considering you as a potential resource. When I forgive you, I continue to recognize that you have flaws, but I do not define you completely in terms of your flaws. I allow for the possibility that you have strengths that I can draw on in the future.

Without forgiveness, human life is virtually impossible. Intimate relationships with friends, family, and co-workers cannot exist without forgiveness. Without forgiveness, a leader's organizational performance is artificially capped. The effective leader forms a relationship with followers with forgiveness at its core. The forgiving leader's message to followers is essentially this:

> **You might as well know in advance that I will make mistakes, and so will you. As your boss, there are times when I won't be doing my best work. There will be days when**

you're not in top form, either. If you can't forgive me for not always being your perfect boss, our relationship will be ineffective. It will be not only emotionally hurtful, but neither of us will perform as well as we should. If we can forgive each other for not being perfect, we will both be able to use each other as a valuable resource. We will be able to help each other be happy and perform at our best.

In the previous three chapters, we have talked about the specific moral competencies we need to live in alignment with our principles. Taken together, our moral competencies are the behavioral glue that binds together all the frames of the alignment model. Though we've considered them one by one, it's rare to find moral competencies in isolation. The moral competencies overlap because the universal principles themselves overlap. It's hard to imagine someone who has integrity but lacks responsibility or someone who has compassion but lacks forgiveness. Our moral competencies act synergistically to keep our day-to day actions lined up with who we want to become and what we hope to achieve. We each have relative strengths and weaknesses in our moral competencies. The more competent we become across the full spectrum of moral competencies, the more we will live in alignment. The more aligned we are, the happier we will be, and the more productive and successful our organizations will be.

8

Emotions

Usually, we know the right thing to do (using our moral compass), and frequently, we know how to do the right thing (using our moral competencies). What then stops us from doing what we know is right? Moral challenges usually provoke highly charged emotions. How can we manage our emotions in a positive way? This chapter explores how our emotional intelligence competencies can help us reinforce our moral intelligence. By acting together, our emotional and moral competencies can enable us to conform more deeply to universal human principles and gain greater moral intelligence.

Recall the potential obstacles to staying in alignment. When destructive emotions and moral viruses threaten, our emotional skills help us stay connected with our values. There is nothing necessarily moral about emotional competencies. But emotional competencies are essential tools for the morally smart leader.

Keith Reinhard, chairman of DDB Worldwide tells this story:

> **I can remember being excited when my boss decided that he wanted me to be his successor. But there was a hitch. Charlie, the guy everyone thought would get the job, figured he had it all wrapped up. So my boss decided that he would create a new job for Charlie and sell it to him as a promotion, thereby getting him out of the way so I could have clear shot for my boss's job. Then after I got my new job, my boss would find a way to get Charlie out of the company. I wouldn't accept it. I told my boss that Charlie had always been straight with me and I couldn't do this to him. I thought it would be better for my boss to be straight with Charlie. I even quoted him some of his own public statements about integrity. So he was honest with Charlie after all, and things worked out fine.**

How tempting it would have been for Keith to let his promotion play out the way his boss originally planned. Keith could have stood by quietly while his boss cleared the playing field by offering a bogus job to the heir apparent. Keith wanted that job, and he knew he could get it without being personally responsible for sidelining Charlie. All he had to do was keep his mouth shut. But as much as he wanted the job, Keith knew that his personal integrity was at stake. So he told his boss that he wouldn't take the job if it meant treating Charlie badly. Some executive power players may not have taken that message kindly. But Keith was no fool. He gave his boss a way to deal with Charlie that was aligned with values—both his and his boss's. Keith's goal of advancement could have easily overcome his values had he not tapped into his moral and emotional skills to find a morally acceptable way to get promoted. Keith needed the moral competencies of acting consistently with values and telling the truth. But he also needed the emotional skill of self-awareness to recognize two conflicting emotions—both his strong desire for the job and his discomfort about how Charlie might be treated. He needed the confidence that he could handle a negative reaction from his boss if he challenged him about his treatment of Charlie. He needed the interpersonal savvy to convince his boss to deal with Charlie in a morally competent manner.

Self-Awareness

Every waking moment, we face the world from within an **experiential triangle** of thoughts, emotions, and actions. No matter what is going on, we are always *thinking*, *feeling*, and *doing*, and we are doing all those things simultaneously. As leaders and decision makers, many of us are more comfortable operating in one of those three domains. Some of us are thinking types who tend to rely on logic and ideas; others are feeling types who tend to make decisions based on emotion, or some are physical types who want to *do*, to take action, as a way of responding to a problem. Research on work styles shows that American business leaders tend to be thinking and doing types, rather than feeling types. It's not that business people don't know they have feelings. It's just that many feel uncomfortable expressing them. Why the discomfort? English-speaking cultures place a high value on the products of the cognitive mind. No doubt thoughts *are* powerful. What we think certainly affects how we feel and what we do. But emotions are equally powerful. How we feel strongly affects what we think and what we do. Fear may paralyze us into inaction; anger may prompt us to strike out; optimistic beliefs may give us courage. Life's experiential triangle is an endless loop in which thoughts, feelings, and actions are continuously and mutually influencing one another.

Whether or not you are aware of your own experiential triangle, people around you see the outward behavior that results. What your colleagues notice about you and how they interpret what they see have enormous impact on your work relationships, for good or ill. Because those around you can't read your (thinking and feeling) mind, it is easy for them to misunderstand your actions. If you want to be an effective leader, you need your colleagues to accurately understand what you mean and why you do what you do. Without self-awareness, you will remain a mystery to yourself, and you'll be in the dark about how you come across to your colleagues. If you are unaware of your feelings, you are at their mercy. Without self-awareness, your capacity for self-correction is extremely limited.

Modern Survey's Don MacPherson is seething. Earlier today, he was presenting a software demonstration to a new client, and the demo didn't work. "I can be very hard on my partners. They are the ones who create what I sell. If something goes wrong with the technology, it upsets me. And I'm the one who has to deal with the fallout. I handle it professionally with the client, but then I go back to my partners and get angry with them." Don pauses, leans back in his chair, and then continues, "I haven't told my partners yet about the problem today, and now that I'm talking about it I'm sure I will handle it better and not blame them. I know they'll get it fixed, and the fact that the demo didn't work won't be a big deal. Sometimes, the software is complicated and mistakes happen."

Don's story illustrates the power of self-awareness. He recognized that his typical pattern when angry about technical problems was to haul off and blame his partners. But this time, he reflected on the situation. He became aware of his frustration. He had time to put some distance between how he felt and what he would do about it. That self-conscious pause—between reaction and action—made a big difference. It allowed Don to plan how to talk constructively with his partners about the failed demo. He was even able to change his attitude about it: Instead of thinking "woe is me" because he had to deal with clients when things go wrong, Don was now able to see technical problems in a way that was both realistic and optimistic. That moment of self-awareness will pay dividends in reduced personal stress and a smoother relationship with his partners.

Recognizing Feelings. When a moral choice is at stake, self-awareness is essential. Recall Keith and his promotion. Keith's awareness—of his excitement about a likely promotion *and* discomfort about the impact on a trusted colleague—was crucial to communicating with his mentor in a way that produced positive results. Without awareness, Keith's desire for advancement might have overridden any moral reservations he had. Without sensitivity to the pain his colleague would feel at being passed over in a manipulative way, Keith might have remained silent. If emotions—Keith's and Charlie's—had been factored out of the decision process, Keith's promotion would have played out in a way that was morally suspect and likely damaging to Keith's credibility in his new role. All business decisions have wide audiences. Keith and Charlie's colleagues would have known that Charlie had been manipulated. Charlie's closest colleagues probably would have resented Keith, even though he was not directly responsible for Charlie's bad fortune.

Inner Feelings Affect the Outer World. Awareness of your feelings is also vital to your ability to create a positive work climate for your employees. Because emotions are contagious, you need to monitor your feelings so that the mood you project is a stable one. Leaders accomplish far more when they don't put their people in a position of wondering what kind of mood their leader is going to be in each day. If you can save your colleagues the trouble of having to navigate around your unexamined emotions, you will liberate more creative energy for performance that would otherwise be sapped by your employees' anxiety.

Understanding Your Thoughts

Tune in to your thoughts, and you will realize that you are in constant conversation with yourself. Listen in while you head to work: You pass a Jaguar and think, "I'd love to have a car like that." You're stopped at an endless red. When the light changes you accelerate and someone cuts you off. "What a jerk!," you say to yourself. That constant internal dialogue is often called "self-talk." Whether we are alone or not, our minds are full of ideas and attitudes that we express in the inner language of self-talk. That self-talk, in turn, has a major impact on our emotions *and* our physical state. Thoughts are powerful. We may shed tears when we think of a lost parent or smile when we think about our last vacation. We did not decide to cry or smile; our physical reaction happened spontaneously in response to our thoughts.

Effective leaders tend to be highly conscious of their internal thoughts, like Safeco's Mike Hughes. Mike's self-talk comes in the form of frequent warnings, which he believes are key to his success. "My inner dialogue is very, very conscious, and it's usually geared toward thinking about how other people feel about a situation. When I pay attention, I am able to handle the situation with sensitivity. Sometimes, I don't show as much empathy as I should, but the inner dialogue is always taking place." Ed Zore, Northwestern Mutual's CEO, is constantly aware of his feelings and reactions, adding, "I sometimes have to sort them out from the objective facts because my feelings and the facts about a situation can be very different."

We need to understand our thoughts so that we can monitor and manage their emotional and physical effects. Our thoughts are not random, and we are not at their mercy. As we'll see shortly, we can choose our thoughts. When we change our thoughts, everything changes.

Time Out to Tune In: A Self-Awareness Break

Pick a few times during each day to perform a mental check. Ask yourself:

- What am I thinking right now? What am I saying to myself?
- What am I feeling about that? Am I excited, frustrated, peaceful, annoyed?
- What am I doing physically at this moment? How is my breathing? Are my jaws clenched? Am I hungry or thirsty?

Personal Effectiveness

We don't cultivate self-awareness for its own sake, but because it provides us the data we need to manage ourselves and our emotions. Managing emotions, by the way, does *not* mean trying not to feel, denying hurt, or even necessarily concealing strong emotions. We are not meant to be unemotional automatons (like *Star Trek's* Mr. Spock). It is human to feel uncomfortable emotions. Personal effectiveness helps us channel our emotions so that we are able to spend more time living in alignment. The goal is not to increase our emotional awareness and emotional skills per se; it is to increase these competencies so we can achieve greater alignment and moral intelligence. Personal effectiveness encompasses all the skills we use to perform well in the face of strong emotions. These include

- Changing self-defeating beliefs that lead to upsetting emotions

- Deciding to behave well under trying circumstances

- Rolling with the punches when things don't go our way

- Taking care of ourselves so we can better handle stressful situations

Deciding What to Think

If your thoughts are self-critical, you will notice that your emotions are negative, your body is tight, and you are not able to perform at your best. If you spend a few minutes to replace your critical thoughts with statements of realistic confidence in yourself, your mood lifts, your body relaxes, and your work performance improves. Negative self-talk is a program for failure, while positive self-talk frees you to do your best. A caveat: We are not advocating that you mindlessly allow only positive self-talk or that you ignore fears or failings. There are negative thoughts that are realistic and must be confronted seriously. But no matter how dire the situation at hand, realistically positive self-talk is the best way to get your mind and body ready to perform effectively. If we *think* we can't run a marathon, we won't even try. Now imagine replacing that belief with a different thought—"If I train hard, I'll bet I can finish the marathon." Our new thought makes it far more likely that we will ultimately reach the finish line. Why? Because now we have created the motivation we need to get ready for the race.

When you are in a morally charged situation, it helps to remind yourself of your principles, values, and beliefs. Self-talk about your beliefs allows you to counteract disruptive emotions that can drive you out of alignment with your moral compass. When Cray Inc.'s Lori Kaiser is really troubled or searching for direction, she thinks about the three principles that she tries to live by: "First, if I don't speak up, nobody will—don't assume it will be handled by someone else. Second, Winston Churchill said, 'Never, never, ever give up!' That kind of tenacity is important in business. Third is a quote from existentialist philosopher, Albert Camus, 'In the midst of the darkest day of winter, I find within myself the eternal day of summer.'"

Lori's practice of mentally recalling her principles is an example of the value of deliberately interrupting negative thought processes or feelings. Once our minds are clear, we are ready to tackle the situation at hand. Then we can ask ourselves, "What do I need to think about to deliver what I need? There is a bonus that comes with changing our self-talk: When we alter our internal thoughts from negative to positive ones, any emotional and physical discomfort we may feel usually lessens or goes away entirely.

Self-Control

Effective leaders rely on self-control to maintain alignment with principles. Most successful leaders know from experience that losing emotional control is bad for their self-esteem, their reputations, and their business performance. A healthcare executive we'll call Ellen understands the importance of emotional control. "I've blown up at someone only twice in my career. In the heat of the moment, I felt there was such an injustice, and I felt so 'in the right' that I justified my actions. But in reality, I violated my moral code—I certainly didn't treat them the way I'd like to be treated. Of course, they were treating me badly too, but that's no excuse. In both cases, it damaged my relationships, and that has had its costs." Asked what she learned, Ellen says, "When I get really angry, I now know to say, 'I need some time to think about this; let's talk tomorrow.' I've also learned when to consult with someone who's not personally involved before I decide what to do."

An emotionally intelligent leader knows when *not* to trust gut reactions. A marketing executive says this about self-control: "I conscientiously think about exercising self-control over my emotional responses. A few months ago, I had a job opening and knew someone in another department would be perfect for that spot. I started to recruit him, but then got a call from his boss telling me, 'No way.' My first thought was, 'Okay, fine—someday I'll do the same for you.' But then my self-control kicks in. I know better than to retaliate."

Nurturing Emotional Health

Leaders need emotional reserves to deal effectively with moral challenges. It's hard to manage stressful situations without a baseline level of emotional well-being. You can't expect yourself to deal with the demands of leading morally if your emotional tank is empty. You can't expect to influence others to be morally competent if they don't respect the way you live your life. Dan Marvin (pseudonym), CEO of a large retailing business, told us this story of a failed executive:

> **Recently, I had to let go our chief operating officer. He was probably the brightest and hardest working human being I'd ever worked with. He is the first person I've ever told that they worked too much—I've never been the poster child for personal balance myself. He would come in at 9:00 AM and leave at 1 in the morning. When he got home, his wife would get up and serve him dinner and talk to him for an hour and then go back to bed. For the two years he was here, he never got to a soccer game or baseball game of his kid. He never did anything with his wife. He'd leave early—at 11:00 at night—on birthdays and anniversaries. People hated working for him. He'd call them at 10:00 at night, and he did nothing to develop them. He lost three VPs who worked for him. Though he worked a ton of hours, he really didn't do a good job, and he put his entire family and marriage at risk.**

Balance. One of the best emotional nutrients is a balanced life. Balance means achieving equilibrium in the amount of time and energy you spend on each of the many dimensions of your life. You establish emotional equilibrium by allocating personal resources—such as time, energy, and money—to life areas in a way that makes sense to you. There is no rule for creating balance. Only you can determine how much time and energy you spend on which areas of your life. Only you know the right mix of pursuits for each stage of your life.

Human resources executive Judy Skoglund, was the first professional to work part-time at the financial services company IDS. Judy was a role model for women who saw that she was highly productive *because* of her decision to spend more time with her family, not in spite of it. Today, Judy coaches women on managing their careers. "I don't call it work life balance any more," Judy says, "I call it work life *happiness*. People don't necessarily care about balance; they want to be happy."

Women are not the only folks who care about the quality of their whole lives—men do, too. Consider the case of Frank, a successful broker who makes over $200,000 per year. Although Frank works hard, he also values family time, taking one week off every seven weeks to spend uninterrupted time with his family. His schedule was so personally rewarding that he started thinking about taking one week off every five weeks. But after planning to reduce his work hours, he then launched a new business partnership, a decision that would require he keep to his current work schedule. Frank was excited about his new business but wondered if he was copping out on his plan to spend even more time with his family. We don't think so. We think he made the decision he did because he had already achieved equilibrium. His work and family life were balanced in a way that worked both for him and his family.

Ecolab's Doug Baker works hard to keep his time expenditures aligned with his values. "Family, marriage, career, and community are all important to me. I barely have time for those four. So friends get the short end of the stick. I may only have three golf games a year that are just for fun with friends. Guys will call me and want to go golfing for two days—I'd love to but can't. I can golf or I can see my kids."

Despite the importance of creating balance, many managers, and executives in particular, do it poorly. Corporations may offer lip service about work/family balance, and some companies provide flexible work schedules or family-friendly services to enhance retention. But American business leaders rarely recognize the positive business benefits of encouraging employees to lead fulfilling and balanced lives. If they did, balance-enhancing strategies would be mandatory rather than tolerated.

Companies that support balanced lives among their employees soon discover the business benefits. They attract high performing people who are happy and productive in multiple roles. Those content employees produce excellent business results independent of how many hours they spend at work. Consider American Express, which enjoys an enviable history of strong financial performance. The company employs about 80,000 people, some of whom are undoubtedly workaholics. But the American Express executive team doesn't believe it's reasonable to base a business model on an assumption that most of its employees are workaholics. The company bases its business model on the assumption that people care about other aspects of their lives beyond the office. The American Express workforce is energized because they know that the company they work for recognizes that they have lives and that the company's leaders really want their total lives to be successful and joyful—and by the way—they do want their employees to "work their butts off" when they are at work.

Recharging Your Emotional Batteries. You are your most precious asset. When you prioritize your activities, it's important to carve out time for yourself. Physical fitness, for instance, is a key contributor to emotional health. Aerobic exercise triggers the release of brain chemicals that are associated with feelings of pleasure and well-being. Evidence of the emotional importance of exercise is that medical research has found that regular aerobic exercise (such as brisk walking) is as effective as medication in reducing symptoms of moderate depression. Your emotional well-being will be enhanced if you choose activities that you enjoy, rather than activities that you only do because you think they are good for you. Daily relaxation activities also can contribute significantly to emotional and physical well-being. Medical research underscores the benefits of planned relaxation—from lowered blood pressure to faster healing and greater pain tolerance. Dr. Herbert Benson in his best-selling book *The Relaxation Response*, provides an easy and efficient method for achieving a relaxed state.[1] Just as people need a unique balance in their life endeavors, each of us differs in the kind of activities that promote relaxation. Many people find deep breathing and meditation to be effective in calming their minds and bodies, while others may find it maddening to sit down and meditate, preferring a yoga class, a massage, or a relaxing after-dinner stroll. The important thing is to choose some daily practice that allows you to recharge your body, mind, and spirit.

Managing Emotions for Peak Performance. The self-awareness competencies and personal effectiveness competencies we have discussed here are clearly synergistic. Taking charge of your emotions means mustering all of your emotional resources to manage the competing demands of work and personal life. Most of us will never get to a state in which we perform at the absolute peak regardless of how we feel. However, the more we practice self-awareness and personal effectiveness skills, the more often we will outperform ourselves, and the more often we will find ourselves conforming our behavior to universal moral principles. Rehearsing for emotional challenges is critical to effective performance. You cannot control what will happen to you in the course of a day. But you can imagine it. You can prepare for it. You can get ready to be successful. As the old saying goes, *"Good luck happens when preparation meets opportunity."* Coping effectively will keep you from being knocked off course by destructive emotions and ensure that your behavior stays in alignment with your goals and beliefs.

Interpersonal Effectiveness

Personal effectiveness skills such as *deciding what to think* and *self-control* are obvious aids to moral competence. We know we need emotional control to do the right thing. But why do we need people skills to

1. Herbert Benson and Miriam Z. Klipper. *The Relaxation Response.* New York: Random House, 1993.

be morally competent? To serve the needs of others, we have to understand them. To be compassionate or forgiving, we need to be able to see the world through another's eyes. Interpersonal effectiveness is an indispensable leadership tool. Leaders get very little done by themselves—they rely almost completely on the energy, strength, and commitment of the people who work with them. If we want to influence others, we must understand the complex emotional worlds of others and communicate to them in ways that satisfy their emotional needs.

Northwestern Mutual's Ed Zore knows this as well as anyone, "If you're oblivious about your impact on others you'll hurt people. So you have to make an appropriate response, and that means first being aware of the wake you're leaving."

Empathy

Empathy is a kind of "as if" mental state in which you experience a challenging situation through the eyes of another person. It is as though you put on a virtual-reality headset that instantly gives you the emotional mindset of another person. Empathy is critical to moral competence because it neutralizes destructive emotions that can interfere with living in alignment. Take college President James Norwell (pseudonym), for example. When James was the VP and Dean of another liberal arts college, he found himself in an awkward position. The college president at the time had been a highly popular appointment but turned out to lack the depth needed to meet the challenges the institution faced. Frustrated with his inadequacies, the board of trustees turned to James as a sounding board, problem-solver, and potential presidential replacement. James recalls, "It would have been easy to let the board push the current president aside and put me in his job. But I knew how much he was struggling and wanted to do well. And because I was able to look at the situation from his point of view, I decided to take myself out of consideration so that I couldn't be used by the board in their attempt to resolve his limitations. I had to lay my own ambitions aside for him to be treated the way I would like to be treated in that situation."

Empathy as a Conflict Antidote. When we are at odds with others, often the last thing we want to do is to consider the situation from their point of view. Nevertheless, empathy is a powerful tool for managing conflict in a way that produces the best outcomes for you and your adversary. Recall the experiential triangle of emotions, thought, and action. If you have been clashing with a work associate, you are probably caught up in a high-energy negative emotional state that is clouding your thinking. Without empathy, you are limited by your own subjective view of reality. If you can see only your side of the conflict, you risk lashing out in anger. You may decide you have to win the battle at all costs; you may try to retaliate; you may make hurtful accusations—all actions that are inconsistent with your moral compass, actions that will also damage your reputation as a good leader.

After you experience a conflict from the perspective of another person, it is then possible for you to stay in alignment. With the expanded perspective that includes your feelings *and* the feelings of others, you can think more clearly, and the odds that you will make an aligned choice improve dramatically. Your ability to help your partner in conflict stay in alignment also improves because empathy activates both forgiveness and compassion. If you can imagine how someone else feels, you can understand why they acted as they did. With that understanding, you are more willing to let go of their mistakes and more disposed to help them accomplish their goals.

Misplaced Compassion

Empathy for another's life situation often inspires us to want to help them. It's important to distinguish between understanding another's world and being controlled by another's needs and preferences. It's possible to go too far in translating our empathy into unproductive care-taking. Pam Moret, executive vice president of Marketing and Products at Thrivent Financial for Lutherans demonstrates how to be empathetic without compromising your business. When two companies merged to form Thrivent, Pam decided to consolidate her dispersed workforce into a single location. Some employees were upset by the prospect of the move, and though Pam empathized with their feelings, she was convinced of the need to locate her group together. Though her empathy didn't change her business decision, it did cause her to engineer softer landings and lengthier transitions than many companies offer.

Listening. Leaders are generally rewarded for being decisive, for taking action, for being the experts, for having something to say. That action orientation can make it difficult for leaders to value what may seem like the passive act of listening. Hearing may be passive, but listening attentively is an active skill requiring concentration and emotional intelligence. Thrivent's Pam Moret says, "Active listening is an unbelievably powerful personal skill. If you signal to someone that they're fourth priority on your list…for example, by canceling one-on-ones or doing e-mail while you're meeting with them…it can really adversely affect them and the situation." To counteract her natural inclination to multi-task when with others, Pam has established informal contracts with her direct reports that commit her to giving them her undivided attention. When she meets with them, she tries not to sit behind her desk, look out her window at her secretary, or take a quick glance at her computer. That, says Pam, keeps her from hurting someone or missing important information.

Listening attentively is essential to moral competence. Careful listening demonstrates respect for the values, beliefs, goals, and emotions of others. Listening skillfully also makes empathy possible because it provides the data on which compassion and forgiveness are based. Very little of the meaning of what is said comes from the words themselves.

What people really mean when they speak is found in their tone of voice and the physical movements ("body language") that accompany their spoken words. That is why active listening is so much more important than passively listening to words alone. You can get the message if you get the *whole* message. Suppose you get a call at work that your daughter is sick and needs to be picked up from school. As you rush out the office, your boss says, "Are you leaving again to pick up your daughter?" Stripped of your boss's tone of voice, the words themselves could represent a simple request for clarification. But you heard the way she made that statement. Embedded in the words was a point of view. Her tone suggests she thinks you are not getting your work done. Listening carefully allows you to form a useful hypothesis that your boss is not happy with you. But active listening goes a step further. Instead of simply assuming that you have correctly assessed your boss's attitude, you check with your boss about what she meant. If your boss was just asking for information, then you can let go of the anxiety that your interpretation of her message caused. If she really is annoyed with you, testing your assumption gives you and your boss an opportunity to resolve a problem and keep you both in alignment.

Listening to Understand the Contents of all Three Frames. Active listening is typically used to uncover underlying emotional messages. But listening well can provide information about all three frames. It is important to listen in a way that allows you to discover others' values and goals. If you listen only for emotional messages, you might be missing clues that can help you stay in alignment, as well as help you to help others to stay in alignment. If you simply listen to another's emotions without understanding their values and goals, you don't know whether or not they are in alignment.

Michael Connolly, Heartland's CEO, was upset when Deborah, one of their senior executives, left abruptly to work for another multi-unit fast-food company. When he learned that Deborah was also trying to recruit other Heartland employees by bad-mouthing the Heartland management group, Michael got angry. Imagine that Michael had gone to you for advice. If you listened only to his feelings, you might be tempted to help him plan a counterattack that could damage his company's reputation and encourage employees to jump ship. Now imagine what might happen if you also listened to Michael's goals. By asking him about his goals, you would probably have learned that he wanted all of his employees to stay. By carefully listening for information about all of Michael's frames—his values, goals, and feelings, you would then have been able to encourage Michael to choose a strategy that would give him the best shot at keeping all his employees. In fact, Michael did go on to develop a plan that matched his values and goals. He called each of Heartland's employees and told them this: "We know some of you are being contacted by a former employee, and we know she wants you to consider working with her. We certainly understand why she might want you. We want you to know we appreciate everything she did, even though she has chosen to leave. But we are still here, and we really value what you do. We have nothing bad to say about Deborah. We want you to stay. And we want you to know we are committed to making Heartland a strong and healthy company."

Respecting Others

It's easy to work with people we like, or whose views match our own. But we all must work with some people we don't enjoy or who express opinions with which we disagree. Disrespect is a product of our inability to understand that each of us sees only part of what is true or real. We think we have all the facts, so when someone disagrees with us, we assume they are wrong. Respect comes when we understand that truth has many colors and we can't see all of them. Our view of the world is necessarily incomplete. None of us has perfect seats in the theater of life. When we realize that our sight lines are limited, we can then respect those who disagree with us—because we then appreciate that their opinion is based on seeing what we cannot see.

Respect is the glue that allows people of different backgrounds, perspectives, and habits to work together. Moral leaders know that they can only inspire people they respect. Respect is a tricky skill. It goes beyond the easy task of appreciating people whose ideas you like or the bogus politeness of "respectfully disagreeing" with someone. Respect comes from our deep appreciation of another's ideal self. When we say that we respect someone, what we are really saying is that we connect with the best intentions of that other person. When we respect another, we establish a relationship with their ideal self, a positive relationship that is independent of our judgments about their current opinions and actions. Our respect for their positive intentions becomes the basis for our work together. When you respect a coworker, you open yourself to the possibility that your coworker—who you might not like and who sees the world very differently—has something important to teach you that will help both of you succeed. When you genuinely respect another—when that other person feels respected by you—only then is that person open to the possibility that your perspective may also have merit.

It's not easy to stay connected to the ideal self of an obnoxious or seemingly wrong-headed co-worker. But you can keep the channel of respect open if you also call on your capacity for empathy and listening. To see what is ideal in another's mind, you have to listen. You need to observe. When you visit a co-worker's office, what do you see? What is there, and what is not there? What do those family pictures, trophies, or pieces of art tell you about what your coworker cares about? You might not agree with their approach to a customer's problem, but your ability to connect with their ideal values allows you to negotiate from a position of respect.

Respecting Differences. Imagine that you have hired a team that thinks a lot like you do. You like their ideas, and they like yours. Staff meetings are pleasant and convivial. Decisions are made quickly, and you are confident in those decisions because so many people agree. When you are right, things work out very well. But because you share the same blind spots with your colleagues, before too long you make a big mistake that could have been prevented or you lose a significant business opportunity that could have been identified with more diverse views on board.

Very few leaders would deliberately hire their own clones, and most leaders intellectually understand the value of diversity. In an emotionally charged situation, however, it is tempting to over-rely on the opinions you trust the most—yours. That is why you must consciously cultivate an appreciation for others' ideas. You do that by ruthlessly challenging your own views, while aggressively looking for the wisdom in others' ideas.

By doing this, you will discover that the existence of differences creates great opportunities for synergy and gives people who work together the potential to accomplish far more than individuals can achieve on their own.

When financial planning was first coming into its own in the 1980s, most financial planners were paid for selling financial products, such as stocks or insurance policies. Industry critics had pointed out that commission-based financial advisors could be tempted to push certain profitable products, even if they were not in their clients' best interests. Martin Levy (pseudonym), division vice president of sales for a growing financial services company, vehemently objected to a proposal to charge clients for developing their financial plans. Martin thought the financial plan should be a free, relationship-building activity that would demonstrate the sales person's competence and set the stage for subsequent sales of financial products. Only one thing disturbed Martin's argument. Jerry Masters (pseudonym), one of his sales managers, was as vocal an advocate of fee-based financial planning as Marty was an opponent. Over time, Martin decided, "If Jerry thinks it's a good idea, I have to find out what he sees that I don't see." Martin asked Jerry to convince him, and he did. Jerry laid out his rationale about the importance of charging for objective advice because of the integrity that brings to the equation and the increased confidence that customers have in the financial advice they get when they pay for objective information. Jerry also pointed out that other disciplines, including medicine, have emerged as respected professions because they acquired a body of knowledge and were then able to charge for what they knew. Martin was convinced. Because he respected Jerry and had learned to listen to divergent views, Martin was able to let go of a strong personal bias and clear the way for a new product that led to significant revenues increases in years to come.

Getting Along With Others

Because leaders need others to accomplish their goals, they have to get along with them. Empathy, listening ability, and respect are hallmarks of individuals who get along well with others. Leaders who get along exceptionally well with others share four additional qualities: They show genuine interest in other people's lives; they are open and approachable; they are flexible in accommodating other's preferences and needs; and they enjoy the differences among us. When people are skilled at getting along with us, we like them. And because we like them, we are more apt to view their ideas positively and more likely to cooperate with them. So personal likeability is an asset to moral competence because when we need to enlist others to help us do the right thing—especially when it's a hard thing to do—people who like us will be more motivated to join us. Politics is an arena where we see how personal likeability can influence actions for good or ill. Political consultant and community leader Karen Lane, a native of Washington State, recalls how former Seattle mayor Norm Rice capitalized on his personal appeal to inspire others to do good:

> **Sometimes, especially in local politics, a person will come along who genuinely cares and reaches out to people. They talk about things in ways that tend to "make the tent**

bigger." Norm was one of those people. I used to love to go to his political events because one saw the enormous richness and diversity of our community. People of color came because Norm was one of them. Neighborhood advocates came because Norm had worked for their causes. The "movers and shakers" came because Norm had earned not only their respect, but also their affection. It was spectacular to see what he could do by bringing everyone together.

While Norm was Mayor, the Rodney King riots broke out in Los Angeles. He rightly recognized that, as Mayor, he had to lead our city constructively and inclusively so that the anger and fear caused by the verdict in the trial of the police officers involved would be turned into opportunity and hope for the young people of Seattle. He got on the phone with several business leaders and, in less than a week, raised more than a million dollars to expand summer employment opportunities for low-income youth of all races. He also went on TV and radio to make it clear he would not tolerate violence of any kind against anybody. It was a remarkable piece of leadership that kept Seattle violence-free and moved our community forward.

Being Approachable. Positive personal connections with your co-workers fuel highly committed and creative approaches to the work at hand. It might seem obvious that good leaders need to be approachable, but it is striking how often leaders make themselves inaccessible. Some maintain distance from their employees as a matter of personal style. Others may discourage contact unintentionally because of work overload. As managers are promoted to higher levels, there is a tendency for them to become invisible—they disappear to more remote offices or spend most of their time traveling or attending meetings with other senior managers. Even when you are in a high-pressure leadership job, it is vital to make time to deliberately cultivate warm and approachable relationships with others. We've all read books advocating the "open door policy" or "management by walking around." These are simple tools that are very effective if actually applied.

Being an approachable leader begins with your willingness to share the contents of your moral compass—your principles, values, and beliefs. You add to your approachability by sharing your personal interests and human foibles. Do you play in a rock band on the weekends, sing in a church choir, or fix up vintage cars? Sharing your interests and asking about others' interests sets the stage for warm work relationships.

Being approachable does not mean "telling all." Each of us has a private zone of personal information that should not be shared indiscriminately. Neither does approachability require that you become a raving life-of-the-party extrovert. But you do need to actively help people feel comfortable around you because your approachability is an important element of a positive, highly productive work environment.

Being Flexible. People who get along with others don't get stuck on doing things their way. Whether you are a work peer or leader, your success depends on your willingness to let others have a say about how work gets done. You also need to be able to accept mid-course changes that affect how work gets done. What happens when your teammate who was slated to give a big presentation gets laryngitis and asks you to fill in at the eleventh hour? How do you handle an employee's request to work at home for the next few weeks? What if your boss asks you to head a project that you think the company doesn't really care about? Rolling with the punches may not always get you exactly what you want in the moment, but over the long term it will cement important work relationships and help you cultivate inventive ways of solving inevitable problems.

Enjoying Differences. People who are seen as getting along with others usually have a diverse network of people with whom they have positive relationships. It's easy to get along with people we like, but if our network is limited to people who are just like us, then we will be seen, not as emotionally skilled, but as interpersonally biased.

Appreciating differences goes beyond respecting or valuing the diverse perspectives that others bring to the table. It is the capacity to savor those differences among us that makes us interesting. People who get along well with others don't merely tolerate differences; rather they feel enriched by the unique personalities and perspectives that people of different backgrounds offer.

PART THREE

MORAL LEADERSHIP

By now, you no doubt recognize that it's not just organizational leaders who need moral intelligence. Leaders can't make their businesses succeed through their own efforts alone. They succeed by doing things that motivate others to design, build, and deliver their companies' products and services. No matter how morally intelligent a leader you are, your moral skills are only valuable to the extent that they inspire morally smart behavior in others. Given that many members of an organization have non-managerial leadership responsibilities, it's crucial that both formal and informal leaders possess strong moral skills that they can impart to their co-workers. In this section, we concentrate on the strategies leaders use to create morally smart organizations.

9

The Moral Leader

Dick Harrington is CEO of The Thomson Corporation, a global electronic information company that sells the financial information systems that help power the New York Stock Exchange. On September 11, 2001, Dick was in London for a meeting of his Board of Directors. He was talking on the phone with his Connecticut headquarters when he got word of the attack on the World Trade Center. Harrington, along with the other members of his executive team in London, was thunderstruck. Over 2,200 Thomson employees worked in the neighborhood of the World Trade Center, with offices of about 200 employees in the twin towers themselves. It would be days, even weeks, before they knew for certain that 11 of their employees had been killed, including one who had been a passenger on the plane that struck the North Tower.

In the early hours following the terrorist attack, nothing was clear. But Dick and his team quickly shook off their shock and prioritized: people first, business second. They mobilized cell phones and Blackberries to track down missing employees. They commandeered limos from Connecticut to pick up employees who had escaped uptown or across the river to New Jersey. As they confirmed who was missing, they contacted family members, they sent cash and catered meals, and they arranged for transportation so family members of victims could be together.

Beyond that, Dick and his team extended generous benefits to victims' families that they are too modest to publicize. What's more, even while they attended to the needs of victims' families, they didn't miss a beat when it came to serving their other constituencies—employees, shareholders, and customers across the globe. They communicated early and often. They comforted traumatized employees. They reassured investors and customers.

The moral leadership that Harrington exhibited was the norm for him and his fellow executives—and it was reciprocated with the same degree of loyalty from Thomson's employees. One employee's first act after escaping from the World Trade Center was to race to the back-up facility in New Jersey. Other employees talked their way back into condemned buildings near Ground Zero to rescue critical financial data. By September 13, Thomson was able to announce that the financial information technology so crucial to Wall Street was up and running.

Other leaders demonstrated powerful moral leadership in the crucible of the 2001 attacks. Nine days after the World Trade Center towers collapsed, American Express CEO, Ken Chenault, gathered nearly 5,000 New York employees for a meeting at Madison Square Garden. Eleven American Express employees had died in one of the towers, and the company's headquarters across the street from the World Trade Center had been seriously damaged. Employees were shell-shocked and suffering from the loss of relatives, colleagues, and friends in the financial services community. Although business continuation was vital, Ken's first priority was his employees' well-being. The meeting wasn't about "busting butt" to keep the company on track. Instead, Ken expressed his grief about those who died in the attacks and invited his employees to share their own feelings of loss and remembrance. He encouraged people to reflect on all they were grateful for and to spend time attending to the parts of their lives that mean the most. Then he communicated his sense of hope and confidence in the face of tragedy. He told the gathering how the company was helping those who were affected—employees, customers, and the New York community—in their recovery. Ken's employees didn't need to be told to work hard. They needed to hear that their leaders cared about them. That is what allowed American Express employees to move forward in the aftermath of the attacks.

How did Ken Chenault manage to inspire and comfort his employees at a time when he was personally grieving and facing unprecedented threats to his business? Ken made hundreds of conscious decisions— and every one of them required not just business skills, but moral skills. Though we all need moral skills to be effective in our lives, as leaders we have a special responsibility to use our moral intelligence to ensure that the people and groups we lead act consistently with the principles of integrity, responsibility, compassion, and forgiveness. As leaders we have influence and power that we can use to communicate the importance of moral skills to the rest of our organizations.

Not all CEOs affected by 9/11 responded like Dick Harrington or Ken Chenault. Some had to consult professional handlers, PR firms, or legal experts before they did anything. Some took so long that when they finally did respond with compassion for victims' families, it came across as artificial and forced. Harrington and Chenault succeeded where others dropped the ball because they both operate from a set of principles, values, and beliefs that factor into every business decision they make. The result? Morale and job performance has remained consistently high in both companies. Thomson employees say their company is a place they're proud to be part of. "No matter what my job level," said one information specialist, "I know that Dick Harrington respects me enough to communicate about significant issues. I'm going to stay, and I'm going to recommend Thomson as a great place to work." With the kind of moral leadership that engages their workforce to do their best, The Thomson Corporation has continued to produce enviable returns during both economic recession and recovery.

Leveraging the Spotlight. When you are a leader, you are always on stage. Everything you do is scrutinized, analyzed, and interpreted by those around you. Celebrities and politicians recognize that visibility is a double-edged sword. On the one hand, you can use the spotlight to promote worthy causes. On the other hand, it's nearly impossible to hide bad behavior from the public eye. Sam Bronfman, former senior executive with Seagram Company, recalls a time when he eviscerated a marketing manager for presenting a merchandising plan that Sam thought was ridiculous. "Everyone was shocked. I eventually apologized for it—but people still remember the incident. I hope they remember the apology, but I think people remember the outburst more."

Sam's incident reminds us that a leader's high profile requires a particular sensitivity to those emotional states (in self and others) that have the strongest potential to stimulate either moral alignment or moral breakdown. Greed, jealously, envy, hate, and anger can all easily disrupt alignment, while emotions such as love, compassion, happiness, and joy have a tremendous capacity to enhance moral competence. Leaders who consistently display negative emotions tend to get involved in negative behavior, and by example encourage negative behavior in those around them. Leaders who act out of love, who demonstrate respect and regard for people, tend to encourage moral competence in others—like the CEO we know who spends $1,500 a month more on his commercial cleaning service than he could negotiate with another vendor because the woman who owns the cleaning business has been loyal and responsible, and he knows that their family relies on that income.

There is an upside to your visibility as a leader—you can capitalize on it by modeling moral skills for others in your organization. To communicate moral messages effectively, it might be necessary to stand up for what is right in an exaggerated way. In live theater, for instance, actors' makeup is plastered on thick so that their faces can be seen throughout the audience. You as a leader may need to "lay it on thick" to make your values clear to all of *your* audience. You may think that it should be obvious to others that certain business tactics are wrong and that you would never approve of it. But to avoid saying so is to miss an opportunity to underscore the importance of integrity to everyone's success. Harvey Golub, retired Chairman of the Board and CEO of American Express agrees. "I made it a practice," Golub says, "to always model the behaviors I wanted others to show…I didn't just hope they observed well, but would point out behaviors to make sure they understood."

Leveraging Power. Power is another leadership asset that you can use to influence your organization to adopt moral skills. Leadership and power are virtually synonymous, as evidenced in the characterization of leadership as "being in power." A common definition of power is that it is "possession of control, authority, or influence over others." Power, like visibility, is a double-edged sword. Certainly, you can use power to accomplish worthy goals through others that you could not reach on your own. But there is something about power that makes it potentially as dangerous as it can be helpful. Power is addictive. Using power activates brain chemicals called endorphins that create a highly enjoyable physiological state. Power can provide pleasure much like the satisfaction offered by food, sex, or vigorous physical exercise. Most people in formal leadership positions value power. But some leaders crave it. It is easy to get accustomed to the perks of the leadership role. It feels good to have people with less organizational power defer to our ideas and desires, so unlike our experience with family members who treat us like the fallible humans we actually are.

Leadership power is not just asserted by the leader—it is given to leaders by followers. Followers allow leaders to be powerful. Because

leaders have power, followers are careful about how they present information to their leaders. Research has demonstrated that the higher one
goes in an organization, the more distorted the information they receive.
Followers provide information that they believe leaders want to hear
and censor information that they fear would upset or anger leaders. The
more heavy-handed a leader is in his or her use of power, the more distorted the information they are given. But even benevolent leaders who
are careful in their use of power have trouble establishing accurate communication channels because of followers' strong tendency to defer to
the leader's position power, independent of the leader's actual behavior.

Deference to power affects not only the quality of "hard" business
data related to financial reports, product quality, and customer attitudes,
but deference to power also limits the amount and quality of "soft data"
available to the leader. When leaders make mistakes, it is difficult for
followers to tell them so. Many organizational cultures discourage interpersonal feedback, even among peers, so imagine how reluctant most
followers would be to openly criticize the actions of someone with
greater power. This leaves most senior leaders operating in a feedback
void. Their accomplishments might be praised, but their personal flaws
are not brought to their attention. The absence of appropriate negative
feedback about our leadership behavior can leave us with the mistaken
notion that we are far better leaders than we really are. Without accurate
information about the business and about our own capacities, we are at
risk making a big mistake that can lead to a devastating business outcome. Workaholism can reflect a subtle abuse of power. When you
insist on doing everything yourself rather than delegating work, you
deprive others of opportunities for development and their own share
of power.

So use power with caution. It's not a drug you can quit cold turkey.
Like food, power can't be eliminated completely from your life. For
a formal leader, power is inescapable; it comes with the territory.
But power, like food, can be used carefully to promote health and

well-being. You can leverage your power to accomplish morally positive goals that also produce higher business performance. As a moral leader, you can use power positively by modeling the moral skills that keep you in alignment. You also can use your power to encourage followers to live in alignment with their own moral compasses.

Higher Standards. When you are highly skilled in all the moral competencies, you are able to use your leadership power and visibility to produce the best business results. We do know business leaders who are quite effective despite some gaps in their moral competencies. But we have never known a consistently successful business leader who was not highly skilled in the integrity and responsibility competencies. Many effective and honest senior executives are respected because they demonstrate integrity and responsibility, even though they lack notable compassion or forgiveness. But leaders who inspire their followers' best efforts are compassionate and forgiving as well. When followers see that such leaders actively care about them and are willing to let go of mistakes, they forge a bond with their leaders that just doesn't happen otherwise.

Why does emotional bonding between follower and leader matter? When leaders show compassion and forgiveness, they create a safe emotional environment. In this positive climate, followers feel free to be creative because they know their leaders will tolerate the inevitable mistakes that come from creative risk-taking. When followers believe their leaders care about them, they want to give their best efforts to the work at hand. It is as though the integrity and responsibility competencies come from the "head," while the compassion and forgiveness competencies come from the "heart." The most effective moral leaders are those who have both the head and the heart fully engaged.

It is interesting that moral competencies of the "head" are necessary and sufficient for a minimal level of leadership effectiveness, but moral competencies of the "heart" are not sufficient for effective leadership. A leader could seem to actively care for others ("I feel your pain!"), could forgive himself or others, and be open about mistakes, but if he or she does not tell the truth, doesn't keep promises, and doesn't act consistently with the values, beliefs, and principles of the organization, then he or she will not be an effective leader. Leaders who are known for their compassion and forgiveness, but who lack integrity and responsibility are often considered "nice people" but by virtue of their lack of integrity, do not command the respect and trust required for high performance.

How Moral Leaders Look at Followers. So far, we have seen why moral leaders need to operate at the top of the moral competence scale. Because of their power and visibility, their behavior has a major impact on the behavior of those around them. In addition to high proficiency in moral and emotional competencies, the most effective leaders operate from a central organizing belief that informs their transactions with followers. Everything they do is inspired by a belief in the essential goodness of people. It can be summarized as follows: *Even though people are not perfect, and even though they make mistakes, most people have good intentions.* This belief is the moral leader's key to inspiring the best in others because your belief that people are essentially good has a profound impact on your leadership behavior. Knowing that the person with whom you are working has an *ideal self* (who they would like to be at their best)—and that the person would rather be their ideal self than their current flawed *real self*—allows you to practice compassion, forgiveness, and integrity. When you believe in a person's essential goodness, you cannot help but commit yourself to helping them become who they most want to be.

Belief in the goodness of people is not a "technique." It is a potent frame of reference that, paradoxically, allows you to be as tough as nails in managing individual performance. Why? When followers sense your deep belief in their ideal selves—their potential to be their best—they are much more receptive to your feedback about their mistakes and failures. Similarly, when good performers recognize your belief in their ideal selves, they are inspired to give even more effort to your shared work.

Tom Perrine is vice president, Enterprise Systems, with Cardinal Health, the largest health care products distributor in the United States. Tom demonstrates his belief in the goodness of people when he says, "Helping others create who they want to be is a way of life for me." Tom adds, "Number one value to me is *people matter most,* and they deserve to be treated with respect, consideration, understanding, and empathy. Do you brighten their light bulbs or dim their light bulbs? How are you managing the energy of your people? The greatest job of leadership is not personally doing things but helping others do things, and managing the energy of the workforce is what it's all about. If you do that well, you can accomplish great things as a company or in the world." Tom also notes the cost of temporarily losing touch with his positive beliefs about people. When Tom was chief development officer at Coca-Cola, he was forced to make a unilateral decision about an important issue because the team responsible was argumentative and uncooperative. Tom thought the resulting decision was not as good as it could have been if the team had focused on solving the problem instead of fighting with one another. So he convened the team and told them what he thought of them. "No one likes to be called on the carpet," recalls Tom, "and I called the group on the carpet. The manner in which I delivered the message was culturally unusual at Coca-Cola because people there weren't used to being reprimanded as a group. I didn't name names, but I was clearly angry and upset. After that, many of them decided they couldn't trust that wouldn't happen again, so for quite a while, they avoided coming to me with issues. My comments about their poor teamwork were factually true, but I delivered the message in the wrong spirit and mismanaged the energy of the group."

Developing Employees. The moral leader's approach to performance management and development is guided by the leader's belief in the essential goodness of the people who report to him or her. It is an approach that encourages employees to live in alignment, releases their positive energy, and inspires their best efforts.

As a moral leader, you hold yourself responsible for helping others stay aligned with the ideals that are important to them. How? First, you do so by believing in employees' potential to do wonderful things for themselves and your organization. Second, you can use performance discussions to discuss the life goals that your employees care about—*not* just their business goals. Third, hold them accountable for meeting all their personal and professional goals.

When you acknowledge your employee's whole selves—ideal and real—they are energized by your support. Because you care about them and believe in them, employees are inspired to give you—and your company—their best efforts. Employees do not have to be coerced into performing—over the long term, you can't really force anyone to produce. You cannot create a good employee. You can only create conditions that spark their talents into a bonfire of innovative thought and action.

Developing employees is *the* central building block of moral leadership. Why? It's because people development is the way you create a workforce committed to the moral principles necessary for the sustained success of your organization. When a moral leader invests in an employee's development, he or she goes beyond the typical focus on technical skills and behaviors that produce short-term corporate results. Development plans that lead to lasting business performance are comprehensive—they include actions that help employees realize not just business goals but *all* their important personal and professional aspirations. An effective development plan is not the sole responsibility of your employee—it is a shared plan for the employee's growth to which both you and you employee are committed. You and your employee collaborate to achieve goals that are important to the employee and at the same time are intended to produce desirable organizational results.

Leaders who accept responsibility for helping employees achieve their development goals spend substantial amounts of time coaching employees. Leaders who are too busy meeting among themselves to spend time helping employees grow miss golden opportunities for better business results. Investing time in developing employees may seem daunting, but the payoff is exponential. Every hour we spend coaching employees translates into countless hours of enhanced performance.

Each element of a performance development discussion—communicating belief in the employee, reciprocal disclosure of beliefs and goals, contracting for mutual feedback, and mutual accountability—should be discussed and negotiated with every employee for whom you are responsible. If you are a leader responsible for a large organization, it is important to ask all supervisors in your organization to use this approach with their direct reports.

Communicating Belief in the Employee. Actions may speak louder than words, but communicating a belief in the goodness of the follower needs to be actively *spoken* as well. In reality, most of us are starved for affirmation. We appreciate any genuine communication of caring. The effective leader affirms an employee most powerfully by acknowledging his or her strengths. Verbal references to the employee's accomplishments and abilities reinforce the notion that the leader believes in the employee's best self. Beyond acknowledgement of strengths, the leader should look for opportunities to state directly: "I believe in you. I know that you are capable of even more than you have already achieved." In our hard-nosed Western business culture, such a message may sound saccharine. When an employee makes a serious mistake, however, stating your belief in that employee's ideal self helps him or her deal more productively with the fallout of his or her real self failure. Even when employees under-perform, the wise moral leader concentrates primarily on how to improve performance by leveraging their strengths. Emphasizing an employee's weaknesses is rarely useful, as London Business School Dean of Research, Nigel Nicholson, reminds us:

> **...emotions can never be fully suppressed. That is why, for instance, even the most sensible employees cannot seem to receive feedback in the constructive vein in which it is often given. Because of the primacy of emotions, people hear bad news first and loudest.**
>
> **Managers should not assume they can balance positive and negative messages. The negatives have by far the greater power and can wipe out in one stroke all the build up credit of positive messages. In fact, because of the primacy of emotions, perhaps the most discouraging and potentially dangerous thing you can do is to tell someone he or she failed. Be careful, then, of who you put in charge of appraisal systems in your organization. These managers must be sensitive to the emotional minefields that all negative messages must navigate.[1]**

Reciprocal Disclosure of the Manager's and Employee's Respective Moral Compass and Goals. Sharing your beliefs and goals and inviting your employee to do the same provides the basis for both to support the other's actions. You may want to introduce this idea to your employee by saying something like this:

> **In order to be a good manager, I need to know where I am and disclose that to you. I also need to know where you are at, and our shared knowledge of each other will give us the foundation for a trusting relationship.**

---

1. Nigel Nicholson. "How Hardwired is Human Behavior," *Harvard Business Review*, July 1998.

Begin by sharing the principles, values, and beliefs that form your moral compass because many employees will not have had a previous experience with a superior who asked for this kind of information. Your willingness to disclose personal beliefs will usually minimize any discomfort on the part of your employee. But you also should make it clear that your disclosure of beliefs and goals is not a formality. You are sharing your beliefs and goals because you also want help from your employee. You can tell your employee that you hope that together you can be enablers of each other. After you have discussed your own beliefs and goals, your dialogue as manager might sound something like this:

> **My job as your boss is to help you develop the necessary habits and routines that will help you achieve your goals while honoring your principles and beliefs. I start with a belief in you, but if we are going to work together closely, I need to do more than imagine greatness in you. I want to know what you really want your life to be about—the things that really matter to you. What roles do you play, and how good do you want to be at each of them?**

Contracting for Feedback. Managers often assume that they have a unilateral right to dispense feedback by virtue of their position. Unsolicited feedback is neither welcome nor effective. Managers are often frustrated to discover that negative feedback frequently results in further performance deterioration rather than improvement. This performance drop is caused by the negative emotions that uninvited feedback causes. Employees who receive unsolicited negative feedback feel unappreciated, misunderstood, and powerless. These are destructive emotions that cause further breakdown, not alignment. In contrast, critical feedback that is solicited in an environment in which the employee feels empowered is likely to enhance performance. The manager should seek permission to offer feedback and to solicit feedback from the employee about the manager's own performance. Seeking permission to give feedback and asking for feedback levels the emotional playing field for the employee. Because receiving feedback is part of a contract and because the employee has the opportunity to provide feedback to the manager, the employee feels empowered rather than ashamed. If the manager has been successful in communicating deep caring and belief in the employee, the employee can calibrate the negative aspect of the feedback in the context of feeling positively valued by the manager. Finally, if the manager can characterize the feedback as an opportunity to help the employee accomplish important personal or professional goals, the employee will see the feedback as a performance aid rather than an attack.

In contracting for mutual feedback, you might want to say something like this:

> **I know we will both make a bunch of mistakes. I want us to agree to help correct each other. I'm going to mess up. Would you be willing to let me know when you see me making a mistake?**

Now who would not agree to that? When you have their agreement, you may then ask this:

> **If there are times when your performance is not consistent with the goals you have shared with me, may I let you know about that?**

Now you have set the stage for discussing performance problems in the context of goals that are important to your employee.

Mutual Accountability. Contracting for feedback sets the stage for confronting performance gaps that will inevitably arise. Because you have invited your employee to call you on your own behavior, the way you respond to their first attempt will affect the quality of the relationship going forward. In short, you need to make it easy for your employee to offer feedback in the future, by responding well to their feedback. Responding well to employee feedback does not necessarily mean that you agree and instantly change your behavior. It does require at a minimum that you actively listen to their feedback, play it back to ensure that your employee knows he has been heard, tell them how you plan to respond (even if you plan simply to think about it), and thank him for the respect they showed you by offering their feedback.

When you need to give negative feedback to your employee, it is important to reinforce the context of your belief in them. You might say something like this:

> **Based on everything you've shared with me, I know you want to be great at the work you do. I'm sure that you are aware that [your performance in this area] has not been good, and we need to focus on these few areas to help you reach the goals you agreed were important to you.**

Performance Problems

Focusing on others' strengths and goodness does not mean that the moral leader ignores performance deficits. On the contrary, it is exactly that focus on others' ideal selves as well as the respect created by reciprocal disclosure of beliefs and mutual feedback that establishes an emotional bond between the manager and employee. That bond, in turn, allows a manager to be extremely tough in tackling performance issues.

When Values Collide. Caring for people and believing in their essential goodness does not necessarily make your leadership job easy. Perhaps the most daunting challenge moral leaders face is how to manage individual performance in a way that reconciles competing commitments to their people and their organizations. Jim Thomsen of Thrivent Financial for Lutherans, understands the challenge well. Jim recalls how he dealt with the performance of a direct report who was also a close friend: "I should have decided to get him out of his job much earlier than I did. My personal relationships with the people I work with tend to be very strong. So it took me six months after I had made the decision to act on it. I tried to help him see that he was in the wrong job, but he never came to that conclusion. My decision to let him go damaged our friendship, but letting him stay would have had negative consequences for the organization. People who weren't close to this person thought it was about time we held an executive accountable for under-performing. For those loyal to him, I became the 'evil empire.' Emotionally, it was very hard. Out of integrity and responsibility I had to act, but I also had to be compassionate."

Moral leadership and management techniques. Believing in the goodness of people and managing employee performance consistent with that belief, does not imply abandoning any of the leadership tools you may have found useful in the past. Most organizations provide leadership training and other resources that enhance their effectiveness in the day-to-day management of work and people. Other leadership techniques work best when you begin with your employees' ideal selves in mind, focus at least as much on their strengths as their weaknesses, and invite them to help you improve your personal performance just as you are trying to help them improve theirs. Any leadership technique will be that much more effective when you genuinely care about and believe in your employee and his or her potential. Leadership tools applied in the absence of caring and belief in others often backfire because employees may experience them as mechanistic or manipulative. On the other hand, leadership techniques infused with the spirit of caring tend to work very well, even when not perfectly applied.

10

Leading Large Organizations

The Fabric of Values

It is a blazing summer day outside the conference room in Sedona, where American Express executives Dave Edwards and Brenda Blake have gathered their two teams of international managers. Brenda is stepping to the podium to roll out the company's two new corporate values. Amex had long espoused six values; now it has eight. For the past two weeks, Brenda has been pondering how to make the values memorable so that people will be more likely to practice them.

She has decided to group the values into three categories—moral values, social values, and business values. Pushing aside her concerns about how her audience will react, she reminds them that success depends on a clear sense of what American Express stands for. She explains how values drive both business practices and business results.

Then, before launching into the new values, she puts one more
PowerPoint slide up on the screen. It says this:

**If you don't subscribe to Amex's Moral Values, you proba-
bly shouldn't work here.**

In making that claim, Brenda was out on a limb. It certainly wasn't a
politically correct thing to say. No one had authorized her to say it. She
hadn't even reviewed it with her superiors.

Indeed, it was only following the meeting in Sedona that Brenda e-
mailed the presentation material to her boss. It would be two weeks
before she found out his reaction. Over dinner, the night before she was
to repeat her presentation to a group in London, he approvingly quoted
the new mantra back to her: *"If you don't subscribe to Amex's moral
values, you probably shouldn't work here."*

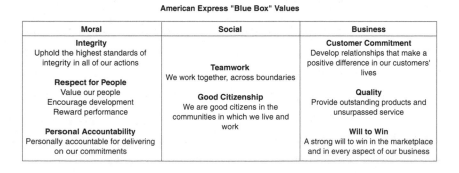

American Express "Blue Box" Values

Moral	Social	Business
Integrity Uphold the highest standards of integrity in all of our actions **Respect for People** Value our people Encourage development Reward performance **Personal Accountability** Personally accountable for delivering on our commitments	**Teamwork** We work together, across boundaries **Good Citizenship** We are good citizens in the communities in which we live and work	**Customer Commitment** Develop relationships that make a positive difference in our customers' lives **Quality** Provide outstanding products and unsurpassed service **Will to Win** A strong will to win in the marketplace and in every aspect of our business

It turns out that Brenda, one of 25 designated "culture champions" at
American Express, needn't have worried about her presentation.
Employees at every level say that when she talks about the three sets of
values—moral, social, and business—they immediately "get it." No one
blinks an eye at the mention of moral values. The only question asked
by some is how to reconcile conflicts between a new business value,
"the will to win," and the longstanding value of "integrity." The Amex
answer comes easily: Amex will win *with* integrity. It is not winning at

any cost. If there is a conflict, integrity comes first. So far, though, the conflict has not come. Any senior manager at Amex will insist they can win in their markets without sacrificing an inch of their other values.

Brenda Blake's presentation captures lesson one about moral leadership of any large organization: Effective leadership depends upon the successful integration of moral, social, and business values. You cannot *just* be a moral leader, even as you cannot *just* be a strategic leader. The values that drive an organization do not work in isolation. Choices about moral values are an intrinsic part of the cultural fabric of every organization. Ask great business leaders about their values and you will inevitably hear them mix "integrity" in the same breath as "beating the competition"; "quality" along with "giving back to the community" along with "honesty."

Is There Such a Thing as a Morally Intelligent Organization?

In the last chapter, you considered the concept that the major task of moral leadership is to bring all of an organization's values to life, so that employees can connect to them personally and understand how to translate those values into action. With that goal in mind, every aspiring leader will at some time ask: Is it my job to influence individuals or groups? Does one lead organizations, or does one lead people? Is it even possible to talk sensibly about a morally intelligent organization?

A morally intelligent organization is one whose culture is infused with worthwhile values and whose members consistently act in ways aligned with those values. A morally intelligent organization's major characteristic is that it is populated with morally intelligent people. After all, if you put enough morally intelligent people in one place, the culture will eventually catch on. But moral leaders realize that their job goes beyond simply hiring others who act in a certain way, just as a morally intelligent organization is more than the sum of its individual members. Moral leaders accelerate and enhance high performance by actively encouraging everyone in the organization to apply their moral principles to their individual actions *while also creating organization-wide policies, practices, and reward systems based on moral values.*

The Morally Intelligent Organization— An Aerial View

Not long ago, PBS aired a program on Italy that consisted of nothing more than exquisite video of the Italian countryside shot from a helicopter. No sound track, no plot, just moving pictures of mountains, valleys, and water as the camera followed the curves of landscape from north to south. Unlike the normal tourist's eye view, the video shot from high above the terrain gave a context for understanding the character of the country in a way that would be impossible from the ground.

If we had an aerial view of the ultimate morally intelligent organization, what would we see? First of all, we would *not* see people being simply moral, or simply social, or simply focused on the technical aspects of their work. We would see moral values lived out in their "natural habitat," interwoven with other social and business values important to a successful large enterprise. We would see leaders who believe that there are some shared human moral values that apply to humankind all over the world and therefore apply both at work and outside of work. We would notice leaders who speak passionately about their beliefs and the values that their company stands for. We would also notice that the leaders are as morally competent as they are strategically gifted.

As we rose higher, so that we could see the entire organization, we would see job candidates being scrutinized to ensure that their beliefs and values are consistent with the beliefs and values the company upholds. We would see employees given opportunities to develop competencies that translate values into action. We would see people solving problems and making decisions in ways that are consistent with the organization's values. We would see managers at all levels sharing their personal values and goals and inviting their peers and employees to hold them accountable to those values and goals. We would watch as employees go the extra mile for their leaders and their company because they feel respected and trusted by their leaders. We would observe employees being rewarded, not for being workaholics, but for results. We would see employees who deliver superior results, while reserving adequate time for their families, for community service, or for other passionate interests. If we looked closely, we would even see people make mistakes. We would also see that mistakes are usually treated as normal byproducts of innovation and growth and that people are given a chance to correct them and move on without being negatively branded.

Higher yet, we would see an organization that does not abandon its values when the economy sours, or a disruptive technology threatens, or a natural disaster strikes. We would see a company that has a long track record of profitable growth. We would see the organization dedicate a certain amount of its resources to helping others in the larger communities where it is located.

If our vantage point were high enough, we would see in the global organization the intertwined threads of moral, social, and business values reaching across countries and continents to join together people of different languages, social customs, and traditions in pursuit of a shared dream of individual and professional performance.

Morally Intelligent Policies

McKinsey co-founder, Marvin Bower,[1] observed that virtually every successful company codifies its culture, rather than letting it grow through an inevitable self-molding process. Many effective leaders have

1. Marvin Bower. *The Will to Lead: Running a Business With a Network of Leaders*, Boston: Harvard Business School Press, 1997.

discovered the wisdom of this advice. A senior management team of a defense laboratory attended a session on managing conflict during an especially stressful period of organizational change. Their workshop leader suggested that one way to prevent conflict in organizations was to develop a "social contract"—a code of behavior that everyone in the organization would agree to. The management team thought that was a good idea. They asked their employees to get together in small groups and talk about what should be in their "social work contract."

Managers admit they were somewhat apprehensive. Most of the laboratory's employees had worked there for decades. They had seen management fads come and go. Would they be cynical about the idea of a social work contract? But when the groups met, they were thoughtful and engaged. When it came time to merge the results of the small groups into a social work contract for the whole laboratory, their managers were surprised and relieved to see that the small groups' proposals were remarkably similar.

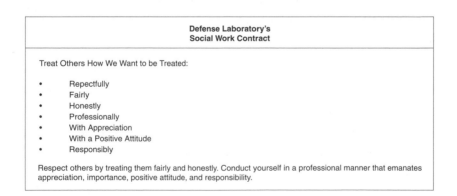

**Defense Laboratory's
Social Work Contract**

Treat Others How We Want to be Treated:

- Repectfully
- Fairly
- Honestly
- Professionally
- With Appreciation
- With a Positive Attitude
- Responsibly

Respect others by treating them fairly and honestly. Conduct yourself in a professional manner that emanates appreciation, importance, positive attitude, and responsibility.

They didn't call it a statement of moral values, but what they developed was clearly a shared moral guidance system. With the support of their leaders, they did the collective work of codifying how they wanted to be treated and how they believed they should treat one another. Many months later, it is clear that the words still mean something to this group. Employees display copies of the contract in their cubicles and on corridor walls—reminders of how they want to be at their best. In a year of massive change and unremitting workload, when people are overtired and tempers could easily unravel, there have been no meltdowns. The people in the laboratory have kept their act together. The social work contract has been a powerful influence on the laboratory's ability to weather the organizational changes that continue to surround them.

The Principles that Matter Most

Earlier, we described the universal principles we believe are key to leadership effectiveness—integrity, responsibility, compassion, and forgiveness. These same principles are essential to organizational effectiveness. The organizations whose values reflect these principles are the most likely to be successful over the long term. Companies that embed these principles into their cultures will succeed because they will keep more than their fair share of the world's most talented employees. These are the principles that resonate strongly with employees, so that they want to stay and are inspired to give their best efforts to the organization. But if integrity, responsibility, compassion, and forgiveness are absent from the life of an organization, there is dissonance between what the organization stands for and its employees' hopes and beliefs. If employees' moral compasses don't line up with a company's code of conduct, it is unlikely that they will give the company their best.

Organizational Integrity

How important is integrity? According to Paul Clayton, CEO of Jamba Juice, integrity is the central requirement for sustainable performance:

Integrity is what keeps successful organizations together.
Every organization will encounter periods when integrity is

challenged. These challenges may arise in the form of having to provide honest feedback during a performance review, or accurately assessing the performance of a marketing program for future learning or resisting the temptation to "borrow" $20 from the cash drawer. Leaders must create an environment where integrity is an important value and the consequences for failing to adhere are severe.

An organization that acts with integrity is more likely to have trustworthy, loyal employees. But integrity is also essential because shareholders relish it. Everyone has heard enough cautionary tales about cooking the books and the inevitable stock price slumps when accounting shenanigans come to light. In contrast, consider this example of how a company's candor helped turn around a company at risk.

Mike McGavick took over as CEO of struggling Safeco Corporation in 2001. Wall Street's confidence in the company had been shaken by its recent performance and Mike knew that he needed to convince the street that Safeco would do what it said it would do. At his first reporting of results, he immediately began to talk to analysts about the need to clean up the balance sheet and reform the business. Mike and his new CFO Christine Mead decided to fully open the company books to the Wall Street community. According to Allie Mysliwy, Safeco's Executive VP of Human Resources, "We wanted to be far more transparent to analysts, so Mike and Chris changed the way we represent our numbers and changed the way we talked to analysts, so they could see deeper into the organization from a numbers viewpoint and see how leaders were interacting with the numbers. Over time, I believe, analysts have grown confident in our ability to do what we say we'll do." Fortunately for Safeco, credibility and candor paid off. Safeco's stock price has nearly doubled since those first few weeks when Mike started.

Cultivating a High Integrity Organization. Companies should assign four to eight values as their "core values"—including among them the very principle of integrity itself. Based on these core values, organizations can use three key strategies that promote and demonstrate integrity. The first is for senior management to plot a communications strategy in which they engage with their employees and the public at large to identify and promote their organization's values. Ideally, the CEO leads this strategy: He or she should talk about the company's values—the core of the corporate culture—at every possible opportunity.

Second, the senior team needs to practice what they preach and enforce adherence to the company's declared values. Managers in many companies fail in this regard. They may not be guilty of fraud or terrible dishonesty but of a common white lie: It is common for managers to give annual performance reviews that fail to confront poor performance or behavior that is not aligned with core values. We've all heard stories of companies giving someone a bonus on Friday for "outstanding performance" and then firing them on Monday, but this behavior pattern has a high cost: Everyone in the company can see that their management does not practice integrity or really believe in it.

The third strategy is for senior management to invite their workforce to hold them accountable. An example of how to establish accountability is to set up a Leadership Alignment Task Force, a group of no more than 12 people from all layers of the organization—from Joe in the mail room to Debbie, a marketing director, or Sam, the head of production—to join this task force on a volunteer basis. The task force is charged with giving the CEO and the senior team an annual "alignment review." During the alignment review, the task force offers feedback from their workforce on their perceptions of how well the CEO and senior managers behavior is aligned with the organization's values. Alternatively, companies can use intranets to collect confidential feedback from their workforce on senior management practices and their integrity.

Integrity produces substantial rewards for organizations who embrace it. All stakeholders—employees, vendors, investors, business partners—prefer doing business with organizations that have strong integrity. It is simply easier to engage with an organization that is honest, that states its mission and values, and does not diverge from them. It's common sense: Organizations that attract employees and customers by virtue of their integrity are likely to be highly successful in the long run.

The Responsible Organization

There are two hallmarks of the responsible organization. First, it embraces its responsibility for being of service to others. Second, it acknowledges mistakes and failures. With respect to serving others, there are two levels of service. The first level of responsibility is that the organization provides worthwhile products or services. This does not mean that your organization is only a responsible one if it invents the cure for the common cold. It is, however, important that your organization has a socially worthwhile mission. In a 2002 letter to shareholders, Jeffrey Immelt put GE's mission this way: "Let me put it as simply as I can. Customers win when we provide better products; they win when we provide better service; they win when we can generate productivity through information management; they win when we can provide needed capital."

Companies that make dangerous products or provide questionable services put their long-term performance at risk. They may be profitable for a time, but eventually will falter. Phillip Morris is an example of a company that struggles with the tension between a dangerous core product and its desire to be socially responsible. Phillip Morris sells cigarettes. No one can ignore the dangers of their core product. But Phillip Morris also sponsors anti-smoking advertising aimed at children and contributes generously to charitable causes. Admittedly, Phillip Morris's social responsibility efforts were court-ordered as a result of litigation. One could argue that the company has not been as aggressive as it should in diversifying its holdings so that cigarettes are no longer their only revenue stream. You might dismiss Phillip Morris' efforts to be responsible as nothing more than a public relations smokescreen. You might be right. But it is possible that Phillip Morris genuinely wants to behave responsibly, rather than creating the disaster for shareholders that an abrupt exit from their core business would provoke.

Another example of a company dealing with adverse consequences of some of its products is Kraft Foods, maker of Oreo cookies, Oscar Meyer bacon, and Easy Mac macaroni and cheese. In 2003, Kraft announced that it would stop selling high-fat foods to schools and launched a series of initiatives to promote healthy eating. As of 2003, it had spent more than $17 million to increase the amount of fruits and vegetables distributed by U.S. food banks. You might conclude that Kraft is simply trying to forestall the kind of litigation first seen by fast-food chains by some obese customers who blame the food purveyors for their health problems. Hopefully, Kraft is making a good faith effort to ensure that its products are used in ways that do no harm. Whatever its full range of motives, Kraft does serve its broad customer base by encouraging people to make wise nutritional choices.

While companies like Phillip Morris and Kraft try to be responsible without altering their core product, other companies demonstrate responsibility by literally changing their product into one that better serves their customers. Harvey Golub did just that as CEO of IDS, a financial advisory company. He transformed IDS from a transactional services company to a company that offered objective financial planning services. To understand how profound a change that was, recall that the 1970s and1980s were a time when the financial services industry had a well-deserved reputation for questionable transactions. Consider the comments of one person who worked for a brokerage house:

It was a hectic noisy place with stock brokers crowded together talking on phones and calling out across the room to one another. Right in front of me, I saw a man on the phone put someone on hold, then yell out, "What do we have for a buck with a half?" Someone yelled back, "XYZ stock." The man got back on the phone and proceeded to extol the virtues of XYZ stock. As I left, I asked my friend to tell me what a buck with a half meant. He told me that it is a stock for which you pay a dollar for the stock with a fifty cent load—meaning the customer paid a dollar for a stock that was only worth fifty cents. It was obvious that the guy who promoted XYZ stock didn't care about gouging his customer and was only interested in maximizing his earnings.

It is no wonder people were suspicious of brokers, many of whom were more interested in lining their own wallets than helping their customers. It was the "me generation," an era of excess, a time when "Wall Street" was synonymous with greed. Enter Harvey Golub, a McKinsey consultant called in by American Express to analyze a promising potential acquisition in the financial advising business. Golub examined IDS, a small company in Minneapolis that focused on creating wealth for its clients by offering long term investment and insurance products. Golub's studies showed that IDS advisors gave good financial advice. Clients could benefit from their advice, even if they decided to purchase financial products elsewhere. They didn't use hard-sell tactics. Their first priority was helping clients reach their financial objectives. Golub thought IDS had the right idea. IDS was small, but its principles were scalable. So he recommended that American Express buy IDS.

American Express agreed, but on one condition—that Golub take over as CEO. Golub grew IDS (eventually American Express Financial

Advisors) by putting its customers front and center. He made a commitment that the financial planning documents prepared for clients would be objective. IDS's recommendations would not be biased towards IDS products. They would recommend IDS products that fit client objectives, but also acknowledge that clients could do well if they chose to go to another company to purchase financial products. He also insisted that financial planning had to be independent from the sale of products, even though he knew the company wouldn't be profitable if it only sold financial planning services. But Golub said, "We are going to be a financial planning company and help customers make financial decisions prudently and carefully." It was curious advice at a time when the financial industry's high flyers were just "doing deals."

A lot of industry insiders thought IDS would fail, especially after his predecessor lowered the sales charge customers paid for each transaction. There was a revolt in the ranks of the sales force. Many advisors threatened to quit. But Golub was confident it was the right thing to do, so IDS lowered its sales load. It lost some advisors, but, importantly, kept those who understood the values that drove Golub's strategy.

Although pundits had their doubts, Golub's values-driven strategies paid off spectacularly. From 1984 until 2000, IDS (later renamed American Express Financial Advisors) increased profits by at least 15% every single quarter, taking the company from 60 million to over one billion dollars in gross earnings. In recent years, AEFA has helped keep American Express profitable through the worst of the post 9/11 doldrums. Providing a valuable service and being a responsible organization is no doubt the morally right thing to do—but, as the success of AEFA demonstrates, values-based business practices are also strategically smart. At AEFA, financial advisors feel energized by providing a worthwhile service for their clients. Most financial advisors would hate having to pressure their clients to buy a product. Clients, in turn, value solid advice that helps them achieve their financial goals. Being a responsible, service-oriented organization resonates powerfully with employees and customers alike.

There is a second dimension that marks the responsible organization: its willingness to admit mistakes and failures. According to Paul Clayton, former CEO of Burger King North American, and current CEO of Jamba Juice:

We owe it to everyone, including shareholders and ourselves, to get results, and to get consistent results; we owe it to ourselves to have open and honest dialogue around what's working and what's not. The leadership team has to convey that it's all right to make a mistake; it's all right to bring up an issue. Sometimes the best we can do is to make sure we are honest about flawed assumptions. If you're not, it doesn't take long for things to go wrong. In our business, we are dependent on young people. If you are going to get people to really commit, then you have to be honest about what is working and what isn't.

If admitting mistakes is crucial to maintaining employee commitment, it is essential to maintaining customer loyalty as well. Some companies seem to know this in their bones; others go down in flames trying to hide the truth about their mistakes. Taking responsibility for mistakes may be painful in the short run, but admitting failure and taking steps to compensate for errors cements customer loyalty. Customers know that they can trust an organization that tells them the truth.

In 1982, the fate of Johnson & Johnson was in the balance when bottles of Tylenol capsules were laced with cyanide, killing seven people. James Burke, CEO at the time, knew exactly where to look for direction—the company's 40 year-old "Credo," a single-page document that began with these words: *"We believe our first responsibility is to the doctors, nurses, and patients; to mothers and fathers; and all others who use our products and services."* Johnson & Johnson ordered an unprecedented recall of all 30 million bottles of Tylenol capsules in circulation. They immediately stopped production of the capsules and replaced them with tamper-resistant caplets. They communicated constantly with the public and the media, and it was their openness and concern for public safety that that helped Johnson & Johnson to overcome its initial losses and recover its market share within a matter of months.

More recently in 2004, drug manufacturer Merck & Company voluntarily withdrew its widely used arthritis pain medication Vioxx after a three-year clinical trial showed a higher incidence of heart attacks and strokes among users of the drug. Merck has a reputation for concern for those who use its products. It developed and distributed at no cost a drug that cures river blindness in underdeveloped regions of the world. According to Thomas Donaldson, Wharton professor of legal studies and ethics,[2] Merck "has always emphasized, in effect, that the company puts the health care of the customer first, and if we do that, we will make money. If we ever just put making money first, we will lose our business." Donaldson adds, "You can question the extent to which Merck follows this, but it's not something that just appears [once in a while]. It is repeated fairly consistently."

Contrast Merck and Johnson & Johnson's handling of product defects with Firestone Tire's handling in 2000 of the recall of tires that were implicated in fatal SUV accidents. Firestone was initially very reluctant to replace the defective tires, claiming that it was the vehicle rather than the tire that was at fault. The media later discovered that Firestone had prior knowledge of the problem and did nothing. It was also reported that Firestone had earlier refused to recall another defective tire sold in Saudi Arabia because a recall would mandate reporting the problem to the U.S. National Highway Traffic Safety Administration. Instead, it had launched a quiet replacement program that left the NHTSA in the dark. The result? Daniel Eisenberg, reporting on Firestone's tire debacle for *Time* magazine concluded, "Thanks to a generally dreadful crisis management, marked primarily by silence

2. Quoted in "Death of a Drug: The Aftermath of Merck's Recall," *Knowledge at Wharton*, October 6, 2004.

and denials, the Firestone brand has very little credibility left. The public is becoming increasingly skittish about any of Firestone's tires—the vast majority of which are safe."

To promote responsibility, CEOs should carefully consider what it means to be a "responsible person," communicate this to managers, and encourage the promotion of responsible people within the organization. A company made up of responsible people is a responsible company. CEOs can assess managers according to the following "responsibility checklist."

Responsibility Checklist

Taking responsibility for personal choices
When I make a decision that turns out to be a mistake, I admit it.
When I make a mistake, I take responsibility for correcting the situation.
When things go wrong, I do not blame others or circumstances.

Admitting mistakes and failures
I always own up to my own mistakes and failures.
I am always willing to accept the consequences of my mistakes.
I use my mistakes as an opportunity to improve my performance.
I discuss my mistakes with coworkers to encourage tolerance for risk.

Embracing responsibility for serving others
I believe and show through my actions that an important aspect of my leadership approach is to find ways to serve and support others.
I pay attention to the development needs of my co-workers.
I spend a significant amount of my time providing resources and removing obstacles for my co-workers.

Rather than simply use this as a tool for self-examination, CEOs should discuss this checklist with senior management and ask them to rate their own responses on a scale from 1 (never does this) to 10 (always does this). The CEO should then discuss his or her expectations with management: which statements are the most important, which need to be adhered to the most closely, and work with them to improve their scores if necessary. The managers can then, in turn, work on responsibility within their individual departments.

The Compassionate Organization

When it's business as usual, acts of compassion are small or subtle in the great organizational scheme of things. But when a major crisis strikes, it is easy to see the difference between the truly compassionate organization and one that gives lip service to values. Aaron Feuerstein is the former president and CEO of Malden Mills, a company best known for producing the revolutionary fabric, Polartec. On a cold December night in 1995, a devastating fire tore through his factory in Lawrence, Massachusetts. In a time of corporate downsizing, many of his peers urged him to re-open operations overseas—a decision that would lead to the loss of 3,000 jobs at home. Shunning their advice, Aaron pledged instead to rebuild the mill at home—*and* to pay his employees during the three-month reconstruction. "I think it was a wise business decision, but that isn't why I did it. I did it because it was the right thing to do," says Feuerstein.

Malden Mills battled insurance companies and government officials not just to rebuild the plant, but also to spend the additional money necessary to build the safest textile plant possible and to take care of his employees while the new plant was under construction. By 1997, just two years later, he had proved to the doubters that it was the right thing to do. Malden Mills was recording $400 million in annual sales—more than it ever had before the fire. Although Feuerstein's sometimes controversial decision-making led to financial problems and a bankruptcy filing, the company has recently emerged from bankruptcy intact.

Sometimes, though, despite a company's best intentions, layoffs must be made for the good of the company—its customers, its shareholders, and its remaining employees. The way an organization handles layoffs says more about its corporate character than any other activity. It is a test of its ability to weave moral, social, and business values into an effective whole. Answering the call of compassion in isolation might tempt an organization to avoid a layoff at the cost of fiscal survival. But a moral organization that doesn't attend to its bottom line won't be around long enough to keep any of its workforce gainfully employed. So the task of a moral leader facing serious financial difficulties is not necessarily whether or not to reduce the size of the workforce, but how to do it in compassionate way that provides a soft landing for those affected and in a way which preserves key talent.

Not so long ago, Safeco was on the verge of extinction when Mike McGavick took the reins. The clock was ticking, so he had to move quickly, cutting the workforce by 10% while consolidating 15 major offices into 5. Although the relocations and layoffs were difficult, they did not blindside Safeco's employees. Mike McGavick decreed that Safeco's leaders would tell employees what they knew when they knew it. When it came to delivering bad news, Mike decided that was his job. So he showed up at every regional office that was closing and told employees what they could expect.

Allie Mysliwy describes McGavick's visit to Indianapolis:

We needed a meeting place that could hold all of our Indianapolis employees, so we rented out the Scottish Rite Cathedral across the street. It was a dark, oppressive, and enormous place, which only intensified the foreboding of the gathering group. Mike took command of the stage. He was completely upfront. He explained the grave situation the company faced, how we had gotten to where we were, and what we were going to have to do to survive. He told them that a large number of them would lose their jobs.

Some employees would be retained, but most would not. When he finished, the audience clapped. Even though the news was bad, Mike communicated in a way that allowed employees to make sense out of a really tough situation.

When jobs were eliminated soon after, reductions were made based on comparative performance. That may have been a blow to the egos of those who left, but it turned out to be a morale boost for remaining employees. Prior to McGavick's arrival, Safeco had been a haven of entitlement. Employees' number one complaint in their employee survey was the company's tolerance for poor performance. Instead of rewarding longevity, Safeco decided to keep its strongest performers, thus solidifying the new performance-based culture it desperately needed to get back on track. According to Allie, those who were asked to leave were treated with compassion and respect. There were none of the all too common layoff scenarios in which notified employees are summarily escorted out of the building, with little or no severance or support. Safeco provided generous severance packages by industry standards, but also tried to individualize its severance offering to meet special needs of employees. Employees who left appreciated how Safeco had treated them. Employees who remained were proud of how Safeco treated their departing employees.

In our high achieving business culture, self-recrimination is very common. We often find that our executives are far more critical of themselves (and less forgiving) than their bosses. One of the best ways a morally intelligent leader can show compassion is to challenge the executive about his or her excessive self-criticism. Of course, this implies that the leader has enough interpersonal skills and rapport with the subordinate to find out what their critical self-talk is all about. Yet, this challenge can be a superb way to embrace compassion and make it central to your organization. To the extent that an employee is spending his or her precious energy engaging in negative and self-critical inner dialogue, he or she is *not* giving it to the company in pursuit of the strategic plan!

The Forgiving Organization

Organizational forgiveness is an organization's capacity to accept mistakes and failures among its workforce. Forgiveness is critical for two reasons. First, employees need to know that they have room to fail. If mistakes are invariably punished, the emotional climate of the organization will be unattractive to your best employees, who will go elsewhere in search of a more favorable work environment. Second, forgiveness is fundamental to innovation and growth. Innovation entails venturing into the unknown, where no formulas exist. Risks will be taken; mistakes will be made. Some things will work, and some things will fail. Organizations cannot pioneer new territory unless they accept that they will spend some time going around in circles or down dead-end paths.

When asked whether 3M's reputation for innovation is legitimate, Ray Langer, a 3M project engineer, says, "Yes, it really is. We're encouraged to try new things in our projects, and if they don't work out, no one is punished. As a result, we have created many, many engineering processes that no one else in the world comes close to."

Interestingly, the United States Marine Corps is an organization that has institutionalized forgiveness. "Most managers like to say they give their subordinates room to fail," says David Freedman, author of *Corps Business: The 30 Management Principles of the U. S. Marines,*[3] "but the Marines practice failure tolerance to a degree that would raise most manager's hair. To a certain extent, they *demand* failure: a Marine who rarely fails is a Marine who isn't pushing the envelope enough, goes the logic."

A final incentive to practice forgiveness is that without a climate of risk tolerance, employees will be too intimidated to acknowledge mistakes or offer feedback, thus perpetuating problems that may be costing your company millions each year. When Safeco began to encourage

3. David Freedman. *Corps Business: The 30 Management Principles of the U. S. Marines*, New York: HarperBusiness, 2001.

employees to communicate about problems with senior management, senior management e-mail from employees went from a few contacts a month to 30 to 40 a day. Everyone, from Mike McGavick on down, takes feedback from employees very seriously. In the process of encouraging feedback, Safeco learned from its employees about long-standing process problems that they were finally in a position to correct. In the last several years, Safeco has saved millions annually thanks to information from its employees, information that they would never have felt safe enough to relay in the old environment.

While the most forgiving companies are often the best innovators, these companies also know how to set limits. If you want to increase forgiveness at your company, establish "curbs" for innovative behavior—for example, set out the percentage of work time team members can use to engage in innovative projects that are their own or their team's creation or set budgetary limits, allowing employees to spend a certain percentage of their department's budget on innovation. But then, if you wish to establish a truly forgiving company, make sure you celebrate this activity—not just the positive results. Honor your team members' mistakes as learning episodes. Edison is quoted as saying something like, "I didn't make any mistakes. I just tried ten thousand things that didn't work;" if you want to build an organization of budding Edisons, celebrate the innovation process and the failures that come with it, not just the results.

Another way to encourage your organization to increase forgiveness is for you to establish a learning organization (rather than a punitive organization). Praise your team members for embracing the learning process. Allow mistakes to be forgiven and analyzed and not punished harshly.

But, as with all values, forgiveness cannot be practiced in isolation. Peter Georgescu of Young & Rubicam recalls a time when some young employees discovered racist jokes on the Internet and began passing them around. In all likelihood, they did not intend to offend anyone;

they were just completely thoughtless. Georgescu struggled and worried over this. Anyone could make a mistake, he realized—but the company also had a policy of zero tolerance for such activity. People's lives and self-respect were at stake. In a move that he judged to be not only best for his business, but also for the moral development of the two employees, he let them go. It was an action that won acclaim throughout the business community. By understanding the implications of each possible choice, Peter demonstrated moral intelligence. By taking the action he did, he demonstrated moral competence. As Peter showed, the leader who consistently puts both skills into practice creates resonance with those whom he or she leads.

Recruiting for Values

The basic unit of your organization is its people. Your organization's ability to engage in principled actions rests squarely on its people. Hiring the right people—the ones who already share your company's values—and have a track record of acting consistently with those values—is the most important lever you have in creating a morally competent organization.

Jim Collins, author of *Good to Great*,[4] found that hiring the right people was a key differentiator of companies that had significantly outperformed the S&P over many years. When *FastCompany.com* asked him what his research suggested was the best way to respond to economic slowdown, he said this:

> **If I were running a company today, I would have one priority above all others: to acquire as many of the best people as I could. I'd put off everything else to fill my bus. Because things are going to come back. My flywheel is going to start**

---

4. Jim Collins. *Good to Great: Why Some Companies Make the Leap…and Others Don't*, New York: Harper Collins, 2001.

to turn. And the single biggest constraint on the success for my organization is the ability to get and to hang on to enough of the right people.[5]

Don't delegate recruitment to your human resources department. Take charge of your own hiring process as much as you can while still conforming to employment law. When possible, avoid anonymous newspaper adds. Instead, network continuously so that you always have a large pool of potential candidates or referral sources. Let your network know what kind of people you are interested in having work for your company. Don't hesitate to talk about your organization's values. Recruiting from your personal network is likely to lead to significant jump in the retention rate, and contribute positively to your organization's performance Why? Because new jobholders who know you or are connected to you through your network, are much more likely to share your values, and are much more likely to stay when the going gets a little rocky.

Reinforcing Values Starts at the Top

In *Primal Leadership: Realizing the Power of Emotional Intelligence*, Daniel Goleman, Richard Boyatzis, and Annie McKee describe their model of leadership.[6] The best leaders, they say, are resonant leaders. Resonant leaders use their emotional intelligence to create a positive emotional work climate in which the best work happens. To that equation, we would add this: The best leaders create resonance through their moral intelligence as well as their emotional intelligence. People naturally wish to follow leaders who demonstrate commitment to moral principles and values. When people believe that their organization and

5. Jim Collins, Web-Exclusive Interview, "Good Questions, Great Answers," *Fast Company.com*, October 2001 (http://pf.fastcompany.com/magazine/51/good-togreat.html).

6. Daniel Goleman, Richard Boyatzis, Annie McKee. *Primal Leadership: Realizing the Power of Emotional Intelligence*, Boston: Harvard Business School Press, 2002.

its leaders practice the values they preach, they become energized. When people work in an organization that operates from a set of beliefs that resonate with their own, they are naturally inclined to give their best efforts to their work.

In the real world of organizations, we never have the luxury of working with a fully morally competent workforce. Maintaining organizational alignment with values is just as challenging as it is for any single individual. That is why leaders should look for any opportunity to reinforce values. Training is key to reinforcing values and enhancing moral competencies. Senior executives may act allergic to training sessions in the misguided belief that they are finished products who don't need further education. But values start at the top, so senior level managers need to hone their moral judgment just like the rest of the workforce.

The 2003 American Express Executive Conference is a case in point. Held during a difficult time in the global economy, you might expect the conference to be focused on financial challenges. But this executive group spent little time talking about money. They talked almost exclusively about leadership and spent an afternoon in facilitated small groups discussing cases in ethics and their recommended solutions. Think about the investment in salaries, time, and travel expense involved in putting that high-octane group together. The message from the top was not subtle. Ethics is important. Making principled decisions is a key leadership competency. It takes practice, even if you are a top executive.

The Power of Formal Rewards

Psychologists tell us that people do what gets rewarded. It is critical that reward systems reinforce morally competent behavior as well as goal attainment. Unfortunately, corporate reward systems that violate the principle of integrity are not unusual. Media reports of fired CEOs laughing all the way to the bank, CEOs who get multimillion dollar bonuses despite staggering year-end losses, and pyramid compensation systems that routinely reward executives far in excess of their relative contributions are common. Contrast that with Best Buy CEO Brad Anderson, who declined 200,000 stock options in 2004. He already owns company stock worth roughly $78 million dollars, and asked that the declined options be distributed to non-executive employees.[7] Anderson's action was an effort to create more equity in the distribution of corporate rewards, although no one—Anderson included—would argue that he will feel too much of a pinch. But his recognition that he does not need more sends a powerful message to other companies' executives about corporate excess—while creating a richer source of rewards for rank and file employees who do the right things.

Paul Clayton is insistent about sending positive messages through meaningful rewards. Paul recalls a time when he was president of Burger King North America, and had to convince his own executive team that he was serious about rewarding employees.

At Burger King, we had a recognition program for the top general managers. Once a year, we brought them to our world headquarters in Miami. During the recognition ceremony, 600 headquarters employees would give the award winners a standing ovation. As they entered the main rotunda, their pictures went up on our "Wall of Fame." As we were giving out awards, it struck me that one GM in particular had been the top performer for five years running. I turned to the HR person next to me and said that we should give him a car. The HR person replied, "We can't do that because we don't have budget and I don't have authorization." I reminded him that I was the president

7. Reported in Patrick McGeehan, "Making a Point By Taking Less," *The New York Times*, May 24, 2004. Also reported in the article was that James Parker, Southwest Airlines' chief executive, recently requested that his salary be significantly lower than suggested by their compensation consultant.

and that I thought that I could authorize the expenditure. When I presented the idea to the finance team, they thought it was fine, but suggested an inexpensive car that wouldn't cost too much. "He'll never know the difference," one finance person said. But I had a different idea. I told them, "I'm thinking about a BMW. I don't care about the budget. I want people to know that we are sincere about the contribution they make." So when I took the stage to announce that I was rewarding the top GM with a fully loaded series 3 BMW, the place went crazy. The GM's wife ran up on stage to hug me and her husband. Then the GM ran off the stage to call his grandmother.

Success Stories

Given that moral values are embedded and intertwined with other values in the conduct of your business, how do you link moral values to performance? American Express does it by storytelling. The Amex team in Australia had just won the prestigious "Chairman's Award." The country manager wasted no time assembling his team to congratulate them. He did it in a way that explicitly linked Amex values to their success. He told stories about how individuals acted on Amex's values and how that contributed to their getting the Chairman's Award. This manager celebrated not only their accomplishments, but the values that led to their success. Leaders in morally competent organizations never take values for granted. They promote them, they apply them, and they make sure that their people see how values translate into business performance.

Ideal Versus Real

Even within an organization that is committed to values, you can always find managers who fail to apply them. Wherever there are imperfect managers, there are cynical employees who look at them and say, "He, or she doesn't live the values, so...why should I follow the values if my boss ignores them?" Or, "...why should I go the extra mile for a management that doesn't respect me?" If employees complain about someone who works for you, it is your responsibility to deal individually with unacceptable behavior. It is also critical that you convey the message that Ken Chenault gives to his employees: "There is no excuse for personal behavior inconsistent with Amex's values. You can't wait for everyone to behave in alignment with values before you do. The only way for people to start acting on values is to do it independently of whether others do. Do not expect perfection from leaders."

Values and the Global Organization

More and more companies not only do business internationally, but are actually global companies with offices throughout the world, employing local workforces in numerous countries. Imagine how difficult it would be to communicate with a multi-national workforce in the absence of some shared beliefs. Without common values, business would be impossible. Common values, based in the universal principles, can knit together a diverse global workforce. In an era marked by international conflict, we believe it will be in the world of business—rather than in the political arena—that people from different ethnic, racial, and religious heritages will discover their common path.

11

Moral Intelligence for the Entrepreneur

Starting from Scratch. Imagine this: You have a great business idea, eager investors, and a prime location for your new company. With every resource at your disposal, you now have the chance to realize your fondest hopes and ambitions. You also have the power to create a high-performance culture from the ground up. No legacy employees, no unnecessary bureaucracy, no history to overcome. How would *you* begin? Would you use your newfound power to build a company based on universal principles, with socially noble goals and a morally competent workforce? Entrepreneurs rarely launch their ventures with an explicit moral focus. They make mistakes, and the most costly missteps are frequently moral, not strategic or operational. When entrepreneurs lack a consistent level of moral competence, their businesses usually falter or fail completely. Even exceptional business models can't survive without morally competent leadership. Entrepreneurs who want to succeed must master not only their business challenges, but must align their businesses with the principles of integrity, responsibility, compassion, and forgiveness.

Morally Clueless in Minneapolis. In the 1970s, a group of entrepreneurs started a telemarketing business named Minneapolis Circulation, which primarily sold subscriptions to *Minneapolis* magazine. Their arrangement with the magazine was that Minneapolis Circulation would own the subscriptions and would pay the magazine $1 for every $5 subscription they sold. The company was very creative about marketing subscriptions, but the partners' greed and irresponsibility doomed them to failure. The partners failed to recognize that the magazine publishers would come to resent their meager share of the profits, and it was only a matter of time before the publisher found a way to dry up the telemarketing company's pipeline and pave the way for a better deal with another telemarketer. When the entrepreneurs got the squeeze, they didn't have the financial reserves to retool their strategy. They had naively thought of the company as their cash cow, and any money they made after expenses went straight into their personal bank accounts. Because their vision of the business was so limited, Minneapolis Circulation's owners didn't even think about their responsibility to their employees or to the sustainability of the business itself.

Poorer, but wiser, or so one owner thought, he launched another company, Twin Cities Telemarketing, with a new business partner. He had learned his lesson about trying to own subscriptions, so his new enterprise sold subscriptions for a fee. Their first client was *Twin Cities Woman*, a struggling newspaper look-alike. When *Minneapolis* magazine got a new publisher and a new name, *Minneapolis St.Paul* magazine, Twin Cities Telemarketing acquired their subscription sales business, too. Then they went after business with *Twin Cities* magazine, a publication that *Minneapolis St.Paul* magazine viewed as a competitor. Twin Cities Telemarketing knew that they could sell both magazines effectively. They recognized that a lot of customers, such as hotels and professional offices, subscribed to both. Their game plan was to help both clients succeed. But they carefully didn't mention their relationship with either magazine to the other. That was a fatal flaw. When the *Minneapolis St. Paul* magazine publisher found out that Twin Cities

Telemarketing was working for their arch rival, he pulled the plug. The owners of Twin Cities Telemarketing never thought of themselves as dishonest, but they were. Integrity would have dictated that they do their best to convince both magazines that representing the two was a win-win scenario—before taking on the second magazine.

Both of these ventures demonstrate that business savvy relies as much on moral intelligence as it does on a good business plan. Both start-up companies were initially successful businesses that unraveled because of gaps in integrity and responsibility. Like most entrepreneurs, it took several false starts for this group to learn the importance of principles and values. Those early business failures also point out just how critical moral competence is to a small business. Failures of integrity or responsibility might not be terminal in a large business which has the resources to absorb a certain number of mistakes. But for most small organizations, the distance between solvency and bankruptcy is painfully short.

Driving Without a Steering Wheel. KRW International, one of the first executive coaching firms in the country, was founded in 1990 to offer premium consulting services to Fortune 500 executives. KRW's owners were strong on integrity and responsibility where their clients were concerned, but those principles were not always extended to their own organization. In the first few years, the owners' attitude was, "Let's have fun and make money." When demand for their services started growing beyond what they could handle themselves, the partners did not think proactively about the kind of organization and workforce they needed. Instead, they reacted to the needs of the moment. They hired contract consultants and discovered that they didn't stick around long. They hired administrative staff at fairly low wages, and worked them really hard. They didn't stay long either. It took some time for KRW's partners to realize that if they didn't act responsibly toward their employees, employees would have no reason to feel responsible to them.

Luckily, KRW hired an administrative head, Kelly Garramone, who became its moral champion. More than once, Kelly confronted the owners, "There is too much work, too few people to do it, and deadlines are impossible." She successfully challenged the company to create work processes that both consultants and administrators could live with. Business grew consistently until 1994 when a major client company abruptly cancelled its contract. KRW's owners were so shaken that they immediately decided they had to lay off most of their employees to preserve the owners' financial resources. That decision was ill-considered, both on business and moral grounds....

It was a beautiful fall day when KRW employees were gathered for the company's annual Octoberfest celebration. When the owners walked into the room, employees expected the festivities to commence. Instead, the owners announced a major downsizing. Soon, people were crying and running out of the room to call their spouses and friends. KRW's owners *were* open and honest, but their approach was a lot like surgery without anesthesia. It turned out to be unnecessary surgery. Everyone was given a good severance package. But soon most employees were rehired as independent contractors because KRW still had work in the pipeline. Before long, their major client reinstituted the contract, and KRW rehired all but a few of their former employees. One employee never missed a paycheck, but she got a windfall—three months off. KRW's owners ended up losing more money by thinking of themselves first than they would have if they had stepped back to take everyone's needs into account.

The mistakes KRW made during their 1994 downturn were the result of destructive emotions and a moral virus. KRW's owners had started their business with the goals to "make money and have fun." As soon as something happened that threatened both goals, fear took over, and they lost their ability to be reflective and self-aware. Further, because their goals were not aligned with a deeper purpose, there was no overriding sense of responsibility that could overcome their impulse to take care of themselves first.

KRW weathered that crisis and soon regained considerable momentum, so much so that during a 1998 company meeting, Kelly Garramone and her administrative staff once again announced that they were so overworked and stressed that if the company didn't make major changes, many would quit. KRW owners and consultants finally got the message. It was a turning point. The strong feelings of the administrative staff prompted the group as a whole to question why they were in business. It became clear that financial rewards were only part of the motivation for working at KRW. Some employees said that their ideal purpose was "to make the world a better place." Many employees resonated strongly with that purpose. Others worried that KRW would lose business if hard-nosed senior executives got wind of such a pie-in-the sky mission statement. Eventually, their collective desire to do something ambitious and wonderful won the day. In subsequent months, Kelly led the effort to define the organizational values that sprung from their newly articulated purpose. "If we are going to be an organization of moral integrity," insisted Kelly, "then we need to behave consistently with our purpose." Eight years after starting the company, "doing the right thing" became an explicit part of the KRW culture. Little did KRW's owners realize that within a few short years, KRW's collective commitment to a shared purpose would mean the difference between extinction and survival.

KRW took a steep trajectory as it gathered media recognition for its approach to CEO coaching and senior executive development. In the year 2000 alone, it increased its revenues by 27%, expanded its consulting staff by a third, doubled its office space, and was actively recruiting for additional staff to support anticipated further growth. By June of the following year, business bookings were so strong that one overwhelmed owner instructed the consultant group to stop marketing until further notice. Only three months later, in the wake of September 11, KRW's revenues crashed. This time, the moral lessons of the past came to the fore. The owners, despite enormous pressure, vowed to keep the company going. They cut their own salaries, mortgaged their houses, and did everything they could to keep the staff together for as long as possible. Each week, they updated their employees on the financial status of the company. For months, the news was grim. Everyone could see the handwriting on the wall, but when two rounds of selective layoffs finally came, laid-off employees were grateful for the lead time they had been given to prepare for their job transition. Employees who remained had almost as tough a time as those who left. Consultant salaries were cut, and administrative employees were given reduced hours. Owners suspended their salaries. With half of the staff gone, the offices looked—and felt—like a ghost town. But no one left who had the choice to stay. Maybe they stayed because the job market was dismal. But if you ask KRW employees why they stayed, they will tell you, "I believe in what KRW is trying to do." If you ask former KRW employees if they would go back if asked, the answer is almost always, "Yes." KRW returned to profitability within a year. Quite a few consulting firms did not survive the economic downturn of 2000–2002. KRW might have started by driving without a steering wheel, but it learned the value of guiding principles along the way, and those values steered it safely through its darkest hours.

Moral Values in Small Organizations

The moral values highlighted throughout this book are crucial to organizations of all sizes and stripes, big and small, for-profit and non-profit. Integrity, responsibility, compassion, and forgiveness are undeniable values, no matter what the venue. Although the four core principles are the same, the moral challenges that dominate an organization are often size-dependent.

Poll a cross-section of employees who work for small organizations, and you begin to see differences in the character of small versus large organizations. Small company employees typically place a premium on decision-making freedom. Some value risk and adventure, while others value the small-town intimacy or the potential to have a larger impact. Another difference lies in the visibility of leadership in small organizations. The entrepreneur or small company CEO lives in a fishbowl—everyone can see everything they do. The beliefs and goals that drive leader behavior are just as clear. So moral competence is particularly crucial to the small company leader because moral gaps can not be hidden—and bad choices lead to more than a slap on the wrist. They could spell the end of the business.

Challenges of Integrity. For small organizations, internal integrity comes more easily than external integrity. Small companies by virtue of their size promote more direct and honest communication. Your boss might be sitting at the desk in the next cubicle, rather than sequestered in a remote executive suite. Fortunately, good information flow is easier to come by in a small company because without it, a small enterprise could go belly up in a matter of weeks. Spenser Segal, CEO of technology start-up ActiFi, says this about the business value of honesty: "When we started, financial viability was not a given, and we felt everyone had to feel responsible for our success. To do that, they had to be able to manage the risk they were personally taking on. So we instituted a policy of sharing detailed financial information on a weekly basis. Now everyone knows how much cash is in our account, what is coming in, and what our pipeline looks like. Instead of managers and employees speculating and worrying, everyone knows what's going on and works together to help us find solutions."

Some hierarchical organizations, on the other hand, produce cultures of intimidation that discourage effective communication. Employees of large corporations often feel pressured to keep distant superiors happy, even if it means concealing a painful truth about poor performance. Ironically, when difficult truths are finally uncovered, the consequences might not be so dire because large profitable companies usually have the cash reserves to weather fallout from internal dishonesty.

While internal honesty might come more readily to small companies, integrity can be challenged when small companies must put on a good face to the outside world. Capitalization is a perennial issue for many small companies. They need to borrow, they need to sell equity shares, or both. According to Paul Clayton, CEO of Jamba Juice, "It is very tempting to hide the truth from potential investors about the health of the company." But resisting temptation is essential. "I've always preached that we have to be open and as transparent as possible about what the issues are," says Clayton. "If you're getting people to really commit—whether they are employees or investors, then you have to be honest about what is working and what isn't."

Challenges of Responsibility. Unlike large companies, which usually are focused on increasing profits, many new or small companies are trying to reach the point of making a profit. Small companies don't have the luxury of irresponsibility. Taking too long to admit a mistake can make the difference between black ink and red ink. But admitting failure can be hard, in part because individuals who work for small companies often feel more intense ownership for the decisions they make and want to keep plugging away to make it work. Unfortunately, that can spell doom for an emerging business. New companies are successful, not because they don't make mistakes, but because they know how to make a lot of mistakes quickly. The sooner the organization acknowledges a mistake, the sooner it can change course.

ActiFi's Spenser Segal reflects on the cost of denying mistakes: "In a small business that doesn't have a long history of results, it is critical that you stay firmly grounded in reality without giving up hope for the long term. We initially developed some sales assumptions for our first product. Our projections exceeded our results by a factor of five. It was four months before we were ready to reexamine our assumptions. The truth was staring us in the face, but no one said anything—maybe because I was a big part of making the mistake. Fortunately, we were able to recover, but we lost three months of valuable time by not admitting that our assumptions were flawed and our targets were unrealistic."

Spenser then adds a note about the benefits of admitting mistakes: "Because we had a very experienced management team, we were over-confident about our business model and our projections. After we admitted our miscalculation, we got better at admitting that we don't know what we don't know and therefore could look at things more like experiments. That took a lot of pressure off of everyone thinking that everything had to succeed."

Contrast ActiFi's rocky start with giant American Express, which had the financial resources to stay with a troubled business venture that its executives mistakenly thought would work—eventually. American Express finally closed the business at a loss, but the company as a whole was never at risk of going out of business because it delayed coming to terms with a bad business decision. Executives of large companies might produce higher profits if they heeded the lessons of responsibility that come from small organizations.

Small Companies Teach Some Big Lessons about Responsibility

In large organizations, we often encourage people to take lateral assignments that broaden their experience. Companies would be even smarter to encourage their high potential managers to spend a year or two working in the small business world. What they would learn would make them far more disciplined financial managers. They would know how to pay more attention, when to maintain support, and when to pull the plug on a struggling business. They would be more responsible with the company"s resources. They would appreciate that five million dollars is a lot of money and should not be squandered.

Challenges of Compassion. Compassion comes more easily in a small organization. Recall the compassion of BWBR Architects, the firm that went out of its way to give a struggling Chinese and Malaysian firm business when they most needed it—with nothing expected in return.

Within the walls of a small enterprise you know people better, and you are likely to know all of your co-workers. In a small organization, no one is anonymous. Small companies more closely resemble the interdependent tribal groups that were so important to survival of our human species. Membership in smaller working groups seems to activate our hard-wired tendency for altruism. We take interest in our workmates. We feel bonded to them. We see their success and ours as interconnected. When they need help, we want to help them. That does not mean that smaller organizations are immune from rivalry or deception or dislike. No human community is perfect. We may see the dark side of connectedness when we work in a small organization, but we rarely see indifference. If the small company headquarters is big enough to have an elevator, it will not be a silent ride.

But compassion is a double-edged sword. Too little compassion—as in the hard-edged and ultimately unnecessary lay-off in KRW's early days—and business may suffer. Too much compassion, as in KRW's post 9/11 protracted subsidy of employees, and business may also suffer. Business judgment without compassion can be as equally damaging as compassion without business judgment. Just as in the last chapter when we emphasized the fabric of values, skillfully interweaving business and moral values is even more critical for the small organization that commonly lacks the financial cushion to absorb mistakes and downturns.

Challenges of Forgiveness. Because small organizations rely on their ability to cycle rapidly through mistakes, it is equally important for small organizations to forgive mistakes. Spenser Segal believes that forgiveness is critical to the success of a new business, adding, "Every startup makes tons of mistakes. We have built our business model assuming mistakes and bad assumptions. By being aligned around our mission and core values, we are able to look at various strategies as tests and hypotheses that we are seeking to prove or disprove. By ensuring that an environment fosters trying new things and doesn't cause bad feelings when tests or hypotheses fail, we are able to learn much more quickly—and that results in much better business models going forward. We need to learn to avoid four-month mistakes. It's better to make lots of small mistakes than any big ones." Amazon.com credits its growth from small online bookseller to e-commerce giant to its encouragement of innovation. David Risher, former SVP of Marketing with Amazon.com, describes what the company did to foster innovation:

> **Three times a year, we presented the "Just Do It" award. We wanted to explicitly reward people who have pride in doing something innovative. It had to have been well-thought through—not just something silly—truly innovative and focused on customer need. But it didn't have to work! And a third of the time they didn't. The reward? A used Nike sneaker—the bigger the better.**

When it comes to letting go of mistakes and failures, small organizations have an edge. It can be hard to forgive a stranger. Forgiveness works best when you and I know each other and therefore are willing to give each other the benefit of the doubt when we make mistakes. Therefore, letting go of mistakes and moving beyond them happens more easily in a smaller organization—luckily so. In a small organization, you work in close quarters with all the people who might do something to hurt you. When you are angry at someone who has done you harm, or when you have done something to hurt another, there is nowhere to hide. Without the capacity for forgiveness, you would be surrounded by the tension of the unresolved hurt. Not only would a tense work environment prevent you from giving your best efforts, it would keep you from being able to take advantage of the resources your colleague would normally offer. In a small organization, it is difficult to work around a contentious relationship. For example, when you are in conflict with your colleague who is the company accountant, there is usually no department full of other accountants you can go to for help. In small companies, we are stuck with one another. That is ultimately a good thing. Knowing and accepting the foibles and failings of our fellow workers sets the stage for "getting over it" and moving forward.

The Moral Impact of Small Organizations. Small businesses (companies of 500 employees or less) represent about 99% of U.S. employers, employ about half of the private sector workforce, and provide nearly 75% of new jobs. Even during the economic recession of 2001–2003, job growth surpassed job losses among small companies. During the first quarter of 2002, 36% of jobless managers and executives started their own businesses, with a majority of laid-off managers moving to small companies.[1]

Some workers, disenchanted with the legacy of mega-company scandals or simply weary of large corporate bureaucracies, are looking to smaller organizations to provide a greater sense of meaning and purpose. KRW's Chief Financial Officer Don Waletzko, is a case in point. Don left an executive finance position when he couldn't approve his former employer's plan to go on an acquisition binge that would produce substantial layoffs. Don's moral compass wouldn't allow him to be financial architect of a strategy that he feared would cause great personal disruption to his fellow employees. His former company's loss was KRW's gain. Don arrived with a financial pedigree that a small company like KRW could ordinarily never have afforded. Fortunately, salary was not Don's top priority. He wanted to work for a company whose values reflected his own, and he found that in KRW's commitment to leadership development as a way to improve human lives.

1. Challenger, Gray & Christmas study, May 2002.

When the aftermath of 9/11 threatened KRW's survival, Don's stead-fastness and financial savvy saved the day. He was a key player in the reorganization and recapitalization that stabilized KRW on its way back from the brink.

Don is one of many managers who believe they can have more positive impact on people and organizations by working in a small business. The large organization, like a lumbering ocean liner, can be hard to turn in the direction of increased moral competence. In contrast, small organizations, like a 25-foot sailboat, can turn quickly and efficiently when the compass and prevailing winds dictate. Small companies are fertile ground for shaping a morally intelligent culture—one that provides value simultaneously to its customers, employees, owners, and the community it inhabits. For those of us who are concerned about the welfare of all the world's peoples—small ventures offer great hope for the future. The path of economic development isn't from the sweatshop to the boardroom. It is from poverty to small locally based sustainable businesses. Everyone who invests in a new venture or small company has a golden opportunity to infuse the business world with more principled, more humane, and ultimately, more financially stable businesses.

Five Maxims of Moral Entrepreneurship. Start-ups are excellent laboratories for moral leadership. Because resources are tight, mistakes have more immediate consequences. If you falter, there is no elaborate infrastructure to cushion you from disaster. American Express can write off millions in bad junk bond debt without going out of business. The owner of a new company does not have that luxury.

Entrepreneurs by definition choose paths to success that are both risky and rewarding, both exhausting and exhilarating. Your success as an entrepreneur, like that of any leader, depends on following the same four principles of integrity, responsibility, compassion, and forgiveness

that underlie any sustainable enterprise. Here are five additional pieces
of advice:

1. **Build a business that helps others. If your product or service doesn't make the world a better place, why bother?**

   Frankly, the world just doesn't need any more pet rocks, reality
   TV programs, or 2,500-calorie cinnamon buns. Starting a business
   is hard work. Doesn't it make sense to unleash your passion
   on something that will improve the safety, security, or
   comfort of fellow humanity? Knowing that you are building a
   socially worthwhile business can sustain you and your workforce
   through the rockiest times. Consider this model of a
   profitable business that exists to help others. Mark Oja runs
   ACTIVEAID, Inc., the medical devices manufacturing company
   founded by his father 40 years ago. ACTIVEAID is a
   small company by most standards. But to the 37 employees in
   the small town of Redwood Falls, Minnesota (population
   5459), it is a big business. Employees know what their work
   means to customers—disabled people who rely on their products
   for mobility, comfort, and dignity. Quality is paramount.
   Everyone takes pride in the fact that what they do helps people
   in their daily lives.

   There is no scarcity of business ideas with service at their core.
   Heartland Juice, the regional partner of Jamba Juice for Illinois,
   Wisconsin, and Minnesota had a vision—to offer a quick,
   healthy alternative to the usual fast-food establishments. It is
   now selling thousands of smoothies and fruit drinks a week to
   happy customers, employing hundreds of young people, and
   developing leadership talent for the company and community
   at large.

   Modern Survey is another small enterprise with service at its
   core. Early on, its founders discovered that their real product

was not the business information software solutions they provided, but the service they offered their customers. According to co-founder, Don MacPherson, "Service to others is very important. That's what we do as a company. It's helped our business effectiveness because if we put our clients' goals first, we achieve our goals. We have loyal clients, and we do virtually no advertising.

Even if your business fails—most entrepreneurs do fail several times before finally developing a successful venture—you will have the satisfaction of knowing your intentions were good. When you ultimately succeed—by staying true to universal principles and following the maxims of moral entrepreneurship—you will reap the combined rewards of service and profit.

2. Choose Your Partners Wisely

If you work in a large organization, your professional relationships tend to form through networks of work associates, industry colleagues, mentors, bosses, and acquaintances. If you work in a small organization, your professional relationships often overlap with personal networks of family and friends. Small business entrepreneurs are more likely to enter into partnership arrangements with family members, friends, and friends of friends. Choosing friends as business partners carries a host of dangers. No matter how objective you think you are, it is hard to evaluate a friend or relative's moral strengths and weaknesses. The success of your partnerships depends on shared principles and values. Looking at close personal associates through the rose-colored glasses of your affection, you may not notice moral gaps that could spell doom for your mutual venture. Rowland Moriarty, noted chairman of Charles Rives Associates, said this about a previous business partner. "I made a 25 year commitment to a friendship then watched him take actions that led to the collapse of our company."

Choosing a friend as a business partner can make it difficult to address the business problems created by one or the other. What *do* you do when a partner-friend betrays your trust by putting the business at risk? Though it's hard to contemplate, your best response would be to remind yourself of your friend's ideal self. By considering how your friend wants to behave ideally, you are able to give your friend the benefit of the doubt and avoid being overcome by destructive anger. When you believe that your partner and friend shares your values, you are able to discuss and jointly recommit to your vision and goals for your business. You forgive, and then you move on. You try again. You trust again. Keep in mind, however, that shared values lose meaning when ongoing behavior is inconsistent with those values. Forgiveness is not synonymous with stupidity. You can't look the other way when a partner continues to violate your mutual commitment. It's bad for your bottom line, and it sends the wrong message to employees who see that you are afraid to confront deceptive behavior. Remember that your emotional blinders are even stronger when your partner is a family member. Consider the experience of Janet Smith. Twenty years ago, her husband started a home renovation company. Business was booming, but cash flow was tight. Janet, a bright special needs teacher and mother of two, did not know that her husband was keeping his employees' social security and tax withholdings, until the IRS summons arrived. Janet and her husband declared bankruptcy, but that did not protect her from the legal liability to the IRS. They avoided imprisonment but ended up with massive penalties that took many years to repay. Meanwhile, her husband started a second small construction company, after assuring his wife that he had learned his lesson and would faithfully make employee tax payments. A year and a half later, Janet discovered that her husband had once again failed to make the proper employer payments to the IRS. Angry but still desperate to believe in her husband, Janet agreed to become his partner in a new business that designed, produced, and sold diagnostic equipment for chiropractic offices. The company had some success, was on the way to profitability, and had attracted the interest of a potential buyer. But the succession of business pressures had taken its toll on their marriage, and Janet and her husband finally divorced. Only after he signed over the business to her, did she discover that the potential investor was a phantom, and her husband had saddled her a third time with a set of enormous tax liabilities. Janet was an intelligent woman, with good analytic skills. But her overwhelming desire to trust her husband blinded her to his persistent ethical lapses. Ten years after her divorce, she is a successful financial advisor to small businesses, having built a second career out of the painful lessons of her business partnership with her former husband.

Because start-ups are so fragile, it's especially important to choose partners who share your values. "I can't say enough about this," says Spenser Segal. "Understanding that the first few years would be filled with adversity, it was critical that we hired a leadership team that shared common values and believed that working on something they believed in was the best possible use of their time. By coming together with a team who shared that commitment, they were assured of personally being successful *even if the business failed*."

3. Hold on tight to your core values.

Small business entrepreneurs need to be vigilant about maintaining their alignment with core values. Most entrepreneurs we know are highly morally intelligent. They are notably articulate about the principles and beliefs that guide them. ACTIVEAID's Mark Oja, for instance, endorses the importance of remaining true to one's principles. His moral compass is deceptively simple. "Honesty and family are the values that mean the most to me," says Mark, adding "If you don't mean it, don't say it. If you know or think or feel that something is improper, immoral or illegal, don't do it." But even though Mark is strongly committed to those values, business pressures can begin to lure a company away from its moral foundation. "It can be tough competing with companies who go offshore for their products. When we had an opportunity to sell a low-priced cane that came from outside the U.S., we took it. Then our distributors complained about how bad the canes were. Our distributors and customers count on us for high quality products, and we had violated their trust. When we realized what we had done, we cancelled the deal. It took some time to repair the relationships that had been completely trusting before."

4. **Surround yourself with employees who share your values.**

When it comes to human talent, do not confuse the "best" with the "brightest." Values fit is a stronger contributor to performance than technical skill. We all have known "values misfits" who were expert in their fields but couldn't advance because they did not operate effectively within a particular organizational culture.

Mark Oja recounts this experience: "One time, we knowingly hired someone we didn't trust. We needed a certain skill that was in short supply in our area. Our only skilled candidate in this small town was a man with a minor rap sheet and a reputation for bad relationships. But we felt desperate, so we thought we could handle him. We were wrong. He was impossible to work with, and we had to let him go."

KRW International is obsessed with hiring employees who resonate with its purpose and values. Before job candidates are invited for an interview, their technical credentials are carefully scrutinized. Then the real vetting begins. Candidates run through a gauntlet of individual and group interviews in which the spotlight is almost exclusively on "fit" and values. The KRW community as a whole must agree that the candidate shares key values and will effectively represent them to customers and stakeholders. An owner once violated the recruitment protocol by hiring a consultant who had not run the full interview gauntlet. His colleagues were angry, and the unwitting new consultant wondered why some of his new associates were less than friendly.

Although resonance with organizational values is key for successful hiring, be sure to preserve diversity. Organization cultures have strengths as well as weaknesses, and if you hire only clones of your current workforce, you will lose the opportunity to energize your company with new employees who bring novel approaches to your products and services.

5. Put your people—and your organization—first.

The United States Army has a saying, "The leader eats last." *The New York Times* offered an illustration of this maxim a few years ago when it published a photograph of an Army general serving Thanksgiving dinner to his combat troops in Afghanistan. Army leaders know what every entrepreneur needs to know. Followers must be able to absolutely trust their leaders to do what is best for the unit.

Putting people first also means investing in the development of employees. Small businesses are notorious for neglecting to invest in employee development. Their financial struggles usually leave little cash reserve, and it's easy to drop the ball when it comes to "overhead" expenses such as training. Studies indicate that large company employees are more than twice as likely as small company employees to be offered employer-

subsidized educational programs.[2] Given the lower average
wages offered by small companies,[3] it is even less likely that
employees of small companies will have the financial resources
to maintain and update their job skills. Bucking this trend is
ACTIVEAID's Mark Oja, who used the productivity increases
generated by a new production system, not as an excuse to
downsize, but as an opportunity for employee development.
Several years ago, ACTIVEAID transformed its manufacturing
process from batch production to packet production—
essentially it changed to a "just in time" production method.
Mark knew that packet production would be more responsive to
their customer, but it also meant there would be times when
employees were not occupied making inventory during the
transition. When employees were first told not to make products, they were worried, fearing that down time would mean
layoffs. But Mark had no intention of laying people off or
reducing work hours. Today, when orders come in, production
gets busy. When no inventory is needed, employees use the
time for training. Mark is firmly convinced that the investment
in training creates not only more skilled employees but a more
motivated workforce that will enhance their business performance in the months and years to come.

Last Words About Business Start-Ups

Despite many differences in the culture and operations of small and
large enterprises, the basic requirements of moral leadership are the
same. Moral skills are intrinsic both to successful entrepreneurship
and successful management of established companies. If you are an
entrepreneur, it may seem more difficult to stay true to principles when

2. *International Foundation of Employee Benefit Plans*, June 2000.
3. *Bureau of Labor Statistics*, March 2000.

the stakes are high and the cash flow is low. But your new venture simply will not survive unless it is anchored in core principles. Moral competence is essential for the small business leader. The small organization rarely has the excess resources to weather a major moral lapse, nor does it typically offer the golden handcuffs that could keep employees tied to a morally bankrupt enterprise.

So in the end, the small organization and the large have this in common—doing what is right morally and doing what is right for the business are inseparable. No matter the size of the territory, the morally competent leader weaves business and moral values together—and that makes all the difference.

EPILOGUE

Becoming a Global
Moral Leader

Undoubtedly, you want your business to succeed, *and* you want to do the right thing. The good news of this book is that you are not alone. A large number of business leaders want to do the right thing, and they believe doing the right thing leads to organizational and personal success.

Like many leaders, you feel deep responsibility for your businesses and your workforces. Your challenge now is to accept an even larger responsibility. Whether you realize it or not, the future of our planet is in your hands. Why? Because you are part of the most powerful social force on the planet today. In the last half-century, the corporation has assumed a central role as *the* iconic institution of many cultures across the globe.

Business is rapidly assuming a role as *the* most influential force in the lives of the world's 6.4 billion people. Religions, families, ethnic groups, and governments still matter and thankfully will continue to

207

matter, but unless business leaders and their workforces bring moral values to work, none of those other institutions will matter enough. If you are not sure just how influential you really are, consider the importance of the consumer economy to the well-being of your friends, family, employees, and the world itself.

As a business leader, you are de facto a moral educator. The moral lessons you and your company teach are lessons more powerful and more pervasive than that of churches, schools, and families. If you do the right thing, you will teach moral behavior to your employees. If you cook the books, fire someone unfairly, or use deceptive business practices, you will be teaching others to do the same thing, or you will be misleading others into believing that's just how business is done.

Your workforce is learning right and wrong at your workplace and is learning that "right" is sustainable and "wrong" is not. If we want current and future generations to care about the welfare of others as well as the prosperity of the business and the survival of the planet, we who lead today's businesses will have to show them the way. When it comes to moral values in the workplace, a lot needs to be said, and more needs to be done!

You may not have signed up to be a global moral leader, but you are. And with the inescapable power of your role comes a daunting responsibility. It is a responsibility that includes and yet goes beyond profitability. It is a responsibility that encompasses and goes beyond more obvious notions of corporate social responsibility.

Raising the Stakes

This book argues that moral intelligence and moral skills are critical to sustainable business performance. It has proposed a set of essential moral skills and highlighted the moral mechanics of interacting with the usual organizational stakeholders, especially customers, employees, and owners. Like most leaders, you recognize that you are accountable to those three groups, but there is another constituency that is equally important—the communities beyond your organization.

Every organization lives within at least one community: whether it is the neighborhood surrounding the corner grocery store or the world community in which a major multinational corporation operates. How well do you serve the community that hosts your business? Consider these three different levels of responsibility you have for your external communities:

- The responsibility to do no harm

- The responsibility to add current value

- The responsibility to add future value

Watch Your Wake

Boaters entering harbors are often greeted by signs saying, "Watch Your Wake." Traveling too fast creates lines of turbulence—the wake of the boat—that can capsize smaller vessels. You also need to watch your wake. You need to understand the potential negative consequences of your presence in the communities where you operate. Some of the most admired corporations in the United States and in the world have been slow to acknowledge the catastrophic side effects of their business processes.

Businesses have knowingly and unknowingly polluted oceans and rivers and lakes. As Erik Peterson and Jay Farrar from the Center for Strategic and International Studies[1] have pointed out in their presentation on the "Seven Revolutions" that will shape the world in the next 25 to 50 years, strategic resource management of food, water, and energy

---

1. As presented at http://www. csis.org.

will become an even greater challenge as the overall population of the world balloons to 8.8 billion by mid-century, while simultaneously the population of developed countries contracts.

Too few of the world's biggest companies take seriously their responsibility to do no harm. Alison Maitland reported in the June 23, 2004, issue of *Financial Times* that, "the world's 100 largest companies have a poor record of accounting for their impact on society and the environment." Maitland drew her conclusions from a recent research report published by AccountAbility, a UK-based social responsibility institute. Had traditional philanthropy and community involvement been included in the report, big companies would have been rated more highly. Nevertheless, their relatively poor showing illustrates large companies still need to be convinced to do no harm to the environment.

Although environmental protection is an obvious responsibility for business organizations, other more subtle forms of pollution need to be remedied, and other challenges need to be addressed. If you work in the media industry, you may need to watch your wake in the behavioral messages you send to children and adults alike. Just about every business has to concern itself with the potential negative consequences on family life of a 24/7 work culture.

Give Back

In addition to doing no harm, you also have a responsibility to "give back" to your communities in exchange for the varied resources that they provide—desirable locations, good employees, attractive living conditions, raw materials for manufacturing, customers, and so on. Business-sponsored social responsibility programs are one good way to add value to your communities at large. Your personal efforts and contributions of time and money are another.

There are likely a number of ways that you and your business have contributed positively to your local communities—perhaps by supporting programs in education, the arts, and health/well being or by mentoring programs for at-risk youth or fundraising for medical research. If you and your organization are adding value in these and other ways, good for you and good for your company.

Giving back is more than a public-relations tool. It is vital for maintaining thriving local, regional, and world communities and the more you can do, the better. As the world's economy continues to globalize and as communication and travel technologies continue to "shrink" the world, each of us and the businesses we lead and/or work in will have the opportunity to become even better at giving back.

Create the Future

Your third level of responsibility, to add future value, is the most challenging. Accepting responsibility for the future can be difficult in a business environment that is so attuned to the short term. It is relatively easy to contribute to the cause of the month because the need and the benefits are usually obvious. Figuring out how to add future value is less intuitive. Caring about the future impact of your business on the community and the world requires a different mindset. Consider this illustration of the kind of mindset that we would have to cultivate: At the 1998 State of the World Forum (founded in the mid-1990s by Jim Garrison and Mikhail Gorbachev), participants had the fascinating experience of participating in a ceremony led by a Polynesian tribal chief from Hawaii. After the ritual, the chief was asked, "What is your advice for those of us in businesses who are concerned about both the short term and the long term? There is a lot of pressure on quarterly and annual results." The chief answered, "You need to understand how we think about responsibility and accountability. In our culture, we help people realize they are *accountable to the three generations that preceded them and responsible for the seven generations that follow them.* When we make decisions, we take into consideration the impact of that decision on someone seven generations from now."

Imagine what your company's strategic plan would look like if Polynesian decision-making criteria were incorporated into your analysis. We have seen the harm done by managers who optimize for the short term. What kind of good could your company do if its performance objectives were designed to contribute to results a hundred years down the road?

A Global Business Opportunity

Like all the moral competencies discussed in this book, serving your external communities is not only morally right, but essential for sustainable business success. The business case for global moral leadership is strong. There are profits to be made. Here lies the opportunity: As you provide the people of the world with good jobs and fair pay for their work or fair prices for their products and services, you simultaneously expand the opportunity for yourself and your business.

Global business is less about expansive holdings and more about expansive thinking. Consider this: *Businesses that work to increase the welfare of the global community simultaneously increase the market for economic goods and services.*

A recent *Business Week* article chronicled how new technologies could help alleviate chronic poverty in India. It pointed out that "many of the educated elite responsible for the success of India's tech and software houses—or who have helped U.S. multinationals prosper—decided to turn their energies to helping India's poor."[2] They see both the opportunity for *compassion* and the business opportunity for profit that comes from helping the poor move up the economic ladder.

2. "The Digital Village," *Business Week*, June 28, 2004.

The article quotes management strategist C.K. Prahalad, who says,"If you can conceptualize the world's four billion poor as a market, rather than as a burden, they must be considered the biggest source of growth left in the world."[3] Every person on the planet is a potential customer or partner or supplier or employee. Large companies today may compete aggressively for dominant share of a ten million customer market or for a relatively small number of highly educated and technically competent prospective employees, when the actual potential market and the potential workforce is the entire world's population.

Today, markets are constrained by the economic status of regional populations, and education and development is typically available only for those who can afford it. But people lacking education are not dumb, and people without economic means still have material needs and the intelligence to create economic value (through jobs) in exchange for the ability to buy products that will satisfy those needs. Many people in underdeveloped regions can't afford the consumer products they are hired to produce (think designer athletic shoes.) Wouldn't it be good for business if they could? Henry Ford asked that question about an infant American car industry more than half a century ago. Henry Ford may not have been a saint in many respects, but he knew how to do well by doing good. He figured out how to create customers for his new-fangled automobile by paying his workers well above the going rate. He wanted people making the Model T to be able to afford one. He created a market for his products through enlightened self-interest. Henry Ford's workers won, and Ford won.

Prosperity need not be a zero sum game. Why couldn't we increase our markets by financing business start-ups in third world regions? The micro-lending movement is a good example of the economic effectiveness of business creation in undeveloped regions. But those economic experiments are largely the province of academics and non-profits. Why

3. Ibid.

aren't those of us in the for-profit sector doing more to develop communities that will, in turn, sustain us and our businesses through the balance of this new century and beyond?

We need to stop thinking that we can only win if others lose. Ultimately, none of us will do well unless all of us do well. We may be feeling pretty comfortable in our plush executive suite or on the porch of our summer home. But our grandchildren and great grandchildren will not have the benefit of our well-appointed lives if we don't help all the world's people do better.

Conclusion

Mark Twain once said, "It is curious that physical courage should be so common in the world and moral courage so rare." It is time for moral courage to take center stage in business and for business to accept the responsibility that comes with its prominent position in the world. The ball is in our court.

EPILOGUE

Update on
Moral Intelligence's
Cast of Characters

The moral intelligence framework presented in this book was based on research that included interviews with leaders and public information about companies and their executives. This research was completed in 2004, the year before *Moral Intelligence* was first published. For this edition, we were given the opportunity to update information as of March 2007 about some of the book's "characters"—companies and leaders who helped us shape the business case for the importance of moral intelligence to business performance.

Our cast of characters was of two sorts: companies and leaders who demonstrated the devastating financial consequences of moral stupidity (think of the headliner accounting scandals of 2000–2001); and companies and leaders who displayed a high degree of moral intelligence in pursuit of their companies' success. At the time we originally interviewed some leaders, the jury was still out on whether their values-based leadership really would make a difference to either their

individual leadership effectiveness or the performance of their enterprises. If this were a morality play, all the bad characters would suffer,
and all the good characters would flourish. Reality is a bit more
nuanced: many of the high profile executive offenders were treated far
more gently by the courts than seemed fair and just. Though fewer of
them are in jail today than we might have imagined, none of them so far
have been "reborn" into respectability. Their lives are permanently
impaired (we say this not out of sympathy, but to underscore that moral
stupidity results in bad *personal* outcomes). And, they have left a lot of
damage in their wake. In many cases, their former companies no longer
exist, while those that survived are struggling. Employees are without
jobs or pensions. Shareholders hold worthless stock.

But the picture is much brighter when we turn to the leaders and
companies who taught us so much about moral intelligence. For example, when we got back in touch with several leaders of young entrepreneurial ventures, we discovered that their approach to leadership was
paying off, sometimes beyond their expectations. Their employees were
happy and productive, their businesses were becoming profitable, and
they were able to manage demanding, high-stress jobs with the composure that comes from living in alignment with one's values. Our morally
intelligent large companies were thriving as well. Consider American
Express Financial Advisors, 18 months after its spin-off to become
Ameriprise: its leaders and employees have navigated the landmark
transition well—not perfectly, of course—but with a good deal of moral
intelligence. And as you'll see later in this Epilogue, they have done so
with remarkable financial results.

Where Have All the Scandals Gone?

To demonstrate the business costs of moral incompetence, earlier we
discussed five companies who were among the many embroiled in legal
actions because of accounting fraud. Their stories have progressed in
the last three years.

Mitsubishi Motors

By 2004, its former president and ten other executives were in jail after being arrested on charges that they suppressed information about widespread vehicle defects. In December of 2006, a Japanese court acquitted three former Mitsubishi Motors executives who had been charged with covering up a design flaw that led to a fatal accident. Although the court recognized that the executives had, in fact, concealed the data, it determined that the company had no obligation to report defects under Japan's road and transport laws. The court also acquitted the company over another fatal accident.

Although Mitsubishi Motors had reached a settlement in December 2004 with the family of yet another victim of an accident caused by a design flaw, as of December 2006, four former Mitsubishi Motors executives were on trial in that case.

In February 2007, the company reported its first quarterly profit since 2004, although some of the credit was given to the impact of Japan's weak currency.

Adelphia Communications

In July 2004, Adelphia founder and former CEO, John Rigas, and his son Timothy were found guilty of conspiracy, securities fraud, and bank fraud. Charges against them had included concealing $2.3 billion in loans and embezzling, bankrupting what was then the nation's fifth-largest cable company. On June 20, 2005, a year after their convictions, John Rigas was sentenced to 15 years in prison and Timothy Rigas was sentenced to 20 years in prison. As of early 2007, both are free pending appeal. In July 2006, as part of its plan to wind down operations, Adelphia completed the sale of the majority of assets and transferred its customer base to two other cable television companies. It plans to emerge from bankruptcy protection in March 2007 and to distribute its remaining assets to creditors.

Lucent Technologies

In 2004, the Securities and Exchange Commission charged the company with fraudulently recognizing more than $1 billion in revenues and $470 million in pre-tax income during fiscal 2000. It also charged individual executives for their alleged roles in the case. Lucent settled the SEC Enforcement Action in May 2004, paying a $25 million penalty. Ten executives who were charged in the matter reached individual settlements involving sizable penalties over the course of the ensuing two years.

In September 2006, Lucent merged with its French competitor, telecommunications equipment-maker Alcatel. The new Paris-based company, Alcatel-Lucent, posted a fiscal year 2006 fourth quarter loss, with revenues sliding almost 16 percent to $5.74. To curb losses, in February 2007 the company announced plans to cut 12,500 jobs, roughly 16 percent of its workforce, over a three year period.

Enron

Energy company Enron became the poster child for corporate corruption in 2001 when it was revealed that its financial status was fabricated through deliberate and extensive accounting fraud. In May 2006, former CEOs Ken Lay and Jeffrey Skilling were convicted of criminal fraud and conspiracy. In a dramatic twist, Ken Lay died—before he could be sentenced—in July 2006 of "natural causes" related to cardiovascular disease. In October 2006, Skilling was sentenced to 24 years and four months in prison. He is one of nine ex-Enron executive to serve prison time, and one of seven who are currently behind bars—including ex-Enron CFO Andrew Fastow, who pleaded guilty to fraud in 2004 in exchange for a ten year prison sentence. In November 2006, Enron executives Andrew Fastow and his former chief aide Michael Kopper, received sharply reduced sentences because of their cooperation with prosecutors to help convict Ken Lay and Jeffrey Skilling.

As of this writing, jury selection in a $40 billion Enron shareholder civil lawsuit was expected to take place in April 2007. Meanwhile, Enron is in the process of liquidating its remaining operations and distributing assets to creditors.

HealthSouth

In 2005, HealthSouth former CEO Richard Scrushy was acquitted in a $2.5 billion fraud scheme to overstate earnings and inflate stock prices during a period between 1996 and 2002. The acquittal was surprising to many, because there had been extensive testimony that he was knowledgeable about the fraud, and because 15 former executives had already pleaded guilty and a 16th had been convicted by jurors. But Scrushy's legal woes were not over. In August 2006, the Alabama Supreme Court ruled that Scrushy must repay $48.8 million in bonuses he received during the period of the fraud—and a time when company was sustaining massive operating losses.

A few months earlier, in June 2006, Scrushy, along with former Alabama Governor Don Siegelman were convicted of federal bribery and fraud charges. The charges were in connection with a $500,000 payment by Scrushy to defray Seigelman's campaign debts in exchange for a seat on a state hospital regulatory board. As of February 2007, sentences had not yet been made, and the case is under appeal.

Also in February 2007, HealthSouth former ex-CFO Malcolm "Tadd" McVay got a miraculously light sentence of six months home detention and five years probation, after pleading guilty to taking part in the accounting scandals.

HealthSouth is still trying to recover from the accounting scandal. It narrowly escaped bankruptcy. According to Morningstar, "compared to its industry peers, [HealthSouth] stock has been one of the worst performers over the past five years." As of February 2007, its share price, while fluctuating during the prior 12 months, stood at approximately the same price as it did in February 2006. Perhaps not coincidentally, in February 2007, the company announced plans to sell 600 outpatient rehabilitation centers for about $245 million, in order to reduce its long-term debt.

These corporate scandals, as painful to all participants as they must be, don't seem to act as deterrents. These 2006 news stories attest to the continuing prevalence of bad business behavior:

- **Wal-Mart** will face a lawsuit claiming pay discrimination against more than one million female U.S. employees after a court approved the action. (BBC News February 6, 2007)

- Antivirus and security software provider **McAfee** fired President Kevin Weiss, and announced that CEO and Chairman George Samenuk will retire after a stock options investigation found accounting problems that will require financial restatements, (*USA Today* October 11, 2006)

- **Hyundai Motor Company** Chairman Chung Mong-koo was convicted in February 2007 of embezzlement and other charges and sentenced to three years in prison. Mong-koo continues to run the company while his case is appealed. Meanwhile, Hyundai is grappling with labor unrest that cost more than $2 billion in lost production in 2006. (Associated Press, February 7, 2007)

- David C. Wittig, the former CEO of Kansas utility company **Westar Energy Inc**. was sentenced in April 2006 to 18 years in prison for conspiracy, wire fraud, money laundering, and circumventing internal controls. Wittig served 13 months in prison before he was released on bond in January 2007, following a Federal appeals court reversal of several convictions. In an unrelated case, Wittig was found guilty of bank fraud, but remains free pending his appeal of that case. (*Washington Post*, April 4, 2006; Kansas City Star, February 21, 2007)

Moral intelligence could have kept each of these companies, and their leaders, out of the courts. Now they, their companies, employees, and shareholders are all at risk. One can only wonder why corporate crime is still seen as such a desirable route to personal wealth and power. Why don't the massive devaluations of companies like HealthSouth and Lucent convince more top leaders of the wisdom of following a moral compass?

Good Leaders—Good Results

Since the first edition of *Moral Intelligence* was published in 2005, a number of the leaders interviewed have moved into new assignments or new companies, consistent with the overall trend of CEO and executive churn in corporations. Fortunately, all who have made changes have done so to satisfy personal or career preferences, and none has come anywhere close to needing an electronic monitoring bracelet. Of the 76 leaders interviewed:

- Nine either already were or are now retired

- Forty-one remain with the same organization in the same capacity

- Nine remain with the same organization in a different capacity, most of them promoted

- Sixteen changed companies or left the corporate world together

Sadly, Ken Kaess, formerly CEO of DDB Worldwide, passed away in 2006.

We have maintained contact with a number of leaders featured in the book. Their companies' ongoing success validates the relationship between moral intelligence and sustained business performance.

Thrivent Financial for Lutherans

In 2001 Thrivent Financial for Lutherans was formed out of the merger of Lutheran Brotherhood and AAL (Aid for the Association for Lutherans). Assets under management grew from $52.3 billion in 2002 to $67.5 billion in 2005 (most recent numbers available.) Net income grew from $252 million in 2003 to $498 million in 2005.

But these numbers tell only half of the story. Thrivent is known for its substantial contributions to helping needy people from around the world. In 2005, the financial value of the community and regional outreach programs, sponsored by Thrivent Financial and its three million chapter members, exceeded $420 million. Its charitable projects included support for the tsunami victims in Southeast Asia as well as Hurricane Katrina victims in the United States. Perhaps the most dramatic example of Thrivent's ethical commitment to its member clients is the "Professional Office Practice" (POP) initiative launched early in 2007.

As Jim Thomsen, now Executive Vice President of Distribution explains the POP concept:

> We're working hard to better align the interest of our members [clients] and our advisors. We're spearing some of the sacred cows of the financial service industry, and one of those sacred cows is commission-based compensation. We are introducing a business model where advisors are paid salaries and bonuses based on things like client satisfaction and that helps our members realize advisors' interests are better aligned with their own.

Thrivent's desire to create an even stronger client-driven workforce reinforces its commitment to integrity and responsibility. Its move away from commission-based compensation has the potential to spur significant competitive advantage—and ultimately could revolutionize the entire financial services industry.

The Thomson Corporation

Dick Harrington continues to demonstrate visionary leadership as CEO of The Thomson Corporation. He has led the transformation of this former newspaper and travel company into one of the world's largest publishers of electronic data. Thomson maintains its reputation as highly desirable employer, and by all accounts appears to be a winner in the "war for talent." Shares of The Thomson Corporation stock have increased from about $30 per share in 2004 to approximately $42 per share in the first quarter of 2007.

Safeco Corporation

The choppy waters Safeco navigated to avoid almost certain dissolution have required many painful decisions, including layoffs. However, all of these difficult business acts were undertaken with moral intelligence and courage. Mike McGavick left the post of CEO at Safeco in December 2005 to run for the United States Senate in the state of Washington. His successor, Paula Rosput Reynolds, took the helm in January, 2006 and continued the tradition of high-integrity leadership spearheaded by Mike McGavick. When Mike McGavick assumed the CEO role in early 2001, Safeco stock was trading at roughly $18 per share. When he left five years later, it was trading at approximately $55 per share. Stock value has continued to grow under Paula Rosput Reynolds' leadership to the current price in the first quarter of 2007 of about $68 per share.

BWBR Architects

Jay Sleiter, CEO of BWBR Architects, retired shortly after we interviewed him, but he positioned his successor, Steve Patrick, to do well. The architecture firm continues to grow and thrive under the new CEO. Patrick's vision is to make BWBR "the regional leader in Knowledge and Process Design in their five key market segments, and to be the employer of choice for architecture professionals in the Twin Cities [Minneapolis and St. Paul, Minnesota] area." According to Steve Patrick and his executive team, that vision is well on the way to fruition.

The Russell Investment Group

CEO and President Craig Ueland, featured in the book's Introduction, has done extremely well since 2004—his first year as CEO. The Russell Investment Group has continued to produce outstanding financial returns for its parent company, Northwestern Mutual. Since Craig took the helm, assets under management have more than doubled. The company is growing at a rate greater than the average of their peers. The Russell Investment Group has become a truly global firm with slightly more than 50 percent of profits coming from outside the United States. In 2006, *Fortune* magazine once again included the company on its list of the "Best 100 Companies" in the United States.

Ecolab, Inc.

Doug Baker is still the CEO of Ecolab and has guided it to outstanding financial success with all measures, including net sales, operating income, and return on equity increasing significantly. The Ecolab stock in 2004 was trading in the vicinity of $26 per share. In the first quarter of 2007, it was trading at approximately $43 per share.

Business Ethics magazine named Ecolab one of the "100 Best Corporate Citizens" for six consecutive years. As Jim Baker noted in a recent annual report, "Corporate integrity and good citizenship are essential pillars of our business, and recognition like this reaffirms our ongoing commitment to conducting our business the right way for our customers, our shareholders, and our associates."

Ameriprise Financial Services (Formerly American Express Financial Advisors)

When the first edition of *Moral Intelligence* went to press, American Express Financial Advisors was an American Express company. In October 2005, American Express Financial Advisors (AEFA) spun off to become an independent company, Ameriprise. AEFA and some of its leaders are featured prominently in the book (at times to our publisher's dismay!). AEFA was the first company to develop an extensive program to train financial advisors in emotional intelligence skills, and was the company in which author Doug Lennick formed his initial ideas about the relevance of moral intelligence to business performance. In addition, Ken Chenault then—and now—CEO of American Express, was noted in the book for his morally intelligent leadership in the aftermath of the September 11, 2001 terrorist attack, which killed 11 American Express employees in the World Trade Center and severely damaged its corporate headquarters across the street from the World Trade Center. Although AEFA produced significant financial results between 1984—when it was acquired by American Express—until 2000, it had several difficult years in the aftermath of the stock market slide that began in 2000, and was intensified by the 2001 terrorist attack. In the context of those difficult years, Ken Chenault's decision to spin off AEFA, announced early in 2005, was met with some understandable cynicism. Some critics, inside and outside both companies, assumed that Ken Chenault was trying to unload an underperforming business unit. Where was the integrity and responsibility that *Moral Intelligence* had lionized in Ken Chenault? The authors' view is that Chenault led the spin-off in a morally intelligent manner. For example, when the spin-off was announced, extensive attention was paid to the communicating the rationale for the divestiture to all stakeholders—especially to AEFA employees. Chenault expressed his appreciation and regard for the contribution AEFA had made to American Express. He also expressed his belief in the growth prospects of both firms. American Express provided

Ameriprise with substantial capital. This gave Ameriprise a very solid initial financial position that allowed Ameriprise to invest heavily in establishing a new brand. Employee concerns regarding compensation, retirement plans, insurance, and so on were all addressed. The authors' relationships with American Express and Ameriprise prevent them from being completely objective in their assessment of how the spin-off was managed. Therefore, Ken Chenault offers this perspective on the business decision to spin off AEFA—and the reasoning behind the decision:

> A leader has to make tough decisions, but the execution of those decisions has to be done with integrity and compassion. A good example was our decision to spin off our financial advisory business, AEFA. Many of our colleagues at AEFA felt a close connection to American Express and it was a hard decision for them to accept, because they felt we did not have confidence in them. That isn't how I viewed it. The payments business had high growth and high return prospects while the AEFA business also had high growth prospects, but lower returns. The best way for both businesses to get the capital they needed for growth was to have two separate companies.
>
> We set them up well from a capital standpoint. We did it in the right way for employees, customers and shareholders. We were operating from a position of strength and common values.
>
> The acquisition of IDS [in 1984 IDS became AEFA] was hugely successful and so has been the spin-off. The need existed for us to make another transformational move for both companies. In certain quarters it was very difficult, but following our values allowed both organizations to deal, successfully, with the stress and anxiety.
>
> This was not done for short term reasons, but the short term results have been very good.

> This was not an issue of good and bad. This was two goods. We unlocked shareholder value for both companies. This couldn't be done by vote or consensus. I had to make the decision. I considered customers, shareholders, and employees.

How has Ameriprise performed in its short history? In the 16 months that followed the spin-off, Ameriprise's stock price soared 70 percent. Ameriprise executives attribute their early success to their corporate values. At a February 2007 company leadership conference, Jim Cracchiolo, Chairman and CEO said:

> Our success as a company depends on managing the business with the highest standards of integrity. I want to win, but not at all costs. If we base our decisions on our values and principles, we'll do the right thing by our clients, our advisors, our employees, and our shareholders.

In Their Own Words: Selected Moral Leaders Two Years Later

During February 2007, we again interviewed several of the leaders profiled in earlier chapters. The news is good, and the trajectory of leaders at the helm of start-ups is especially heartening. Unlike leaders within large, established businesses, who may have trouble swimming against the tide, entrepreneurial leaders have an opportunity to put their money where their moral mouths are—to infuse their enterprise with moral values from the outset. When we first interviewed some of the entrepreneurial leaders, we knew that their hearts were in the right place, but often had no hard data on whether their moral stance would pay off for their businesses. Their updates add heft to the business case for moral intelligence. What follows are recent reports from several of our favorite moral leaders.

Lynn Fantom, CEO ID Media

Lynn: We're just celebrating our fifth anniversary, and we've grown profits 200 percent in that time. Although there's been remarkable change in our industry and our company, we continue to work with the world's best marketers, including American Express, HBO, and Verizon.

Q: What were your secrets to that success?

Lynn: We embrace change. Because of that, we're profiting from it—literally and figuratively. In the five years since our roll-up, the media business has experienced greater change than any other area of marketing. Digital media channels have exploded. New ways to entertain and inform have emerged— podcasting, RSS, social media like Facebook, interactive TV, much more granular online search, mobile. But what has remained constant is our respect for our people. That's evident in our training programs, employee communication, everything. It's helped us attract and retain the best talent in the business and that's the difference. When we were being interviewed by Sony Electronics for a new product launch (which we won), the first thing the head of media at Sony said was, "I hear people love working at ID Media!"

Lynn continues to use "Ask Lynn," and she continues to see it as a very effective way to demonstrate she values employee perspective and input.

Lynn: "Breakfast with Lynn and Gaye" is something new, a way for new and old employees to get together monthly to get to know each other, ask questions, share ideas. I leave those breakfasts, and *I'm* the one who's all pumped up.

Lynn offered the following observations regarding industry turnover and ID Media's success at keeping or re-attracting key employees:

> Lynn: Turnover in professional services is high across the board. But believe it or not, corporate culture can provide glue. We had several talented employees leave and come back within a year because of the culture. They say "I missed the people. I missed the openness." That says a lot.

Lynn acknowledges ID Media is known for innovation:

> Lynn: ID Media wasn't on the map five years ago. This year our Director of Emerging Media was chosen by *Advertising Age* as one of the "40 under 40" marketing stars to watch…along with others from Google, Pepsi, P&G, YouTube, Levi Strauss, Verizon Wireless, and Citibank. That made me very happy. Not only because it put ID Media in the company of such great marketers, but also because it acknowledged one of the young stars we'd been mentoring. That's my job…to provide a platform for success.

Spenser Segal, CEO ActiFi

ActiFi was incorporated in the summer of 2003. In the years 2004–2006 ActiFi experienced revenue growth of 135 percent per year and has posted five consecutive quarters of profitability. Workforce headcount has grown from five in 2003 to 41 (26 full time employees and 15 independent contractors) in 2007.

> Q: What has contributed to your growth?

> Spenser: Our core values (Exceeding Customer Expectations, Teamwork, Integrity, Responsibility, and Valuing Clients, Shareholders, and Employees) have had a huge impact.

We don't just have them on a wall. We actually use them in deciding how to work with a customer. A lot of our revenue comes from exceeding customer expectations.

There's been a correlation between reasonable profitability and exceeding customer expectations by adding value and doing work we weren't paid to do. I will always take lower profitability to ActiFi in order to exceed the expectations of the customer.

We're in business to produce great client results and financially improve their businesses.

I need to continue to communicate what we mean by the values. New people don't necessarily know what our shared definitions are, and when they don't know they will default to their own definitions.

We've done a good job of attracting talent. We're looking for people who want to make meaning and not just make money. Our people are attracted to a shared vision. We attract people who don't answer job ads. These are people who want to make a difference. Of course, we're a for profit business, but that's not the driver.

Q: Can you give me an example of exceeding customer expectations?

Spenser: One of the things we did with one client is a review and an update with them a year after we had worked with them. This was done at no cost them. We helped them construct a scoreboard to look at the impact of the work we had done. Just last week the client commented on how much they appreciated the fact that we took the initiative to check on whether they were getting the success they and we had hoped for. We try hard to make the biggest impact for the client.

Lynn Sontag, CEO MENTTIUM Corporation

MENTTIUM celebrated its 15-year anniversary in 2006. Lynn Sontag and Kim Vappie acquired the company in 2002, and 2006 was the first year of profitability since the acquisition.

> Lynn: Now that we're global...we launched 450 partnerships in 2006, and that's up 200 partnerships in just one year, we need to broaden our curriculum and offerings to include multiple languages.
>
> The mentor/mentee relationship that we facilitate provides perspectives that they can't get in their own organization.
>
> We had a very challenging year in 2006. We did some restructuring that allowed us to provide more services to our primary markets and also go global. We exceeded our revenue goals for the year by 20 percent, and we had a profit on the bottom line for the first time since Kim and I acquired the company in 2002.
>
> Q: What has contributed to your success?
>
> Lynn: Focus on the client and focus on training and developing our own people. The employees love it. We just had a company meeting, and the number one comment we heard is "I personally feel valued by this organization." Our passion around servicing clients is noticed, and this is a direct result of our committed staff. We've been told by our clients on a regular basis that our service exceeds what other vendors provide.
>
> Q: Can you give an example of your client focus?
>
> Lynn: A mentee called. She was concerned about the mentor we matched her up with. The client service manager did some investigating. Initially the mentee couldn't understand why we

had made the match. The client service manager helped her understand why we the saw the connection. She stayed with the mentor and two months later she reported the relationship was so strong and she was benefiting so much. When the client service manager can help in a real personal way like that they know they're making a difference. MENTTIUM pays attention to the whole person.

Lynn noted that following a recent kickoff event she was contacted by a client who said, "I saw you at your kickoff and I was so inspired by your story."

The story the client was referring to was the story behind Lynn leaving her job with a major corporation to buy and become CEO of MENTTIUM. Lynn herself had been a mentee, and the mentor she had "helped me hold the mirror up. He helped me understand what I'm capable of, and he helped me gain confidence. I eventually decided to buy MENTTIUM. He said, 'You have potential!'"

Lynn summarized how she feels about her employees:

I have a responsibility for my employees, and I don't take that lightly.

Don MacPherson, Co-President Modern Survey

Modern Survey was founded in 1999. Since 2004, revenues have quintupled and profits have soared.

Q: What has contributed to that growth?

Don: We give a very high level of quality service at a fair price. We're not the highest or lowest priced. We let clients and employees know they are valued. I'll give you an example. My favorite day to work is Thanksgiving. I go to the gym early in the morning and then I go to the office. I call my immediate family and friends to let them know I love them. Then I call many of our clients and I thank them. I tell clients how much I appreciate them. I want them to know how important they are and how they have changed my life. I also call our employees and let them know how much I appreciate them. Sometimes I reach the person I'm calling, and sometimes I leave a message. Clients and employees both know how much they mean to us and that has resulted in amazing employee and client loyalty.

We spend a lot of time making sure whoever we hire is the right person. With big companies personalities don't matter as much as they do here. We treat our employees well. We empower them to make decisions, and we give them opportunities to shine. We work with over 50 of the Fortune 500 companies. Our people really enjoy working with high profile companies. Our goal by 2010 is to be working with all 500 of the Fortune 500, and I know we can do it.

I find I get so involved in the lives of our employees. There's a lot of pride in helping employees grow as people and achieve their goals in life. By employing them, we're helping them achieve their goals and provide for their families. Their families are part of the team too. I sometimes joke that I don't have kids but I do have employees. Their problems become your problems. It's a lot of responsibility but you take it on and you enjoy doing so.

Q: Who is the right person?

Don: Someone who has an entrepreneurial spirit even though they might not be the entrepreneur themselves. Someone who is well motivated and able to figure things out when there isn't a lot of clarity. People who respect other people—all other people. Someone who doesn't feel entitled, all three partners despise entitlement.

We have an employee meeting every month, and I could tell we had an employee who wasn't on the bus. In the end he chose to leave after nine months, and that turned out to be good for him and us.

We want people who understand that when the organization is successful, they will benefit too.

Mark Oja, CEO ACTIVEAID

Mark: Over the last two years our results have been phenomenal! We had been growing at a rate of five to ten percent per year. In Fiscal Year 2004–2005 our net sales were up 16.5 percent and our net income was up 50.6 percent. In Fiscal Year 2005–2006 our net sales were up 13.4 percent and our net income was up another 34.9 percent!

Q: What do you think is behind those incredible numbers?

Mark: Our mission statement contains a focus on the customer and the quality and value of our products and service. It also says we want to provide every employee with the opportunity to learn, grow, and prosper. Competitive return for the company comes after all of that.

Mayo Clinic has been a long-time customer. A lot of our first ideas and products forty-two years ago were launched at Mayo and the University of Minnesota. They choose to work with us because of our product ingenuity, dependability, and integrity. We provide the quality, durability, and value they need.

We accomplished those great growth results with the same permanent workforce. The fun part is we were able to present special bonus checks and additional paid vacation to everybody for their efforts. We have not lost one key employee and total turnover is very low. The average tenure of our workforce is over 15 years. I don't even remember the last time we lost a key person. The workforce has to be taken care of because they have brought us to where we are today. It's not a one-way street. They take care of us, and we take care of them.

Sometimes you have to fail on some projects in order to grow and succeed over the long term. Profitability needs to be in the structure of the success. I focus on the accounting and management, and my brother-in-law Chip Nearing (Chip is a shareholder and company COO. and Vice President of Marketing) focuses on the sales and marketing. The result is the two of us can accomplish the work of three or more people.

Gary O'Hagan, President of Coaches Division, IMG

IMG is the world's largest sports talent and marketing agency. It was founded in 1960 by Mark McCormack. McCormack passed away in 2003, and IMG was acquired by Forstmann Little for a reported $700–750 Million. Gary O'Hagan, whose clients include the legendary John Wooden, reports:

The market for coaching services has grown. There's much more volatility in the profession than ever before. The ability for coaches to maintain their own mental and emotional balance is critical. Your strength as an individual is directly related to how you react to praise and criticism.

The volatility and pressure on coaches creates heightened opportunities for moral and ethical breakdowns. College coaches especially have a tremendous responsibility to treat their athletes in ethical ways. Some coaches actually offer more scholarships than they have available and then they find ways to get rid of some of the players. That's wrong. We make an effort to make sure all of the coaches we represent understand the need to have integrity and act ethically toward everybody— including other coaches (assistants, etc.) and all players.

Charlie Zelle, CEO and Chairman, Jefferson Bus Lines

Last, but not least, Charlie sent this email update to author Fred Kiel:

Hello Fred,

Thank you for contacting me. I enjoyed your book very much and was honored to be a small part of it. Indeed, I am still the CEO of Jefferson Lines. Since we spoke, the bus line has expanded in a number of areas, including many small towns in regions dropped by Greyhound during their past restructuring. Our management team was talking recently about one of our fundamental assets being the trust we develop with rural communities which allows us to stitch together route systems that cross public, nonprofit and private boundaries. In other words, I guess our integrity is becoming a core operating strategy and is paying off. We had a good year last year and expect to be improving in 2007. Good luck on your update. I look forward to seeing it.

Regards,
Charlie

Where We Stand Now

Surveying the landscape two years later reinforces the business case for moral intelligence. It's a deceptively simple case: grounding your business in moral principles produces positive business results. Ignoring those principles can be disastrous. Our research to date is clearly not quantitative. Biases could sneak in to our assessment of the factors that influence business performance. But the qualitative research is revealing. We could not find anyone in our original group of morally intelligent leaders who was not faring well, both personally and professionally. Meanwhile, leaders cited in the media for ethical lapses were wreaking havoc on themselves, their families, and their former stockholders and employees. What's more, at this writing, there is the first quantitative research study that highlights the significance of moral competence to business performance: The Consortium For Research on Emotional Intelligence in Organizations has recently released findings of a study on the key financial advisor competencies that predict return to clients. Seven primary competencies were identified by the research. **Integrity was the advisor competency that had the most impact on financial returns for clients.** The consortium was not looking for any particular kind of competency—although one might surmise that they'd be happy if the most important competencies were in the emotional domain, but in fact, the most significant competency was moral, and the overarching moral competency of integrity, to boot.

Our argument has not changed. It is still time for moral courage to take center stage in business. More than ever, it is time for the business arena to take on the responsibility consistent with its prominent position in the world. The ball is *still* in our court.

A

Strengthening Your Moral Skills

Think of moral skill building as a learning process like any other. Richard Boyatzis, noted leadership development expert, offers a particularly useful way of understanding how we build leadership capabilities.[1] Boyatzis argues that we don't learn to be better people or better leaders by attending training programs. We build our human and leadership capabilities through actual life experiences. Though experience is the best teacher, we don't have to leave what we learn to chance. Boyatzis proposes that we can put ourselves in charge of our learning using a structured five-step process:

1. **Understand your ideal self**—The person you want to be.

2. **Recognize your real self**—Your actual strengths and weaknesses in the context of who you want to be.

---

1. Dan Goleman, Richard Boyatzis, Annie McKee. *Primal Leadership: Realizing the Power of Emotional Intelligence*, Boston: Harvard Business School Press, 2002.

3. Decide how to build on your strengths and reduce the gaps between your real and ideal selves.

4. Experiment with new behaviors and feelings.

5. Develop trusting relationships with people who will support your learning process.

Developing moral skills follows the same cycle of self-directed learning. In Chapter 3, you've already had an opportunity to complete the first step of the process—you examined the contents of your principles, values, beliefs, and your goals, all of which make up the raw material of your ideal self. So you're now ready for the next step of understanding your real self—by assessing your moral strengths and weaknesses. With a full picture of your ideal self and real self, you will then be in position to craft a moral learning plan. Your moral learning plan will be your road map for gaining the moral skills that are most important to you *and* that promote the highest levels of business performance.

A Look in the Mirror

Most of us have some idea of our moral strengths and weaknesses. Our conscience might give us a pang if we exaggerate a business accomplishment. A friend could take us to task for being thoughtless. Or we may feel very secure in our unswerving fairness to our employees. But our data about our own moral performance is usually anecdotal and incomplete. To help you identify your moral strengths and weaknesses, we have developed the Moral Competency Inventory (MCI). See Appendix B.

Using the MCI

The MCI is a 40-item survey that you will find here and in Appendix B. It is a "self-report" survey; that is, you are the person who rates yourself on each item, and you are the person who decides the meaning of the results. Take the MCI when you have an hour to spend. It will take about 20 minutes to complete the survey, about 10 minutes to score, and another 30 minutes to reflect on your results.

The MCI is a self-development tool, not a test, so it does not have the scientific precision of, say the SATs or an IQ test. But leaders who have used the MCI tell us that it helps them capitalize on their moral strengths and strengthen moral skills that are difficult for them.

The Right Frame of Mind for Completing the MCI

The MCI items are all worded in a positive way, so there is no attempt to hide what the survey would consider to be positive behavior. Because you are rating yourself, the value of the MCI will be enhanced if you are as honest with yourself as possible. That means trying to avoid two kinds of self-rating errors:

- The tendency to give yourself a high rating on most items because they sound like positive things to do

- The tendency to give yourself low ratings on many items because you are typically hard on yourself (self-critical)

Scoring and Interpreting Your MCI

You will find scoring instructions in Appendix C and interpretation guidelines in Appendix D.

There are several different ways to look at your MCI scores. You will have an opportunity to consider your overall moral competency profile, and you also will be able to examine specific areas where you have strength or need development. No single interpretation is correct, and no "test" is the last word on your capabilities. If any part of your MCI scores don't ring true to you, keep in mind that you know yourself best. But if you are dissatisfied with your scores, we ask only that before dismissing them, you use your results as a springboard for honest reflection about your strengths and weaknesses.

Prioritizing Your Moral Development Efforts

There are two paths to improving your performance in any arena of life. You can concentrate on removing weaknesses, or you can focus on using your strengths. When you focus on your weaknesses, you try to improve your performance by undoing old behavior and practicing new skills or competencies. When you focus on your strengths, you try to improve performance by finding new ways to use the skills and competencies you already have.

Which path do you think is more effective? We believe you will reach higher levels of performance by capitalizing on your strengths than by trying to remove your weaknesses.

Which path do you think most organizations follow? Most organizations try to improve the performance of their workforce by concentrating on deficiencies. Our experience has been that most of the performance feedback many employees receive is negative, that is, information about perceived gaps. Organizations assume that negative feedback will create awareness of gaps that employees will then seek to improve. Ironically, negative feedback often produces the opposite effect. Studies have shown that performance often gets worse following negative feedback. It can take weeks for performance to recover to previous levels, and months, if ever, to see positive gains in performance. Even though managers regularly observe that negative feedback can be counter productive, most organizations continue to provide an excess of feedback about performance gaps. Focusing on gaps is a well-worn path, but one that rarely leads to the highest organizational performance.

The Road Less Traveled

Most organizations treat positive feedback, that is, recognition of strengths, like a scarce resource. Employees are expected to perform well, and when they use their strengths to accomplish positive results, it often passes without comment. Organizations who fail to acknowledge strengths miss out on a tremendous performance multiplier. That is unfortunate because most employees perform best by spending most of their time leveraging their strengths. It is in our strengths that we most resemble our ideal selves, and the more time we spend using our strengths, the more closely we approach our ideal self. Focusing on strengths may be "the road less traveled," but it is the path that makes the most difference to creating high performance.

The 80/20 Rule

Management consultant Roy Geer, offers this advice: Spend 80 percent or more of your time developing and leveraging your strengths and 20 percent or less of your time "pumping air into your priority flat spots (weaknesses)."

Look for ways to leverage the moral strengths you already have. Actively use those aspects of yourself which are closest to your ideal self. For example, Marietta Johns is a senior executive who knew she

was weak in the financial management aspects of her job. But she did-
n't spend a lot of time trying to learn what she didn't know. She got help
from a corporate financial guru and concentrated on doing what she did
best—connecting with her people and inspiring them to produce enviable financial results.

Moral development is largely a process of developing and leveraging your strongest moral competencies. You will get the most performance equity from using your strengths, but you can also benefit from
spending up to 20% of your development time dealing with your gaps.
By concentrating primarily on your strengths, you can also avoid the
discouragement of trying to remove gaps that are part of your basic personality and difficult to change. So don't ignore your gaps. Allocate
your time wisely on the path to your ideal self.

Your Moral Development Plan

A moral development plan helps you boost your performance by
increasing the odds that you will actually do the things that increase
your moral competence. A moral development plan records your moral
development goals and outlines specific actions you will take to become
increasingly morally competent. This need not be a separate plan from
a professional development plan. If you work in an organization or for
a boss open to discussing principles, values, and beliefs, you may find
it useful to include moral development as part of your overall development plan. The important thing is to write down the moral and emotional competencies on which you want to focus and detail the steps you
will take to use those competencies. Goals for moral development, like
any goals, are more likely to be achieved when you commit to them in
writing.

Step 1: Describe Your Ideal Self

Moral development planning only makes sense in the context of who you want to be. Recall the principles, values, and beliefs that form your moral compass. Given that set of beliefs, what kind of person would you be if you were at your absolute best?

Step 2: Document Your Goals

Again, moral development is only important if it helps you accomplish your most important goals. Recall your goals frame. What are the most significant things you want to accomplish in all of the important areas of your life?

Step 3: Identify the Moral Competencies You Need the Most

Reflect on the moral and emotional competencies that you need the most to reach your goals. If you used the alignment worksheet presented earlier, you have already completed this step.

Step 4: Leveraging Your Strongest Moral Competencies

Now recall your strongest moral and emotional competencies:

- In the course of the next six months, how can you use those competencies to get closer to your goals?

- Can you use your strengths in a new situation?

- How might you become even stronger in your use of some of those strengths?

- If it were possible to use your strengths and use them well enough, how many gaps would you actually have?

Step 5: Reducing Moral Gaps

- In the next six months, what could you do to strengthen those moral competencies in situations that are important to you?

- If you strengthened one competency, what impact would that have on your ability to accomplish your goals?

Finally, consider any other moral or emotional competencies that are highly important to accomplishing your goals:

- In the next six months, what could you do to strengthen those moral competencies in situations that are important to you?

Step 6: Your Moral Development Short List

Putting this all together, what are the three to five most important actions you can take to boost performance by developing your moral competence? Put this on a note card, enter it into your planner, or record it anywhere that you can keep it handy as a reminder of what you plan to accomplish.

Putting Your Moral Development Plan into Practice

Now that you have your short list, moving forward should be easy. But actually doing what you think is important requires that you clear the road ahead. We need to keep our behavior on course with our beliefs and goals. If you recall the alignment model, unproductive behavior is usually the result of *disconnectors*—those moral viruses or destructive emotions that get in the way of positive and aligned actions. So changing behavior begins with *recognizing* your personal disconnectors and then *reprogramming* yourself to stay in alignment even when moral viruses or destructive emotions threaten you.

Breaking Bad Habits

Although moral viruses and destructive emotions are major causes of misalignment, another common cause of misalignment between goals and behaviors is simply a matter of bad habits. Changing our behavior so that we do what we need to do to accomplish our goals usually means overcoming the inertia of doing things the usual way. Anyone who has tried to quit smoking or lose ten pounds knows that reprogramming behavior is not easy. Developing moral competence usually means that you will have to change habits that get in the way of being moral.

Realize that doing something different will not feel natural. Don't wait until something feels right. Do the right thing until it feels right. Expect a new behavior to feel strange or uncomfortable. Be willing to do it no matter what for *x* days. Build in reinforcement to tide you over until the behavior becomes second nature.

Reward Yourself for Positive Change

The best way to reinforce a new behavior is to reward yourself for doing something new. This doesn't mean that you need to sign up for a golf or spa vacation to reward yourself for doing the right thing. It's more along the lines of waiting for dessert until you have eaten your peas. Take the pleasures that are already part of your life and make them contingent on succeeding in the behavior changes that are part of your moral development planning. Celebrate your new behavior by going to that Friday night movie. If you have ignored your development plan for the week, stay home and pay your bills. When setting up your reward system, be sure that you use an optional activity, not a necessary activity such as exercise. You don't want to compromise your health or well-being if you suffer a setback in your change efforts.

Surround Yourself with Positive People

Because we are wired for interdependence, we need help from others to do our best. Within Boyatzis' theory of self-directed learning is the discovery that "you need others to identify your ideal self or find your real self, to discover your strengths and gaps, to develop an agenda for the future, and to experiment and practice." Everyone needs the support of trustworthy friends and colleagues to help them stay true to their goals. Make sure you establish at least a few relationships with people who will tell you the truth about yourself, even when you might not want to hear it. Find trusted people who know your values and goals and will let you know when you are not living up to them. When you are attempting new behavior, let them know what changes you are trying to make and ask them to tell you if they see you falter.

Do I Really Need to Change?

Like any worthwhile activity, living in alignment takes some effort. You might wonder if you really need to change. You are, after all, a decent human being with a good track record of career accomplishment. If you are an experienced manager, you may even believe that you already know all you need to know and don't need to learn anything new. If you are a senior manager, it has probably been a long time since you have gotten any critical feedback about your leadership skills. So why go to the trouble of trying to enhance your moral competence? Developing moral competence is every person's job because when it comes to human behavior, there is no standing still. If you don't continuously work on your moral development, you will lose moral competence. Think about any activity you used to enjoy that you have dropped over the years. It is not quite true that there are some things you never forget how to do, such as riding a bicycle. Get on a bike after 20 years, and you will probably gain your balance, but you certainly won't be able to go as fast, or as far, or turn as smoothly as you did when you were young. You might still be able to pedal, but your performance won't be what it could if you had kept on biking all those years. Maintaining and developing moral competence only happens when we keep pedaling. We need to use our strengths consistently, day after day, in pursuit of our ideal self. As our real self comes to look more and more like our ideal self, we will see the results in our personal lives and in our leadership of others.

Resist the urge to think of yourself as a finished product. Don't let anything stand in the way of becoming your ideal self. Invest time in activities that build on your strengths and enhance your moral competence. You are in charge of your moral development, but don't think you have to go it alone. Take advantage of personal development resources that you might not have considered in the past.

Books, Audio, and Video Media

There are many worthwhile books on the topic of principled leadership and personal growth. Reading such books is one good way to reflect on what is most important to you. For the busy manager with a long commute, books on tape are a useful way to de-stress and maintain alignment.

Workshops

Look for seminars on leadership, emotional intelligence, and values. Many senior managers think they don't need "training." Recognize your human fallibility and invest the time in active learning where you can benefit from the expertise of the presenters and the support of your fellow participants.

Personal Counseling

Some of us find that our moral viruses are so severe that they are seriously limiting our personal and professional effectiveness. The worst moral viruses usually arose out of traumatic childhood events. If some aspect of your life is not working for you, despite your best efforts, find a counselor or psychotherapist who can help you understand the source of your difficulties and work with you to develop more effective behavior.

Executive Coaching

Executive coaches are a particularly helpful resource for high-potential managers who want to accelerate their leadership development and for seasoned managers with moral or emotional blind spots. An executive coach understands the demands of your leadership role and the politics and culture of your organization. A coach can help you get the kind of honest feedback you need to build a development plan, keep you focused on your goals, and advise you on how to increase your leadership effectiveness. Many of the best-known Fortune 500 CEOs have benefited from their use of executive coaching services.

B

Moral Competency Inventory (MCI)

- Please choose one rating in response to each statement by circling the number that corresponds to your rating.

- You will get the most value from this assessment if you respond honestly. It may be tempting to give yourself a high rating because the statement sounds positive, but please do your best to rate yourself accurately in terms of how you really behave.

1. I can clearly state the principles, values, and beliefs that guide my actions.	1=Never 2=Infrequently 3=Sometimes 4=In most situations 5=In all situations

2. I tell the truth unless there is an overriding moral reason to withhold it.	1=Never 2=Infrequently 3=Sometimes 4=In most situations 5=In all situations
3. I will generally confront someone if I see them doing something that isn't right.	1=Never 2=Infrequently 3=Sometimes 4=In most situations 5=In all situations
4. When I agree to do something, I always follow through.	1=Never 2=Infrequently 3=Sometimes 4=In most situations 5=In all situations
5. When I make a decision that turns out to be a mistake, I admit it.	1=Never 2=Infrequently 3=Sometimes 4=In most situations 5=In all situations
6. I own up to my own mistakes and failures.	1=Never 2=Infrequently 3=Sometimes 4=In most situations 5=In all situations
7. My colleagues would say that I go out of my way to help them.	1=Never 2=Infrequently 3=Sometimes 4=In most situations 5=In all situations

8.	My first response when I meet new people is to be genuinely interested in them.	1=Never 2=Infrequently 3=Sometimes 4=In most situations 5=In all situations
9.	I appreciate the positive aspects of my past mistakes, realizing that they were valuable lessons on my way to success.	1=Never 2=Infrequently 3=Sometimes 4=In most situations 5=In all situations
10.	I am able to "forgive and forget," even when someone has made a serious mistake.	1=Never 2=Infrequently 3=Sometimes 4=In most situations 5=In all situations
11.	When faced with an important decision, I consciously assess whether the decision I wish to make is aligned with my most deeply held principles, values, and beliefs.	1=Never 2=Infrequently 3=Sometimes 4=In most situations 5=In all situations
12.	My friends know they can depend on me to be truthful to them.	1=Never 2=Infrequently 3=Sometimes 4=In most situations 5=In all situations
13.	If I believe that my boss is doing something that isn't right, I will challenge him or her.	1=Never 2=Infrequently 3=Sometimes 4=In most situations 5=In all situations

14. My friends and co-workers know they can depend on me to keep my word.	1=Never 2=Infrequently 3=Sometimes 4=In most situations 5=In all situations
15. When I make a mistake, I take responsibility for correcting the situation.	1=Never 2=Infrequently 3=Sometimes 4=In most situations 5=In all situations
16. I am willing to accept the consequences of my mistakes.	1=Never 2=Infrequently 3=Sometimes 4=In most situations 5=In all situations
17. My leadership approach is to lead by serving others.	1=Never 2=Infrequently 3=Sometimes 4=In most situations 5=In all situations
18. I truly care about the people I work with as people—not just as the "human capital" needed to produce results.	1=Never 2=Infrequently 3=Sometimes 4=In most situations 5=In all situations
19. I resist the urge to dwell on my mistakes.	1=Never 2=Infrequently 3=Sometimes 4=In most situations 5=In all situations

20.	When I forgive someone, I find that it benefits me as much as it does them.	1=Never 2=Infrequently 3=Sometimes 4=In most situations 5=In all situations
21.	My friends would say that my behavior is very consistent with my beliefs and values.	1=Never 2=Infrequently 3=Sometimes 4=In most situations 5=In all situations
22.	My co-workers think of me as an honest person.	1=Never 2=Infrequently 3=Sometimes 4=In most situations 5=In all situations
23.	If I knew my company was engaging in unethical or illegal behavior, I would report it, even if it could have an adverse effect on my career.	1=Never 2=Infrequently 3=Sometimes 4=In most situations 5=In all situations
24.	When a situation may prevent me from keeping a promise, I consult with those involved to renegotiate the agreement.	1=Never 2=Infrequently 3=Sometimes 4=In most situations 5=In all situations
25.	My co-workers would say that I take ownership of my decisions.	1=Never 2=Infrequently 3=Sometimes 4=In most situations 5=In all situations

26. I use my mistakes as an opportunity to improve my performance.	1=Never 2=Infrequently 3=Sometimes 4=In most situations 5=In all situations
27. I pay attention to the development needs of my co-workers.	1=Never 2=Infrequently 3=Sometimes 4=In most situations 5=In all situations
28. My co-workers would say that I am a compassionate person.	1=Never 2=Infrequently 3=Sometimes 4=In most situations 5=In all situations
29. My co-workers would say that I have a realistic attitude about my mistakes and failures.	1=Never 2=Infrequently 3=Sometimes 4=In most situations 5=In all situations
30. I accept that other people will make mistakes.	1=Never 2=Infrequently 3=Sometimes 4=In most situations 5=In all situations
31. My co-workers would say that my behavior is very consistent with my beliefs and values.	1=Never 2=Infrequently 3=Sometimes 4=In most situations 5=In all situations

32.	I am able to deliver negative feedback in a respectful way.	1=Never 2=Infrequently 3=Sometimes 4=In most situations 5=In all situations
33.	My co-workers would say that I am the kind of person who stands up for my convictions.	1=Never 2=Infrequently 3=Sometimes 4=In most situations 5=In all situations
34.	When someone asks me to keep a confidence, I do so.	1=Never 2=Infrequently 3=Sometimes 4=In most situations 5=In all situations
35.	When things go wrong, I do not blame others or circumstances.	1=Never 2=Infrequently 3=Sometimes 4=In most situations 5=In all situations
36.	I discuss my mistakes with co-workers to encourage tolerance for risk.	1=Never 2=Infrequently 3=Sometimes 4=In most situations 5=In all situations
37.	I spend a significant amount of my time providing resources and removing obstacles for my co-workers.	1=Never 2=Infrequently 3=Sometimes 4=In most situations 5=In all situations

38. Because I care about my co-workers, I actively support their efforts to accomplish important personal goals.	1=Never 2=Infrequently 3=Sometimes 4=In most situations 5=In all situations
39. Even when I have made a serious mistake in my life, I am able to forgive myself and move ahead.	1=Never 2=Infrequently 3=Sometimes 4=In most situations 5=In all situations
40. Even when people make mistakes, I continue to trust them.	1=Never 2=Infrequently 3=Sometimes 4=In most situations 5=In all situations

C

Scoring the MCI

If you are using the paper version of the MCI that appears in this book, you now need to use the following scoring sheet to produce your survey results:

1. Transfer your ratings for each item to the scoring sheet. Your item 1 rating should be placed next to the number "1" in column A. Your rating for item 2 should be placed next to "2" in column B, and so on. Continue until you have transferred your ratings for all 40 items.

2. Add each column and place the total in the box indicated.

3. Add columns A through J and place the total in the box indicated. Columns A through J are subscores for each of the 10 moral competencies discussed in Chapters 5–7.

4. Divide the total from columns A–J (step 3a) by 2 and place in the box indicated. This is your total MC (Moral Competency) score. The maximum MCI score is 100

5. Using the Moral Competencies Worksheet below the scoring sheet, transfer your scores for each column—A through J —to the corresponding list of competencies that are listed after each corresponding letter.

MCI Scoring Sheet

Item A	Item B	Item C	Item D	Item E	Item F	Item G	Item H	Item I	Item J	3a. Add columns (A–J)	4a. Divide by 2	MCI Score
1	2	3	4	5	6	7	8	9	10			
11	12	13	14	15	16	17	18	19	20			
21	22	23	24	25	26	27	28	29	30			
31	32	33	34	35	36	37	38	39	40			
Add Col A	Add Col B	Add Col C	Add Col D	Add Col E	Add Col F	Add Col G	Add Col H	Add Col I	Add Col J			

Moral Competencies Worksheet

_____ **A.** Acting consistently with principles, values and, beliefs

_____ **B.** Telling the truth

_____ **C.** Standing up for what is right

_____ **D.** Keeping promises

_____ **E.** Taking responsibility for personal choices

_____ **F.** Admitting mistakes and failures

_____ **G.** Embracing responsibility for serving others

_____ **H.** Actively caring about others

_____ **I.** Ability to let go of one's own mistakes

_____ **J.** Ability to let go of others' mistakes

Highest Moral Competencies	Lowest Moral Competencies
1.	1.
2.	2.
3.	3

What Your Total MCI Score Means

Your total score is a measure of alignment. If your score is high, it is highly likely that you typically act in ways that are consistent with your beliefs and goals. If your score is low, it is likely that your typical behavior is out of synch with what you believe and what you want for yourself. Table C.1 shows the distribution of MCI scores from very low to very high.

Table C.1 Total MCI Score (Alignment Score)

Score	Ranking
90–100	Very High
80–89	High
60–79	Moderate
40–59	Low
20–39	Very Low

D

Interpreting Your MCI Scores

There are quite a few different ways to look at your MCI scores. No single interpretation is correct, and no "test" is the last word on your capabilities. We recommend that you reflect on each of these aspects of your MCI scores to see whether they trigger the self-awareness that is so crucial to ongoing moral development. We think you will find your results to be interesting and illuminating. If aspects of the MCI interpretation are confusing or don't make sense to you, we trust that in the final analysis, you know yourself better than any paper and pencil assessment. That said—here are some ways to interpret you scores.

Total MCI Score (Alignment Score)

Score	Ranking
90–100	Very High
80–89	High
60–79	Moderate
40–59	Low
20–39	Very Low

- The maximum possible score is 100. A score of 100 would mean that you answered every item on the MCI with a "5" and would indicate that you believe you are completely competent in all 10 moral competencies assessed by the inventory. Because no human being is perfect, a perfect score on the MCI might mean that you have some difficulty acknowledging areas of weakness.

- The minimum score is 20. Most people have some degree of moral competency; therefore, low and very low scores may reflect excess self-criticism rather than genuine moral incompetence. In our experience, scores below 60 are extremely rare, most likely because corporate leaders do not succeed without some degree of moral competency.

- MCI scores fall most frequently in the moderate range (between 60 and 79).

- Your total MCI score is simply a snapshot of your overall moral competence. If you take the MCI every year or so, your total score can help you see whether your overall level of moral competence is increasing.

Highest and Lowest Competency Scores

- Most people who complete the MCI have one or two moral competency scores that stand out as higher or lower than the bulk of the scores. When you completed the MCI worksheet, you identified your highest and lowest scores in each competency area. Take a look at them now.

- Do your highest scores fit your understanding of your own strengths? If so, these are the competencies that you know how to use to maintain alignment and promote high performance. Are there any high scores that surprised you? If so, they may represent areas of strength that you had not been aware of and are competencies that can further help you to achieve your goals.

- Do your lowest scores fit your understanding of where your weaknesses lie? If so, you have an opportunity to develop your competencies if you decide that improvement in those competencies is important to you. Are there any low scores that surprised you? If so, they may represent blind spots that are keeping you from reaching your goals.

Individual Item Scores

- Go back to the scoring sheet and look for very high and very low scores. If you have a few scores of "5," those items may be areas of particular strength that you should recognize, appreciate, and use. If you have a majority of "5s" you may be extremely morally competent across the board, but you also may have overrepresented your strengths. People with very high scores across the board may need to solicit feedback from others to confirm the accuracy of their scores.

- If you have some scores that are "2" or "1," what weaknesses do those items represent? Given that most people who take the MCI have very few item scores below "3," low item scores usually represent wonderful opportunities for removing obstacles to high performance.

- Take a look at the item scores for your highest and lowest competencies. Was your lowest competency score a result of midrange scores for each of the four related items, or was your competency score low because of one very low item score? If so, you might find that paying attention to that single aspect of the competency could greatly boost your competence in that area.

Reality Testing

How much do you trust your self-assessment of your moral competencies? Most of us have some degree of difficulty seeing ourselves as other see us. As a reality test, we recommend that you share your MCI scores with one or two trusted friends or colleagues. Here are some questions you can ask them:

- How well do my strengths as reported on the MCI reflect your perception of my strengths?

- How well do my weaknesses as reported on the MCI reflect your perception of my strengths?

- Are there other moral competencies that you see as my strengths?

- Are there other moral competencies that you see as weaknesses?

- On a scale of 1 to 10, how would you rate me on integrity?

- On a scale of 1 to 10, how would you rate me on responsibility?

- On a scale of 1 to 10, how would you rate me on how well I show compassion?

- On a scale of 1 to 10, how would you rate me on my capacity for forgiveness?

Do Your Scores Matter?

- All the competencies included in the MCI are important, and all act synergistically. But realistically, we are all human and need to concentrate on developing the competencies that will have the most impact on us and our organizations.

- You already have decided whether your scores accurately reflect your areas of moral strength and weakness. At a deeper level, how well do your scores represent competency areas that are important to you? After all, you can be good or bad at things that you don't care about. So, we encourage you to think about the extent to which the competencies identified are consistent with your moral compass and your goals that you explored in Chapter 3. Completing the *Alignment Worksheet* helps you to decide how much effort to put into developing specific emotional and moral competencies. In the first column, you see the list of competencies.

- In the second column, record your relative scores (e.g., was it your highest, lowest, or midrange score for each scale).

- In the third column, rate each competency in terms of its importance to your personal guidance system. For example, is "admitting mistakes and failures" high, medium, or low in its importance to your principles, values, and beliefs?

- In the fourth column, rate each competency in terms of its importance to accomplishing your goals. For example, is "actively caring about others" high, medium, or low in its importance to your
  ability to accomplish your goals?

Now What?

By completing the alignment worksheet, you have prioritized competencies in terms of their importance to you. You have identified

- Areas of strength and weakness that are important for alignment.

- Areas of strength and weakness that are less important for
  alignment.

- Competency areas that are neither strengths nor weaknesses that
  are important for alignment. Your scores for a competency may
  be mid-range, but because it is a highly important competency for
  maintaining alignment with your guidance system or to accomplish your goals, it is worth your effort to enhance that competency to the fullest.

As an aside, if your rating of a competency's importance to your guidance system is different from your rating of its importance to goal
accomplishment, you might have a disconnect between your moral
compass and your goals that needs to be considered.

Armed with this understanding of your moral competency levels
and their importance to your moral compass and goals, you will be able
to map out a straightforward approach to enhance your moral and emotional competence.

Alignment Worksheet

Moral Competencies	MCI Score (High, Midrange, Low)	Importance to My Principles, Values, and Beliefs (High, Medium, Low)	Importance to Accomplishing My Goals (High, Medium, Low)
A. Acting consistently with principles, values, and beliefs			
B. Telling the truth			
C. Standing up for what is right			
D. Keeping promises			
E. Taking responsibility for personal choices			
F. Admitting mistakes and failures			
G. Embracing responsibility for serving others			
H. Actively caring about others			
I. Ability to let go of one's own mistakes			
J. Ability to let go of others' mistakes			

Index

A

Aberman, Rick, xli
ActiFi, 191, 194, 229-230
actions, behavior frame, 61
ACTIVEAID, Inc., 198, 202, 204, 234-235
Adelphia Communications, 17, 217
AEFA. *See* Ameriprise Financial Services
Alcatel-Lucent, 218
alignment, 63
    behavior frame, 61
    emotional competence, 66-67
    experiential triangle, 74-75
    goals, 59
    misalignment, 68-73
    moral competence, 65
    moral intelligence, 64-65
    preventing misalignment, 76
    scores, MCI (Moral Competency Inventory), 262, 266
    staying aligned, 67-68
Alignment Model, 68
Alignment Worksheet, MCI (Moral Competency Inventory), 269-270
Amazon.com, 195
American Atheists, Inc., 34
American Humanist Association, 34
Ameriprise Financial Services (formerly American Express Financial Advisors), 106, 225-227
    Blake, Brenda, 157
    "Chairman's Award," 182
    Chenault, Ken, 142-143
    emotional competence, 13
    Golub, Harvey, 145, 169

Heath, Brian, 57
importance of balanced life, 126
retention value of servant
    leadership, 102
Woodward, Mike, 106
Anderson, Brad, 181
approachability, emotional
    competencies, 136-137
*The Art of the Deal and The Power
    of Full Engagement,* xliv
Arthur Andersen, 18
assessments, MCI (Moral
    Competency Inventory),
    251-257
interpretation, 265-270
scoring, 259, 262

B

bad habits, breaking, 247
Badaracco, Joseph Jr., *Leading
    Quietly,* 19
Baker, Doug, 4, 125, 224
Baker, Jim, 224
balanced lives, emotional nutrient,
    124-126
Bar-On, Reuven, xli
Bausch and Lomb, 4
behaviors, 61
    experiential triangle, 74-75
    frame, 59-61
    "living in alignment," 39
beliefs, 49-51
    identifying, 51-52
    integrity consistency, 80-82
Bell, David, 67

Benson, Herbert, *The Relaxation
    Response,* 126
Best Buy, 181
bin Laden, Osama, 45
*The Biology and Psychology of
    Moral Agency,* 25
Blackwell, Lawana, 105
Blake, Brenda, 157
Blanchard, Ken, 99
Bower, Marvin, 161
Boyatzis, Richard, xli
    moral skill strengthening,
        239-240
    *Primal Leadership: Realizing the
        Power of Emotional
        Intelligence,* 9, 19, 179, 239
Bradley, Walt, 80
brain
    fMRI image, 29-30
    moral development, 26-29
Bronfman, Sam, 144
Brown, Donald E., 20, 33
Burger King North America
    employee performance truth, 84
    moral responsibility, 170
    positive messages, 181
Burke, James, 170
businesses
    community responsibilities,
        208-212
    environmental protection,
        209-210
    giving back to community,
        210-211
    global moral leadership, 212-214

moral intelligence success, 3-4
    costs of ignorance, 16-17
    differentiating competencies,
        5-10
    influences, 13-15
    learning from mistakes, 11-13
    maintaining talented
        employees, 15-16
    "moral positioning system," 11
    professional rewards, 10
    standing out among
        competition, 5
morally intelligent. *See* morally
    intelligent organizations
startups, 185
    five moral maxims, 197-204
    impact of moral skills,
        196-197
    KRW International, 187-190
    Minneapolis Circulation,
        186-187
    moral values, 190-196
BWBR Architects, 108, 194, 223

C

Campbell, David, *If You Don't Know
    Where You're Going, You'll
    Probably End Up Somewhere
    Else,* 56
Camus, Albert, 122
Capital Professional Advisors
    (CPA), 83, 91
Caplan, Robert, xlii
Cardinal Health, 149
Carlson, Cindy, 83, 91
Carlson Companies, 98

Challenger, 88
*Changing the Game: The New Way
    to Sell,* xliv
Charles Rives Associates, 200
Chenault, Ken, 142-143, 225-226
Cherniss, Cary., xlii
childhood, developing moral
    responsibility, 23-25
Churchhill, Winston, 50, 122
Clayton, Paul
    employee performance truth, 84
    integrity, 163
    moral responsibility, 170
    positive messages, 181
    small business integrity, 192
Clevette, Rick, 98
cognitive behaviors, 60
cognitive intelligence, 5
Collins, Jim, *Good to Great,* 19, 178
communications, leaders belief in
    employee, 151-152
communities
    business responsibilities,
        208-209
    environmental protection,
        209-210
    future responsibilities, 211-212
    giving back, 210-211
    global moral leadership, 212-214
compasses. *See* moral compasses
compassion, 106-109
    misplaced, 129-132
    morally intelligent organizations,
        173-175
    small organizations, 194
    universal principles, 42

competencies. *See also* MCI
   alignment, 65
   moral development plan, 221
confidences, integrity, 90-91
conflicts
   managing with empathy, 129
   values, 48
Connolly, Michael, 131
core values, identifying, 45-46, 48
Corps Business: The 30
      Management Principles of the
      U. S. Marines, 176
Coughlan, Jay, 11
counseling, moral development, 250
Covey, Stephen, xlii, 21
CPA (Capital Professional
      Advisors), 83, 91
Cray, Inc., 66, 122
Curie, Marie, 50

D

Dalai Lama, 105
Danzon, Patricia, 171
Darwin, Charles, 31
Dautheribes, Therese M., 34
DDB Worldwide, 116
DePaul University, 14
destructive emotions, 68, 72-73
development, moral. *See* moral
   development
The Diary of Anne Frank, 85
differentiating competencies, 5-10
disconnectors, 246
disrespect, 132-133

Distribution with Thrivent Financial
      for Lutherans, 96
The Dowry of Miss Lydia Clark, 105
Driven: How Human Nature Shapes
      our Choices, 32, 55
Dylan, Bob, 93

E

Ecolab, Inc., 4, 125, 224
Edwards, Dave, 157
80/20 rule, moral skill development,
      243-244
Eisenberg, Daniel, 171
The Emergence of Morality in Young
      Children, 24
Emmerling, Robert., xlii
emotional competencies, 115-117
   alignment, 66-67
   American Express Financial
      Advisors, 13
   differentiating competencies,
      5-10
   empathy, 128-129
   getting along with others,
      135-138
   interpersonal effectiveness,
      127-128
   misplaced compassion, 129-132
   nurturing emotional health,
      123-127
   personal effectiveness, 121
   positive self-talk, 121-122
   respecting others, 132-135
   self-awareness, 117-119
   self-control, 123

understanding thoughts, 119-120
*Emotional Intelligence: Why It Can
    Matter More Than IQ,* xlii, 5-6
*The Emotionally Intelligent
    Workplace,* xlii
emotions
    behavior frame, 60
    destructive, 72-73
    experiential triangle, 74-75
empathy
    emotional competencies,
        128-129
    neonatal development, 21-22
employees
    communicating belief in
        employees, 151-152
    disclosure of moral compass,
        152-153
    influence of company moral
        intelligence, 15-16
    leader development, 150-151
    leader dispensing feedback,
        153-154
    mutual accountability, 154-155
    performance truth, 84-85
    recruiting for values, 178-179
    resonant leaders, 179-180
    retention value of servant
        leadership, 102-103
    value differences, 155-156
Enron, 17, 94, 218-219
entrepreneurs, 185
    KRW International, 187-190
    Minneapolis Circulation,
        186-187
environments, business protections,
    209-210

excuses, personal choice responsibil-
    ity, 95, 97
executive coaches, moral
    development, 250
exercises, nurturing emotional
    competencies, 126-127
experiential triangles
    alignment, 74-75
    emotional self-awareness,
        117-119

F

failures, admitting responsibility,
    97-100
Fantom, Lynn, 228-229
    alignment, 67
    compassion, 108
    learning from mistakes, 12
Farrar, Jay, 209
Fastow, Andrew, 94, 218
feelings, self-awareness, 117-119
Feuerstein, Aaron, 173
Firestone, 171
flexibility, emotional
    competencies, 137
fMRIs (functional magnetic
    resonance imaging), 29-30
Ford, Henry, 213
forgiveness
    blaming self, 109-111
    letting go of others' mistakes,
        112-113
    morally intelligent organizations,
        176, 178
    small organizations, 194-196
    universal principles, 42

Franklin, Benjamin, 50
Freedman, David, *Corps Business: The 30 Management Principles of the U. S. Marines,* 176
functional magnetic resonance imaging (fMRIs), 29-30
fundamental beliefs, 20-21
    brain moral anatomy, 26-29
    developing responsibility, 23-25
    fMRI image of brain, 29-30
    human drives for survival, 31-32
    influence of childhood nurturing, 22-23
    moral software, 33-35
    natural selection theory, 30-31
    neonatal empathy, 21-22
    neurological growth, 25-26
futures, responsibility to community, 211-212

G

Gage, Phineas, 26
Garramone, Kelly, 187-190
Garrison, Jim, 211
GE, 166
Geer, Roy, xlii, 243-244
Georgescu, Peter, xxxv, 177
Gide, Andre, 50
global businesses
    moral leadership, 212-214
    values, 183
Gnazzo, Patrick, 16
goals, 53-56
    effective leaders, 57
    identifying own, 58

"living in alignment," 39
    moral development plan, 245
    putting in writing, 58-59
Goleman, Daniel, xlii
    differentiating competencies, 5
    Emotional Intelligence: Why It Can Matter More Than IQ, 5-6
    Primal Leadership: Realizing the Power of Emotional Intelligence, 9, 19, 179
    Working with Emotional Intelligence, 8
Golub, Harvey, 145, 167-168
good leaders, 221
Good to Great, 19, 178
Gorbachev, Mikhail, 211
Gowing, Marilyn, xlii
Grigg, Darryl, xlii

H

Hall, Don Jr., xxxviii, 88
Hallmark Cards, 88
Harrington, Dick, 141-142, 223
HealthSouth Corporation, 17, 219-220
Heartland, 131
Heath, Brian
    compassion, 106
    forgiving self, 110
    goal importance, 57
Honda Motor Company, 4, 88
hostilities, truth, 86
Hughes, Mike, 91, 120
Hugstad-Vaa, Jennifer, xlii
Human Universals, 20, 34
Hyundai Motor Company, 220

I

IBM, 112
ID Media, 12, 67, 108, 228-229
ideal self, moral development
   plan, 245
IDS, 124, 167
If You Don't Know Where You're
   Going, You'll Probably End
   Up Somewhere Else, 56
IMG, 106, 235-236
Immelt, Jeffrey, 166
integrity, 237
   consistency, 80
   honoring confidences, 90-91
   inconsistency, 80-82
   keeping promises, 89-90
   morally intelligent organizations,
      163-166
   principled stands, 87-88
   small organizations, 191-192
   truth. *See* truth
   universal principles, 42
International Management Group, 3
interpersonal effectiveness, emotions,
   127-128
Interpublic, 68
inventories, MCI (Moral Competency
   Inventory), 251-257
   interpretation, 265-270
   scoring, 259, 262

J-K

Jamba Juice
   Clayton, Paul
      employee performance
         truth, 84
      integrity, 163

moral responsibility, 170
small business integrity, 192
MacPherson, Don, 198
Jefferson Bus Lines, 65, 107, 236
Johnson & Johnson, 170

Kaess, Ken, 221
Kagan, Jerome, *The Emergence of*
   Morality in Young Children, 24
Kaiser, Lori
   emotional competence, 66
   positive self-talk, 122
   values, 43
Kant, Immanuel, 85
Kantor, Stuart, xliii
Kelner, Stephen Jr., xliii
Kernes, Jerry L., 20, 34
Kessler, Gary, 4, 88
King, Martin Luther Jr., 51
Kinnier, Richard T., 20, 34
Kline, George, xxxi
Kopper, Michael, 218
Kraft Foods, 167
Kram, Kathy, xliii
KRW International, 187-190,
   196, 203

L

Lamb, Sharon, *The Emergence of*
   Morality in Young Children, 24
Lane, Karen, 135
Langer, Ray, 176
Lauer, Dale, 38
Lawrence, Paul, 32, 55
Lawson Software, 11
Lawson, Richard, 12
Lay, Ken, 17, 72, 94, 218

leaders
    author interviews, xxxviii
    communicating belief in employ-
        ees, 151-152
    disclosure of moral compass,
        152-153
    dispensing feedback, 153-154
    employee development, 150-151
    forgiveness, 112-113
    good leaders, 221
    importance of goals, 57
    inspiring followers, 147-148
    mutual accountability, 154-155
    power, 145-147
    resonant, 179-180
    retention value of serving others,
        102-103
    truth, 82-84
    value differences with employees,
        155-156
    view of followers, 148-149
    visibility, 144-145
Leadership Alignment Task
    Force, 165
Leading Quietly, 19
Lincoln, Abraham, 50
listening, misplace compassion,
    130-131
"living in alignment," 37-39. *See
    also* moral compasses
Loehr, Jim, xliii
London Business School, 152
Lucent Technologies, 17, 218
Luskin, Fred, xliii

M

MacPherson, Don, 42, 232, 234
    admitting mistakes, 98
    business to help others, 199
    emotion self-awareness, 118
    forgiving self, 109
Maitland, Alison, 210
Malden Mills, 173
Manning, Mike, 95
Mayer, John, 5
McAfee, 220
McCormack, Mark, 235
McGavick, Mike, 174, 177, 223
MCI (Moral Competency
    Inventory), 251-257
    interpretation, 265
        alignment score, 266
        competency prioritizing, 270
        highest and lowest scores, 267
        importance rating, 269-270
        item scores, 267-268
        reality test, 268-269
        scores, 241-242
    moral strengths and weaknesses,
        240
    scoring, 259, 262
    self-development tool, 241
    self-rating errors, 241
McKee, Annie, *Primal Leadership:
    Realizing the Power of
    Emotional Intelligence,* 9, 19,
    179, 239
McKinsey, 161, 168
McVay, Malcolm "Tadd," 219
Mead, Christine, 164

measurement company, 42
mental checks, self-awareness breaks, 120
MENTTIUM Corporation, 43, 231-232
Merck & Company, 171
Microsoft, 87
Minneapolis Circulation, 186-187
Minneapolis magazine, 186-187
Minneapolis St. Paul magazine, 186
Minow, Newton, 93
misalignment, 68
  destructive emotions, 72-73
  experiential triangle, 74-75
  moral virus
    diagnosing, 69-70
    disabling, 71-72
    managing, 70-71
  prevention, 76
mistakes
  admitting responsibility, 97-100
  forgiving others, 112-113
  self-forgiveness, 109-111
Mitsubishi Motors, 17, 217
Modern Survey Company, 232, 234
  admitting mistakes, 98
  emotion self-awareness, 118
  forgiving self, 109
Mong-koo, Chung, 220
moral compasses, xxxvi, 40
  alignment, 63
    emotional competence, 66-67
    experiential triangle, 74-75
    misalignment, 68-73
    moral competence, 65
    moral intelligence, 64-65

preventing misalignment, 76
staying aligned, 67-68
behavior, 59-61
beliefs, 49-52
disclosure to employee, 152-153
goals, 53-56
  effective leaders, 57
  identifying own, 58
  putting in writing, 58-59
"living in alignment," 39
universal principles, 41-43
values, 43-48
moral competencies
alignment, 65
  moral development plan, 245
Moral Competency Inventory.
  See MCI
moral development
  brain moral development, 26-29
  childhood nurturing, 22-23
  fMRI image of brain, 29-30
  fundamental beliefs, 20-21
  human drives for survival, 31-32
  moral software, 33-35
  natural selection theory, 30-31
  neonatal empathy, 21-22
  neurological growth, 25-26
  plan, 244-247
  prioritizing efforts, 242-243
  responsibility development, 23-25
moral intelligence, xxxiii-xxxvii, 3-4
  alignment, 64-65
  community responsibilities, 208-209

costs of ignorance, 16-17
differentiating competencies,
        5-10
environmental protection,
        209-210
future responsibilities, 211-212
giving back to community,
        210-211
global moral leadership, 212-214
influence on business success,
        13-15
learning from mistakes, 11-13
maintaining talented employees,
        15-16
"moral positioning system," 11
professional rewards, 10
standing out among
        competition, 5
moral leaders, xxxiv
communicating belief in employ-
        ees, 151-152
disclosure of moral compass,
        152-153
dispensing feedback, 153-154
employee development, 150-151
inspiring followers, 147-148
mutual accountability, 154-155
power, 145-147
value differences with employees,
        155-156
view of followers, 148-149
visibility, 144-145
"moral positioning system," moral
        intelligence, 11
moral skills, strengthening, 239-240
bad habits, 247

book and media resources, 249
counseling, 250
80/20 rule, 243-244
executive coaches, 250
MCI (Moral Competency
        Inventory), 240-242
moral development plan, 244-
        247
positive change reward, 247-248
positive feedback, 243
prioritizing development efforts,
        242-243
recognizing need for change,
        248-249
surrounding with positive people,
        248
workshops, 250
moral software, 22, 33-35
moral viruses, 68
diagnosing, 69-70
disabling, 71-72
managing, 70-71
morally intelligent organizations,
        159-160
compassion, 173-175
forgiveness, 176-178
integrity, 163-166
policies, 161-163
principles, 163
responsibility, 166-173
reward systems, 180-182
values, 157-159
        employee recruiting, 178-179
        global organization, 183
        resonant leaders, 179-180
viewing, 160-161

Moret, Pam, 129-130
Moriarty, Rowland, xxxviii, 199
Mysliwy, Allie, 164, 174

N-O

natural selection, moral
  development, 30-31
Nearing, Chip, 235
neurology
  brain development, 26-29
  fMRI image of brain, 29-30
  moral development, 25-26
The New York Times, 203
Nicholson, Nigel, 152
Nicolay, John, xliii
Nietzche, Friedrich, 51
Nohria, Nitin, 32, 55
Northwestern Mutual, 4, 42, 120, 128

O'Hagan, Gary, 3, 235-236
  compassion, 106
  forgiving self, 111
  serving others, 101
Oja, Mark, 234-235
  business to help others, 198
  core values, 202
  employees sharing values, 202
  putting people first, 204
"One Minute Manager," 99
The One Minute Sales Person, xliv
organizations. *See* businesses
Otteson, Orlo, xxxiv

P

partners, selection, 199-201
Patrick, Steve, 223
pay discrimination, Wal-Mart, 220

performances
  deficits, 155
  truth improvements, 87
Perrine, Tom, 149
personal choices, responsibility, 95-97
personal effectiveness, emotions, 121
Peterson, Erik, 209
Phillip Morris, 166
policies, morally intelligent organizations, 161-163
Pomerance, Hy, xliii
positive feedback, strengthening moral
  skills, 243
power, 49, 145-147
The Power of Full Engagement, xliii
Prahalad, C.K., 213
Price, Richard, xliii
*Primal Leadership: Realizing the Power
  of Emotional Intelligence,* 9, 19, 179, 239
primary beliefs, 20-21
principles
  fundamental beliefs, 20-21
  integrity consistency, 80-82
  moral intelligence, 14
  morally intelligent organizations, 163
  universal, xxxiii, 41-43
promises, integrity, 89-90

Q-R

reality tests, MCI (Moral Competency Inventory), 268-269
Reinhard, Keith, 116
The Relaxation Response, 126
reprogramming, 247
resonant leaders, 179-180
resources, moral development, 249-250
respecting others, 132-135
responsibilities, 94
   admitting mistake, 97-100
   childhood development, 23-25
   morally intelligent organizations, 166-173
   personal choices, 95-97
   serving others, 100-109
   small organizations, 192-193
   universal principles, 42
rewards
   morally intelligent organizations, 180-182
   positive changes, 247-248
Reynolds, Kevin, 80
Rice, Norm, 135
Rigas, John, 17, 217
Rigas, Timothy, 17, 217
Risher, David, 87, 195
Rosput Reynolds, Paula, 223
The Russell Investment Group, 224

S

Sadat, Anwar el, 51
Safeco, 223
   Hughes, Mike, 91, 120
   Lauer, Dale, 38
   McGavick, Mike, 164, 174, 176

Sala, Fabio, xliii
Salovey, Peter, 5
Samenuk, George, 220
Schweitzer, Albert, 53
scores, MCI (Moral Competency Inventory), 259, 262
Scrushy, Richard, 17, 219
Seagram Company, 144
Securities and Exchange Commission, 17
Segal, Spenser, 229-230
   forgiveness, 194
   partners, 201
   small business integrity, 191
self-awareness
   emotional competencies, 117-119
   truth, 86-87
   understanding thoughts, 119-120
self-control, 123
self-talk
   positive, 121-122
   understanding thoughts, 119-120
Seligman, Martin, 34
serving others
   compassion, 106-109
   responsibilities, 100-103
The Seven Habits of Highly Effective People, xlii, 21
Shefrin, Hersh, xliv
Siegelman, Don, 219
Sills, Beverly, 50
Skilling, Jeffrey, 218
skills, strengthening, 215-216
   80/20 rule, 219-220
   bad habits, 223
   book and media resources, 225
   counseling, 226

executive coaches, 226
MCI (Moral Competency Inventory), 216-218
moral development plan, 220-223
positive change reward, 223-224
positive feedback, 219
prioritizing development efforts, 218-219
recognizing need for change, 224-225
surrounding with positive people, 224
workshops, 226
Skoglund, Judy, 124
Sleiter, Jay, 108, 223
small organizations, moral values, 190-191
compassion, 194
five moral maxims, 197-204
forgiveness, 194-196
impact, 196-197
integrity, 191-192
responsibility, 192-193
Smith, Janet, 200
social programs, giving back to community, 210-211
Solomon Brothers, 111
Sontag, Lynn, 43, 231-232
Spencer, Lyle, xliv
State of the World Forum, 211
Stewart, Martha, 72, 99
Stewart, Thérèse, xliv
strengths
80/20 rule, 243-244
moral development, 242-243

subordinates, performance truth, 84-85

T

technical competencies, differentiating competencies, 5-10
technical intelligence, 5
Thomsen, Jim, 96, 155, 222
The Thomson Corporation, 141-142, 223
thoughts
behavior frame, 60
experiential triangle, 74-75
positive self-talk, 121-122
understanding, 119-120
threshold competencies, 5
Thrivent Financial for Lutherans, 222
Bradley, Walt, 80
Moret, Pam, 129-130
Thomsen, Jim, 155
Truman, Harry, 94
truth, integrity, 82
exceptions to honesty, 85-86
fueling performance, 87
hostility, 86
leadership, 82-84
self-awareness, 86-87
subordinate performance, 84-85
Twain, Mark, 214
Twin Cities Telemarketing, 186

U-V

Ueland, Craig, xxxi-xxxii, 224
United Nations Declaration of Rights, 34

United Technologies Corp., 16

universal moral compass, 20

universal principles, xxxiii, 20-21, 41-43

University of New Hampshire, 5

values, 43-45
  identifying, 45-48
  integrity consistency, 80-82
  moral intelligence, 14
  morally intelligent organizations, 157-159
    employee recruiting, 178-179
    global organization, 183
    resonant leaders, 179-180
  small organizations, 190-191
    compassion, 194
    five moral maxims, 197-204
    forgiveness, 194-196
    integrity, 191-192
    moral impact, 196-197
    responsibility, 192-193
values log, 47-48

Vappie, Kim, 231

viruses, moral
  diagnosing, 69-70
  disabling, 71-72
  managing, 70-71

W-Z

Waletzko, Don, 196

Wal-Mart, pay discrimination, 220

Warner Lambert, xxxv

Watson, Thomas, 112

WDYWFY (what do you want for yourself), goals worksheet, 55-56

weaknesses
  80/20 rule, 243-244
  moral development, 242-243

Weiss, Kevin, 220

Westar Energy Inc., 220

Williams, Redford, xliv

Winfrey, Oprah, 54

Wittig, David C., 220

Woodward, Mike, 106

Working with Emotional Intelligence, xxxiii, xlii, 8

worksheets
  beliefs, 51-52
  embracing universal principles, 41-42
  goals, 54-56
  identifying core values, 46-48
  MCI (Moral Competency Inventory), 262
  writing goals, 58-59

workshops, moral development, 250

WorldComm, 94

Wright, Frank Lloyd, 50

Yale University, 5

Young & Rubicam, 177

Zelle, Charlie, 236
  compassion, 107
  moral competence, 65
  moral intelligence, 65
  serving others, 101

Zore, Ed, 4
  interpersonal effectiveness, 128
  understanding thoughts, 120
  universal principles, 42